California Fresh Harvest

A SEASONAL JOURNEY THROUGH NORTHERN CALIFORNIA

The Junior League of Oakland-East Bay, Inc. is an organization of women committed to promoting voluntarism, developing the potential of women, and improving the community through the effective action and leadership of trained volunteers. Its purpose is exclusively educational and charitable. The Junior League of Oakland-East Bay, Inc. reaches out to women of all races, religions, and national origins who demonstrate an interest in and commitment to voluntarism.

The Junior League of Oakland-East Bay, Inc.
Lafayette, California 94549
First edition: 25,000 copies June 2001
Second printing: 15,000 copies September 2003
Printed in the United States of America
Production and manufacturing by
Favorite Recipes® Press, an imprint of

FRP

Library of Congress Cataloging-in-Publication Data
Main entry under title:
California Fresh Harvest
00-092342

ISBN: 0-9613744-1-1

Also by the Junior League of Oakland-East Bay, Inc.:
California Fresh (1985)

Any inquiries about *California Fresh Harvest* or orders
for additional copies should be directed to:
California Fresh Harvest
Post Office Box 442
Lafayette, California 94549-0442
(510) 346-COOK (2665)
www.cafresh.com

Cover Photo:
Mudd's Restaurant & Crow Canyon Gardens,
San Ramon, California

California Fresh Harvest

A SEASONAL JOURNEY THROUGH NORTHERN CALIFORNIA

THE JUNIOR LEAGUE OF OAKLAND-EAST BAY, INC.

PHOTOGRAPHY BY STEVEN BRANDT   ILLUSTRATION BY GWEN PRICHARD
FOREWORD BY ALICE WATERS AND GINA GALLO

TABLE OF CONTENTS

The Course at Wente Vineyards, Livermore, California

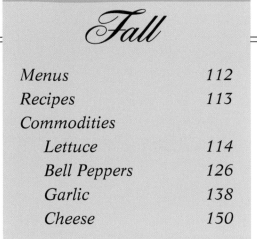

Fall

Winter

Contents

PROFESSIONAL CREDITS

PHOTOGRAPHY
Steven Brandt

ILLUSTRATION
Gwen Prichard

RECIPE CONSULTING
FOOD & PHOTO STYLING
Tami Jewett, Chef-Owner,
Seasons Catering

RECIPE CONSULTING
Sandy Sachs, Executive Chef,
Ingredients Cooking/Lifestyle School
at Andronico's Market

PREPARED FOOD
PHOTO CONCEPTS & STYLING
Joyce Mallonee, Mallonee Associates

TABLETOP CONSULTING
Karla McCormick, Morgan & Company

DESIGN
Barbara Breashears, B3 Design

ART DIRECTION &
PRODUCTION DESIGN
Favorite Recipes® Press

Foreword

by Alice Waters

For thirty years I have been trying to demonstrate the wisdom of an extremely simple formulation: that human beings eat best and thrive most when their diet is fresh, local, and seasonal. To the extent I have succeeded in making this case at my restaurant, Chez Panisse, it is due as much to the qualities of the ingredients we have been privileged to use as to the art and craft of our chefs. Likewise, readers of this cookbook will find that if they shop at local farmers' markets and insist on freshly harvested, organically grown products, their cooking will be transformed.

And not just their cooking! A major part of the pleasure of shopping at farmers' markets is the satisfaction of building lasting relationships with suppliers, so that marketing becomes a rewarding human experience as well as a commercial exchange. As the essayist and ecologist Wendell Berry has written: "A significant part of the pleasure of eating is in one's accurate consciousness of the lives and the world from which the food comes." From farmers we are always learning things that make dinner worth cooking and life worth living. Mas Masumoto, who supplies us with peaches, sends us a box of peach blossom cuttings in the spring just to remind me of the time of year and the delicious peaches to come.

The Junior League has asked me to use this foreword "to discuss the merits of using fresh, seasonal ingredients in menu planning and meal preparation." I would like to believe that these merits are self-evident. But I know that they are not. I have read that 90 cents out of every dollar Americans spend on food is spent on processed food—food that, by definition, is neither fresh, nor local, nor seasonal. But it is within our power to turn this statistic around by shopping locally, cooking sanely, and eating responsibly. This cookbook can help by offering enticing recipes that are oriented toward the food available in Northern California. It makes it easy for families and friends to participate in the preparation of simple and delicious meals. And this ultimately brings them to the very important ritual of sitting and eating together: it is there at the table we learn about ourselves and the richness of our culture.

Alice Waters
Chef-Owner, Chez Panisse

Foreword

by Gina Gallo

Family, friends, community, and tradition. These are the most important things in our lives, and as women and dedicated members and supporters of the Junior League, you understand this better than anyone. My fondest memories are times around the dinner table with family and friends. Two of the things that make these memories so special are great food and great wine. Simply put, the table brings people together. Life takes us all down different paths, but wine and food provide the common threads that enhance our relationships with each other and strengthen the bonds between us.

Something magical happens when you pair food and wine. The most delicious dish is made even better when you add wine to the mix. I like to think of wine as my secret ingredient. Each of us has a favorite recipe that has that one element that makes it special. I believe that for any meal, wine is that special ingredient.

Everywhere you look, there are food and wine pairing recommendations, and everyone seems to have their own set of rules when it comes to choosing a wine for their meal. My only rule . . . drink what you like. There is no question that just the right wine paired with just the right food can create an unbelievable flavor experience. However, when choosing a wine for your meal, don't be intimidated by the rules. Remember that any wine with food is better than no wine with food.

On behalf of myself and Gallo of Sonoma, we are proud to support the Junior League's pride and commitment to developing the potential of women and improving communities through education and empowerment. And from all of us at Gallo of Sonoma to all of you, a toast— to family, friends, community, and tradition.

Gina Gallo
Family Winemaker, Gallo of Sonoma

Preface

Since 1935, the women of the Junior League of Oakland-East Bay, Inc. have made a significant difference in the lives of children and their families in Contra Costa and Alameda Counties in the San Francisco Bay Area. Our members are diverse. We are married, single, childless, mothers, and grandmothers. We work at home and we work outside the home. We live in suburbs and cities and rural settings. We are Caucasian, African American, Latina, and Asian. We are native Californians and California transplants. And we share one abiding belief: women have the power and the responsibility to improve our communities through individual and collective action.

Each year, the Junior League of Oakland-East Bay provides a range of services to East Bay communities. Our efforts include long-term community projects utilizing League resources and volunteers over a period of three to five years, enrichment grants to nonprofit agencies for their special projects, and short-term volunteer-only projects such as staffing a children-focused conference, developing graphic materials, or painting a homeless shelter. Since 1992, our League has focused its funding and volunteer power on improving the lives of *Children at Risk*. In partnership with such agencies as Battered Women's Alternatives, Court Appointed Special Advocates, Newborn Connections, Children's Hospital-Oakland, the Junior Center of Art and Science, Shelter, Inc., Teach for America, and Girls' Incorporated, League members have provided volunteer services and funding to assist children in many ways. They have:

- developed a licensed child care center at a women's transitional housing center
- piloted an award-winning curriculum to prevent teenage violence
- advocated for children in out-of-home placement
- nurtured drug-exposed infants to overcome developmental delays
- provided science and arts enrichment programs for young children living in poverty
- supported volunteer teachers working in inner city schools
- served as home visitors to new mothers who lack social support
- assisted young women to improve their ability to stay in school

At times, new nonprofit organizations are formed to meet critical needs or to expand cultural opportunities. Recognizing these community needs, League members have developed partnerships, raised funds, provided expertise, and garnered community support to establish agencies such as the Oakland Festival of the Arts, Family Stress Center, and Family House at Children's Hospital. These organizations continue to thrive and contribute to the well-being of our communities, children, and families.

The Junior League of Oakland-East Bay's fundraising projects such as Traditions, the Spring Gala, and the Women's Business Conference fund our community grants, volunteer projects, and community leadership training courses. We return 95 percent of proceeds from our fundraisers to our community fund. Proceeds from the sale of *California Fresh Harvest* will support on-going children's services and implement important new programs for *Children at Risk*.

Introduction

California Fresh Harvest: A Seasonal Journey through Northern California is the second cookbook in the *California Fresh* series from the Junior League of Oakland-East Bay, Inc. Capitalizing on the abundance of fresh produce and other regional foods, as well as exceptional seasonal events of the greater San Francisco Bay Area, *California Fresh Harvest* is a cookbook that will appeal to both locals and visitors alike.

In Northern California, we are fortunate to live in an area of agricultural abundance. According to the latest California Statistical Abstract, our farms and farmers are leading the United States in the production of more than thirty commodities, including peaches, chicken eggs, walnuts, strawberries, and artichokes. We have chosen sixteen of those commodities to feature in *California Fresh Harvest* and they are presented throughout the book in the seasons of their peak harvest.

Since the beginning of the twentieth century, food and cooking trends have undergone tremendous changes. In the last decade, technology, combined with an interest in a healthier lifestyle, has led to a greater emphasis on using fresh ingredients to create full-flavored meals. The growing number of farmers' markets have bolstered an appetite for unadulterated, picked-at-its-peak produce. Many foods previously considered specialty items are now frequently found in supermarkets. Menus are inspired by the freshest foods in the market.

Our bountiful harvests are possible in part due to Silicon Valley technology that has changed the science of agriculture. Global Positioning Systems (GPS) and computers have led to Precision Farming. In the field today, a computer mounted on a tractor feeds information to navigational satellites. The GPS plots information so that every square foot of the field can receive customized applications of fertilizer, herbicides, pesticides, and irrigation water. With this information, farmers are producing yields as never before and there is no turning back.

Or is there? Organic farming– using methods of growing and processing foods that rely on the earth's natural resources—is one of the fastest growing sectors in agriculture today. Here again, California is leading the way. The birthplace of certified organic farming in the United States is Santa Cruz, California, where in 1973, the first organization to certify organic farms in North America was created. Organically grown produce is now readily available not only at farmers' markets, but increasingly in local supermarkets.

Northern California is an incredibly rich and diverse region. From thistled artichokes in Castroville and sweet and juicy strawberries in Watsonville to aromatic garlic in Gilroy, fresh and appetizing foods are available year-round. Both Californians and visitors enjoy the many festivals and events that surround the harvest of these products. To celebrate our bountiful harvest, more than thirteen million people attend agricultural festivals and county fairs in California each year. Held in rural, suburban, and urban settings, these events offer much more than cotton candy and carnival rides. They help educate communities about the importance of agriculture and our diverse cultures through cooking demonstrations, tastings, informational hand-outs, recipe sharing, and juried competitions for the best grown produce.

California Fresh Harvest provides information on California's most abundant crops and commodities and the festivals and destinations that celebrate their bounty, coupled with creative menus and recipes to entice both cooks and travelers to expand their horizons. The members of the Junior League of Oakland-East Bay share with you their favorite recipes, triple-tested in our own kitchens, highlighting the best foods our region has to offer. We invite you to turn the pages of *California Fresh Harvest* and take a journey through the seasons of Northern California.

Spring

Spring

Hummingbirds return in frenzied flight to the garden. Lavender wisteria drapes from gazebos, while pansies spill from red clay pots. On lush green hillsides, buttery daffodils spring from the earth. In Northern California it is time to indulge in the pleasures of spring. Along the roadways, fruit stands display flats of plump strawberries, asparagus, and artichokes. Picnickers pack their sourdough bread and goat cheese for an afternoon of wine tasting in Napa Valley. On the last Sunday of April, decorated sailboats parade along the San Francisco shoreline celebrating the official start of the boating season. At PacBell Park, throngs of fans cheer for a homerun ball to be hit into the Bay. It is also time for garden parties—bridesmaids sip mimosas and nibble on crudités while children in linen and lace gather their dolls for afternoon tea. Come with us and celebrate the bounty of spring.

Spring Recipes

Chicken Eggs

California is the leading U.S. producer of chicken eggs with about thirty million prolific hens. The average Californian consumes 240 eggs per year, which is coincidentally the typical output of an average laying hen. California sells over 365 million dollars of eggs annually. In Northern California, Stanislaus County is currently the leading producer of eggs.

Chicken eggs have been marketed as one of the best nutritional buys on the market. Egg protein is often used as a standard by which other protein is measured since it contains all the essential amino acids needed by the human body. Eggs have high nutrient density providing 10 to 13 percent of the Daily Recommended Value of protein, thirteen vitamins and many minerals, in high proportion to their low calorie count of only seventy-five calories per large egg.

Always store chicken eggs in the refrigerator in their original carton. Eggs are generally good for four to five weeks beyond the pack date. The "sell by" date printed on the carton is thirty days after the pack date, thus eggs are usually good for one to two weeks after purchase if refrigerated. To test an egg for freshness, place it in a bowl of water. A fresh egg will sink to the bottom and lie on its side, while an older egg will stand up. A really old egg will bob to the top. As the egg ages, the air cell in the large end becomes larger causing the egg to become more buoyant. As M.F.K. Fisher proclaimed, "Of course, the finest way to know that the egg you plan to eat is a fresh one is to own the hen that makes the egg."

In late April, the Victorian riverfront town of Petaluma in Sonoma County celebrates its poultry and dairy roots with the Butter and Egg Days Parade. The original Egg Days Parade was held from 1918 to 1926 and featured an Egg Day Queen and Ball, a chicken rodeo, and an illuminated night parade with fireworks. Petaluma was known as the "World's Egg Basket" with hundreds of small chicken ranches producing over fifty million dozen eggs annually. The eggs were shipped by train and steamboat to destinations all over the world. In recent years, the parade has been revived with "Butter" added to the title to reflect the increasing importance of the dairy industry to the local economy. Visitors today will see papier-mâché cows, flocks of children dressed as fluffy yellow chicks, and dairy trucks decorated as Victorian buildings and steamboats winding through historic downtown Petaluma.

Photo Opposite: Chicken Eggs, Gary Lawrence's Backyard Chicken Coop, Pleasant Hill, California

OVEN-BAKED EGGS

This recipe from the California Egg Commission is simple to prepare and a nice addition to a brunch menu.

> *2 cups blanched spinach, drained*
> *8 eggs*
> *4 tablespoons crumbled crisp-cooked bacon*
> *2 tablespoons minced fresh parsley*
> *4 tablespoons cream*

Preheat the oven to 400 degrees. Butter four 8-ounce straight-sided ovenproof bowls or ramekins.

Press the excess moisture from the spinach. Place one-fourth of the spinach in the bottom of each bowl. Break 2 eggs over the spinach in each bowl. Sprinkle with the bacon and parsley. Drizzle with the cream. Bake for 10 to 12 minutes or until the egg whites are cooked through.

Serves 4

Petaluma Farms

If hens could talk, they would sing the praises of Steve Mahrt, owner of Petaluma Farms and the man who pioneered cage-free fertile egg production. This Sonoma County farmer is passionate about his eggs—the first certified organic eggs in California. All Petaluma Farms' hens are treated to a specific feed formula that changes with the season and the age of the flock. Most are allowed to roam free in the hen house. The pullet eggs, those from adolescent hens, are some of Petaluma Farms' most flavorful and delicate. A good egg will have a smooth shell, a thick gelatinous white with a greenish tinge, and a yolk that is firm to the touch. When in Petaluma, stop by the Petaluma Farms store and take home the eggs favored by some of the Bay Area's finest restaurants.

FRESH TOMATO BREAKFAST STRATA

Brunch will be stress-free with this great dish. Assemble it the day before and refrigerate overnight.

Pesto Sauce
14 to 16 slices French bread, crusts removed, cut into halves
4 or 5 ripe tomatoes, peeled, cut into 1/4-inch slices (see note, page 99)
1 bunch fresh basil, stems removed

9 thin slices prosciutto (cut from the fullest part of the ham), julienned
8 eggs, beaten
3²/₃ cups milk
3/4 teaspoon salt
1/2 teaspoon freshly ground pepper

Coat the sides and bottom of a 9- × 13-inch baking dish with butter. Spread a thin layer of the Pesto Sauce on one side of each bread slice. Beginning at the short side of the baking dish make standing rows of the bread slices, trimming the bread to fit if necessary. Layer the tomato slices, basil leaves, and prosciutto between the bread slices. The layering is analogous to file folders in a drawer.

Whisk the eggs, milk, salt, and pepper in a bowl until frothy. Pour over the prepared layers, pressing gently to ensure the bread absorbs the liquid. Chill, covered, for 8 to 10 hours.

Preheat the oven to 325 degrees. Bake for 1 hour or until golden brown and bubbly. Let stand for 15 minutes before serving. Cut with a sharp knife.

Serves 8 to 12

PESTO SAUCE

An all-purpose pesto, this sauce can also be used as a topping on pasta by stirring in two tablespoons of the pasta-boiling water to lighten the consistency.

2 cups packed fresh basil leaves
1/2 cup extra virgin olive oil
2 tablespoons pine nuts
2 garlic cloves, minced
3/4 teaspoon salt

1/2 cup freshly grated Parmesan cheese
2 tablespoons freshly grated pecorino Romano cheese
3 tablespoons butter, softened

Combine the basil, olive oil, pine nuts, garlic, and salt in a food processor. Process until blended, scraping the side occasionally. Transfer the basil mixture to a bowl. Stir in the Parmesan cheese and Romano cheese. Add the butter and stir until blended.

Note: To prepare in advance, process the first five ingredients in a food processor until blended. Transfer to a jar and press a piece of plastic wrap over the surface of the pesto; seal tightly with a lid. Freeze until needed. Thaw in the refrigerator and add the cheeses and butter as directed.

Makes 1 cup

Mother's Day Brunch

With this simple, refined menu, treat Mom and the rest of the family to a brunch that brings the best gift of all—a relaxing day conversing and enjoying each other's company. A portion, if not all, of each dish can be prepared ahead, so you'll finish the day with a spring in your step and memories of time well spent.

Fresh Tomato Breakfast Strata 16
Tropical Fruit Salad 18
Garden Spinach Salad 32

·

Toasted Almond Biscotti 57
Lemon, Anise & Walnut Biscotti 57

Fresh Tomato Breakfast Strata

WINE PAIRING BY
wine.com

A dry sparkling wine from Mendocino County's Anderson Valley, such as Handley Cellars or Roederer Estate

California's Mendocino, Lake, Napa, and Sonoma Counties are the wine-producing areas north of San Francisco collectively called the North Coast. The cool coastal microclimates are ideal for chardonnay, pinot noir, and even the tricky German varietals gewürztraminer and riesling, while hotter climates in the hills produce big, chewy zinfandel grapes. Anchored by the towns of Ukiah and Hopland, Mendocino County's best vineyards can be found among the appellations of Anderson Valley, Cole Ranch, McDowell Valley, Potter Valley, and Redwood Valley.

Kiwifruit

A kiwifruit is a berry that grows on a shrub. The kiwifruit shrub requires a warm and gentle climate, consequently kiwifruit is grown in only a few geographic locations, including California, China, New Zealand, Chile, Italy, and France. Originating in China, the fruit was first called Chinese gooseberry. Today, its common name refers to the kiwi bird, the national symbol of New Zealand, primarily because the fruit has a fuzzy skin much like the coat of a kiwi bird.

California produces nearly 100 percent of the kiwis grown in the United States, where the season runs from October through May. Because New Zealand and California produce kiwifruit in opposite seasons, it is always available at the market.

Kiwifruit is packed with nutrients. One serving provides about 230 percent of the U.S. recommended daily allowance for vitamin C. Kiwifruit has a long refrigerator life; it will keep for two to three weeks in the refrigerator if stored apart from other fruits and vegetables in a loosely closed plastic bag.

TROPICAL FRUIT SALAD

Presented in a clear glass bowl, this beautiful fresh fruit salad is enhanced with tropical fruit juices and mint.

Salad (select 4 of the fruits for a total of 4 cups)
Banana, sliced
Pear, sliced
Bing or Rainier cherries, pitted
Mango, peeled, chopped (see note)
Papaya, peeled, sliced
Orange, separated into sections
Strawberries, cut into halves
Kiwifruit, peeled, sliced
Pineapple, sliced
Fresh mint leaves for garnish

Dressing
1 cup mango or papaya nectar, or a combination of both
1/4 cup chopped fresh mint (optional)

Toss the fruit with the nectar and chopped mint in a bowl until coated. Transfer the salad to a glass serving bowl. Top with mint leaves. Serve immediately.

Note: To cut up a mango, slice off a portion of the bottom so it will stand upright. Remove the skin with a sharp paring knife. With the mango standing upright on the work surface, slice down through the fruit starting from the top, passing the knife around the large, fibrous core. Slice down the other sides of the fruit in the same manner.

Serves 6 to 8

GLAZED LEMON BREAD

This quick bread is wonderful for breakfast or tea.

Bread
2 1/4 cups flour
1/4 teaspoon salt
1/4 teaspoon baking soda
1 1/4 cups sugar
3/4 cup (1 1/2 sticks) butter,
   softened
3 eggs
3/4 cup buttermilk
Finely chopped zest of 1 large or
   2 medium lemons

Lemon Glaze
3 cups confectioners' sugar
1/4 cup fresh lemon juice

Preheat the oven to 300 degrees. Combine the flour, salt, and baking soda in a bowl and mix well. Beat the sugar and butter in a mixing bowl until creamy. Add the eggs and beat until blended. Add the dry ingredients alternately with the buttermilk, beating well after each addition. Stir in the lemon zest.

Pour the batter into a greased and floured 5- × 9-inch loaf pan. Bake for 80 minutes or until the bread springs back when lightly touched. Cool in the pan on a wire rack for 15 minutes.

For the glaze, combine the confectioners' sugar and lemon juice in a bowl and mix until smooth. Pierce the top of the warm loaf several times with a sharp, thin skewer. Drizzle with the glaze. Remove the loaf to a cutting board and slice.

Serves 12

Filoli

Twenty miles south of San Francisco in the Crystal Springs watershed lies the magnificent estate known as Filoli. Built between 1915 and 1917 by the well-known architect Willis Polk, the house is resplendent with elegantly carved moldings, marble fireplaces, and inlaid parquet floors. The impressive garden at Filoli was designed as a succession of distinct garden rooms. The Filoli Garden is considered to be one of the finest examples of a private estate garden, representing the "Golden Age of American Gardens." Spring is especially spectacular at Filoli. The home and grounds are open for tours from mid-February through October. Filoli is on Cañada Road in the town of Woodside.

Bay to Breakers

A ten-man centipede running down the street? It must be the San Francisco Bay to Breakers race held each May. The annual event began as the Cross City Race in 1912, but somewhere along the way it took a decidedly different turn. Today the race is as much about costuming as carbo-loading. It is the world's largest foot race, with over seventy thousand runners and walkers traversing the seven-and-one-half-mile course from the city to the sea. Participants are welcome to walk, run, or dance their way to the finish line, and most do it in style. Costumed characters range from "the grasshoppers" dressed in suits of sod, covering the course on pogo sticks, to men dressed in hula skirts, mixing umbrella drinks while pushing a tiki bar up and down the hilly route. There are even a few revelers who bare it all in the spirit of the race. Bay to Breakers benefits the San Francisco Bay to Breakers Foundation, an organization dedicated to improving the lives of the children and residents of San Francisco.

CRISPY PUFFED PANCAKE

Not to be confused with traditional pancakes, a slice of this crispy treat is a welcome accompaniment to fresh fruit and eggs on Sunday morning.

1/2 cup flour
1/2 cup milk
2 eggs, lightly beaten
Pinch of nutmeg

1/4 cup (1/2 stick) butter
2 tablespoons confectioners' sugar
Juice of 1/2 lemon

Preheat the oven to 425 degrees. Lightly combine the flour, milk, eggs, and nutmeg in a bowl; the batter should be slightly lumpy. Melt the butter in a 10- or 12-inch ovenproof skillet. Pour the batter into the skillet.

Bake for 15 to 20 minutes or until golden brown. Sprinkle with the confectioners' sugar and briefly return the skillet to the oven. Remove from oven. Drizzle with the lemon juice, cut into wedges, and serve immediately.

Serves 4 to 6

WAFFLES WITH BANANAS & BERRIES

As light as air, these waffles have a wonderful crunchy texture.

3 eggs
1 cup whole wheat pastry flour
1 cup milk
5 tablespoons vegetable oil
1 1/2 tablespoons baking powder
1 tablespoon cornmeal

1 tablespoon sugar
3/4 teaspoon salt
2 ripe bananas, sliced
1 cup sliced fresh strawberries
1/2 cup fresh blueberries
Maple syrup

Preheat the waffle iron. Separate the egg whites from the yolks. Whisk the egg yolks in a bowl until blended. Add the whole wheat pastry flour, milk, oil, baking powder, cornmeal, sugar, and salt, and stir lightly; the batter will be lumpy.

Beat the egg whites in a mixing bowl until soft peaks form. Fold the egg whites into the batter. Pour approximately 1/2 cup of the batter onto the hot waffle iron. Cook for 2 to 3 minutes or until steam no longer escapes. Top each waffle with sliced banana, sliced strawberries, and blueberries. Serve with warm maple syrup.

Note: The whole wheat pastry flour may be replaced with 1/4 cup whole wheat flour plus 3/4 cup all-purpose flour.

Makes 6 waffles

City Bees

Just blocks away from the bustling sidewalks of San Francisco, hidden in the tiny backyards of city dwellers, lies a little bit of wildlife: honeybees— approximately three hundred thousand of them. Unlike some of their unwanted cousins, these bees are welcome tenants of more than twenty urban landlords who collect a modest rent, about five pounds of honey per month.

San Franciscan Robert MacKimmie has spearheaded this project. "I keep the bees for the sake of supporting the environment because it needs to be pollinated," he says. To make one pound of honey, the bees fly nearly twenty-four thousand miles collectively and visit three to nine million flowers. "I do it to produce diverse and wonderfully different nectars from each neighborhood," MacKimmie explains. "They all taste so unique. The honey from Pacific Heights is buttery and creamy. I can't quite figure out what it is. McLaren Park is cinnamony. It even changes throughout the season." MacKimmie has nearly one ton of honey stored awaiting distribution to local farmers' markets.

Princess Tea

The Princess Tea at the Sheraton Palace Hotel in San Francisco may well be a little girl's dream come true. There, afternoon tea is served to all who attend, but children ages ten and younger get the royal treatment. Upon arrival, they receive a crown and a candy scepter as they are escorted to plush settees. Dainty tea cakes and finger sandwiches, such as peanut butter and banana, and jelly with rainbow sprinkles, are served with a unique blend of fruit tea for Her Royal Highness. The resident harpist takes "royal requests," enchanting the children throughout the afternoon with music that includes all the Disney film favorites. Though girls may be the princesses of the day, little princes are welcome to attend as well.

ORANGE CURRANT SCONES

For variety, substitute other dried fruits or nuts for the currants.

2 cups flour
$^1/4$ cup plus 1 tablespoon sugar
1 tablespoon baking powder
$^3/4$ teaspoon kosher salt
$^1/2$ teaspoon ground cardamom
   (optional)
$^1/2$ cup (1 stick) unsalted butter,
   cut into pieces, chilled

$^1/2$ cup dried currants
1 tablespoon finely grated orange
   zest
$^1/3$ cup heavy cream
2 eggs, beaten
1 egg white, lightly beaten

Preheat the oven to 400 degrees. Combine the flour, $^1/4$ cup sugar, baking powder, kosher salt, and cardamom in a bowl and mix well. Cut in the butter with a pastry blender or two knives until the mixture resembles fine crumbs. Stir in the currants and orange zest. Whisk together the heavy cream and eggs. Add to the flour mixture and stir until a stiff dough forms. Gently knead on a lightly floured surface until the dough holds together.

Divide the dough into two equal portions and place on an ungreased baking sheet. Roll or pat each portion into a circle, 6 inches in diameter and 1 inch thick. Cut each circle into six equal wedges, leaving the wedges in place. Brush the top of the scones with the egg white and sprinkle with 1 tablespoon sugar. Bake for 15 minutes or until golden brown. Re-cut to serve.

Note: For variety, the dough may be rolled $^1/2$- to $^3/4$-inch thick and cut with a round or heart-shaped cookie cutter. Serve with Lemon Curd (page 55) or crème fraîche.

Makes 12 scones

PARMESAN POPPY SEED TWISTS

*Freeze these twists for a ready-made appetizer or
soup accompaniment.*

2 sheets frozen puff pastry
1/3 cup water
1 egg white
1 cup finely grated fresh
   Parmigiano-Reggiano cheese
   (aged Parmesan)

1/2 teaspoon kosher salt
1/4 cup poppy seed
1 tablespoon finely chopped fresh
   rosemary or thyme

Thaw the puff pastry as directed on the package. Whisk the water and egg white in a bowl until blended. Brush the sheets of pastry with the egg wash. Sprinkle each sheet with equal amounts of the cheese, kosher salt, poppy seed, and rosemary. Roll a rolling pin over the top of the pastry to press in the toppings.

   Position one sheet of pastry on the work surface so that the long side is at the top and bottom. Cut the pastry horizontally into halves with a sharp knife, pastry wheel, or pizza cutter. Cut each half vertically into 1/2-inch strips. Twist each strip 3 or 4 times and arrange 1 inch apart on a baking sheet lined with baking parchment. Press both ends of each strip down to adhere to the parchment. Repeat the process with the second sheet. Chill for 15 minutes or longer.

   Preheat the oven to 425 degrees. Bake for 10 to 12 minutes or until golden brown, removing darker twists from the baking sheet as needed in order to get all of the twists evenly brown. They bake fast, so be very attentive. Pale twists will become soggy and overly dark twists will taste bitter.

   Wrap leftover twists in plastic wrap and then in foil, pressing the package gently to remove any excess air. Freeze for future use. Reheat at 350 degrees for 10 minutes or until crisp.

Note: Puff pastry contains a lot of butter. While working with the pastry dough, it is important to not let it warm because the butter will melt. If necessary, chill half the pastry dough while cutting the other half.

Makes 60 twists

Salt

Most recipes call for table salt. However, salt connoisseurs and chefs often prefer to use kosher salt for cooking or as a garnish when the salt is to be seen, and freshly ground sea salt for table use. These salts are more flavorful and complex than ordinary table salt, which is mined from salt deposits left by primordial seas. Sea salt comes from seawater that has been evaporated by the sun. Sea salt can actually vary in flavor, depending on the sea from which it was derived. Kosher salt is coarse-grain, free of additives, and dissolves more slowly than table salt. It is certified to meet strict Jewish dietary standards. Since sea salt and kosher salt are less dense than table salt, a bit more may be needed. The rule is this: the smaller the grain of salt, the less used.

Other specialized salts include pickling salt and the inedible rock salt. Pickling salt, which may be substituted for kosher salt, is free of certain anti-caking additives that may cause pickling liquid to become cloudy. Rock salt is used in the ice cream freezing process and to melt ice on sidewalks and roadways.

*A cooking tip from **Sandy Sachs,** Executive Chef, Ingredients Cooking/Lifestyle School at Andronico's Market*

Pitting Olives

Many of the tastier olives, such as kalamata and niçoise, are sold with pits, and pitting olives by hand can be very time consuming. To speed the process, try this technique used by food professionals: place an olive on a work surface and rest the flat side of a wide chef's knife on top of the olive. Give the knife an abrupt smack, splitting the olive and forcing the pit out. Use caution—if too heavy handed, the pit could very well fly across the room!

TAPENADE, TOMATO & BASIL CROSTINI

This creative combination of tasty Mediterranean ingredients looks festive and colorful arranged on a serving platter.

2 sweet baguettes, thinly sliced
1/2 cup extra virgin olive oil
Tapenade

4 to 6 ripe Roma tomatoes, cut into 1/8-inch slices
1 bunch basil, stems removed

Preheat the oven to 300 degrees. Arrange the baguette slices in a single layer on a baking sheet. Brush each slice lightly with the olive oil. Bake for 15 minutes or until golden brown and crisp. Toasted baguette slices may be prepared several days in advance and stored in a resealable plastic bag.

Spread each baguette slice with a small amount of Tapenade. Top each with a tomato slice and one basil leaf. Arrange the crostini on a serving platter. Serve immediately to prevent the crostini from becoming soggy.

Makes 3 to 4 dozen

TAPENADE

This olive spread may be prepared in advance and stored covered, in the refrigerator for up to one week.

1 garlic clove
1 cup pitted niçoise or kalamata olives (see sidebar)
2 tablespoons capers, rinsed, drained
2 teaspoons chopped anchovies

1 teaspoon grated orange zest
1/2 teaspoon freshly ground black pepper
1/8 teaspoon red pepper flakes
1/4 cup extra virgin olive oil

Process the garlic in a food processor or blender until minced. Add the olives, capers, anchovies, orange zest, black pepper, and red pepper. Process until puréed, adding just enough of the olive oil to make a thick spread.

Makes 1 cup

SMOKED SALMON TEA SANDWICHES

Delicate and beautiful, these miniature open-face sandwiches are appropriate as an appetizer or a tea sandwich.

8 ounces cream cheese, softened
2 teaspoons chopped fresh dill
1 or 2 green onions, white part
   only, finely chopped
1 package cocktail rye bread

8 ounces smoked salmon,
   thinly sliced
1 English (hothouse) cucumber,
   peeled, thinly sliced
1 bunch fresh dill

Combine the cream cheese, 2 teaspoons dill, and green onions in a bowl and mix well.

   Spread one side of each bread slice with the cream cheese mixture. Layer each with a slice of salmon and a slice of cucumber. Top with a small sprig of dill. Arrange on a serving platter. Serve immediately.

Makes 3 dozen

Japanese
TEA GARDENS

Opened to the public in 1966, the Japanese Tea Gardens, located within San Mateo's Central Park, are a peaceful and quiet retreat from the outside world. Children will especially enjoy pretending they are in their own magical world as they pass under the sweeping branches of the Welcome Tree to find the secrets of the garden. Mr. Nagao Sakurai, former landscape architect at the Imperial Palace in Tokyo, designed the tranquil setting of koi ponds, pagodas, and waterfalls. Visitors will enjoy meandering through the garden's intricate pathways, standing on the bridges, feeding the koi, and spending a quiet moment in the teahouse reflecting on the beauty of the garden.

Artichokes

Long before cultivation of the artichoke began in the United States, the plant had its beginnings in the western Mediterranean basin. In the time of Greeks and Romans, the artichoke was an adored luxury item and the wealthy would preserve them in honey and vinegar so they could be enjoyed at any time of the year. In the fifteenth century, the vegetable was grown in Italy, and gradually made its way across Europe where it was a rare, esteemed commodity. The first written mention of the artichoke coming to the United States was in the early nineteenth century. Seeds were offered in catalogs, but the venture was not successful because artichokes grown from seed usually produce inedible buds. It was quickly learned that the artichoke must be cultivated by using existing plant cuttings. In the 1890s, Italian farmers in the California community of Half Moon Bay first began to plant artichokes. Since that time, California has become dominant in U.S. artichoke production. The most recent statistics show California as producing 100 percent of U.S. artichokes with a cash value of nearly fifty million dollars annually.

The farmers of Castroville, in the Salinas Valley, started growing artichokes in the early 1920s and Castroville soon became the self-proclaimed "Artichoke Capital of the World," producing 75 percent of all the artichokes grown in California. Each year for the last half century, Castroville has played host to the Artichoke Festival. Approximately twenty thousand visitors attend this annual event to participate in such activities as a 10K race through the artichoke fields, car shows, recipe contests, chefs' demonstrations, and sampling many different preparations of artichokes. One of the highlights of Castroville's artichoke history occurred in 1947, when Marilyn Monroe happened to be visiting the town. She accepted an impromptu invitation to be "California's Artichoke Queen," and was crowned at a local Kiwanis Club luncheon.

Castroville is also home to The Giant Artichoke, a restaurant that began in 1964 as a small roadside stand selling artichokes and other local produce. The business grew, and five years after its original opening, it began to serve artichoke hearts dipped in batter and deep-fried. The Giant Artichoke became a local favorite, and today many a tour bus makes its stop at what has become a large produce market and restaurant off of Highway One. Smiling tourists fill up on the fried artichoke hearts with a side of ranch dressing.

One artichoke contains only twenty-five calories, and is an excellent source of potassium, vitamin C, folate, magnesium, and dietary fiber. The peak season for artichokes is March through May, though the crop is harvested continuously. When shopping for artichokes, select tight, compact, green heads and avoid those with signs of wilt, dryness, or mold. Do not pass up chokes with leaves that have dark or bronze colored tips—this is a sign that the plant experienced a frost while in the ground, which usually improves the flavor. Store artichokes in plastic bags in the refrigerator for up to one week.

Photo Opposite: Artichokes, Castroville, California

STUFFED ARTICHOKES

An elegant recipe from Ocean Mist Farms.

> 2 large artichokes
> 3 quarts water, salted
> 1/2 cup fresh Italian bread crumbs
> 2 tablespoons freshly grated Parmesan cheese
> 2 tablespoons freshly grated Romano cheese
> 2 tablespoons chicken stock
> 1 tablespoon olive oil
> 1/2 teaspoon minced garlic
> 1/2 teaspoon salt
> 1/2 teaspoon freshly ground pepper
> Chicken stock

Discard the tough outer leaves of the artichokes. Cut off the top third of each artichoke with a sharp knife. Cut the stems flush with the base of the artichokes. Bring the salted water to a boil in a large pot. Add the artichokes and simmer, covered, for 20 to 30 minutes or until a leaf near the center of each artichoke pulls out easily. Drain the artichokes and cool slightly. Preheat the oven to 350 degrees. Remove the center cone of pale leaves and choke from each artichoke and discard. Combine the bread crumbs, cheeses, 2 tablespoons stock, olive oil, garlic, 1/2 teaspoon salt, and pepper. Stuff the mixture in the center of the artichokes and between the leaves. Place in a small baking dish and add enough stock to measure 1 inch. Bake, covered with foil, for 15 minutes. Remove the foil and bake 10 minutes longer. Serve immediately.

Serves 2

WINE PAIRINGS BY
Gallo of Sonoma

*Sonoma County
Chardonnay*

•

Sonoma County Merlot

Gallo of Sonoma, Sonoma County Merlot is 100 percent barrel-aged in a combination of French, American, and European oak barrels for an average of eleven months. This smooth, full-bodied wine has pleasant berry aromas and an excellent balance between ripe fruit flavors and structured tannins.

Gallo of Sonoma wines are aged in barrels from some of the finest European and American coopers. Gallo's winemakers continually experiment with different barrels to add subtle nuances and complexity, without overpowering the true character of the grapes.

An Elegant Gathering

Elegance is found in the pairing of sophistication and simplicity. Start with a creamy soup of California's best known thistle. Follow with rack of lamb enhanced by aromatic lavender, and an abundance of cooked-to-perfection spring vegetables. An impressive citrus dessert rounds out this formal dinner.

Artichoke Soup with Parmesan Croutons 29

•

*Lemon Lavender Rack of Lamb 42
Couscous 41
Array of Spring Vegetables 49*

•

*Caramelized Lemon Tart 54
Fresh Raspberry Sauce 55*

Artichoke Soup with Parmesan Croutons

ARTICHOKE SOUP WITH PARMESAN CROUTONS

The delicate flavor of this soup makes it a great starter.

1¹/2 cups sliced onions
6 garlic cloves, minced
2 tablespoons olive oil
1 tablespoon flour
1 teaspoon chopped fresh thyme,
    or ¹/3 teaspoon dried thyme
¹/2 teaspoon kosher salt
1¹/2 cups water

1¹/2 cups chicken stock
6 artichoke hearts, cooked,
    coarsely chopped (see sidebar)
¹/4 cup heavy cream
Salt and freshly ground pepper
    to taste
Lemon juice to taste
Parmesan Croutons

Sauté the onions and garlic briefly in the oil in a saucepan over medium heat. Cover the pan and cook for 10 minutes or until the onions are tender. Stir in the flour, thyme, and kosher salt. Cook for 3 minutes, stirring frequently.

Whisk in the water and stock. Bring to a boil and simmer for 5 minutes, stirring occasionally. Add the artichoke hearts and simmer for 10 minutes, stirring occasionally. Remove from heat. Purée the soup in batches in a food processor or blender. Return the soup to the saucepan. Bring to a simmer, and stir in the cream, salt, pepper, and lemon juice. Ladle into soup bowls. Top with Parmesan Croutons.

Serves 4

PARMESAN CROUTONS

These savory croutons add a very special touch to soups and salads.

3 or 4 garlic cloves, minced
¹/2 cup (1 stick) unsalted butter
3 cups (¹/2-inch cubes) sourdough or French bread
³/4 cup freshly grated Parmesan cheese

Sauté the garlic briefly in the butter in a small saucepan over medium heat. Remove from heat. Let stand for 10 minutes. Strain into a bowl, discarding the garlic.

Preheat the oven to 350 degrees. Drizzle the garlic butter over the bread cubes in a bowl and toss to coat. Arrange the cubes in a single layer on a baking sheet. Bake for 15 minutes or until golden brown and crisp, stirring 2 or 3 times. Immediately toss the croutons with the cheese in a bowl.

Note: Croutons may be stored in a resealable plastic bag.

Makes 2¹/2 cups

Artichokes

To prepare an artichoke for cooking, cut the stem so it is flush with the artichoke flower. Snap off the small bottom leaves and any tough bruised larger leaves. Lay the artichoke on its side and trim about one inch off the top of the cone. Cut the sharp tip off each of the remaining leaves with scissors. Rub the artichoke with a cut lemon to prevent discoloration. Place the artichokes in a large pot filled with water—one quart per artichoke. Add salt, one bay leaf, and lemon juice to the pot. Bring the water to a boil over high heat. Reduce to a simmer and cook for about thirty to forty minutes or until tender. To test, poke the stem with a sharp knife; it should pierce easily. Remove from the pot with tongs and drain upside down.

Serve artichokes warm with melted butter and lemon wedges, aïoli, mayonnaise, or hollandaise sauce. The leaf is dipped in the sauce, then the lower, tender portion of the leaf is scraped between the teeth. Cut up the heart and dip it in the sauce after removing the fuzzy choke.

To dechoke a cooked artichoke, spread the leaves of the artichoke apart and pull out the center cone of pale colored leaves to reveal the fuzzy choke. Using a spoon, scrape out the choke to expose the heart. This method is used for preparing stuffed artichokes.

Opening Day
ON THE BAY

Each year, at noon on the last Sunday of April, a celebration sets sail to mark the official beginning of a new boating season on San Francisco Bay. Opening Day on the Bay begins with the traditional Blessing of the Fleet ceremony in Raccoon Straits. Spectators on shore delight in the parade of some two hundred recreational boats, representing more than thirty local yacht clubs, competing in the annual decorated boat contest. The parade, on San Francisco's northern shoreline from Chrissy Field to Pier 39, is led by *The Phoenix,* the City of San Francisco's popular spouting fireboat. Receptions and parties ensue onboard sailboats and powerboats, on docks, and at yacht clubs around the Bay. San Francisco Bay is home to some of the most challenging waters and finest sailors anywhere.

CHILLED ASPARAGUS SOUP

A perfect luncheon soup or starter for that first warm spring evening. This soup travels well in a cooler and gives a gourmet flair to picnics.

1 1/4 pounds asparagus	1/2 cup buttermilk
1/2 cup chopped shallots	Salt and freshly ground white
2 tablespoons olive oil	pepper to taste
1 quart chicken or vegetable stock	6 sprigs of fresh dill

Snap off the woody ends of the asparagus spears and discard. Remove the tips and set aside. Slice the stalks into 1/2-inch pieces and set aside. Sauté the shallots in the olive oil in a large saucepan until translucent and golden. Stir in the stock. Bring to a boil and add the sliced asparagus. Reduce the heat and simmer, covered, for 30 minutes or until the asparagus is very tender, stirring occasionally.

Purée the soup in a food processor or blender. Return the soup to the saucepan and add the reserved asparagus tips. Simmer for 5 to 8 minutes or until the tips are tender. Let stand until cool. Stir in the buttermilk. Chill, covered, until serving time. Season with salt and white pepper. Ladle into soup bowls. Top with sprigs of fresh dill.

Serves 6

FAVA & GREEN BEAN SALAD

Favored in Italy and Greece, fava beans have a robust flavor that can stand up to peppery oil, intense herbs, and full-flavored cheeses.

3 pounds unshelled fresh
   fava beans
2 pounds fresh green beans,
   trimmed
1 medium red onion, thinly sliced
   or minced

1/2 cup extra virgin olive oil
6 tablespoons balsamic vinegar
Kosher salt and freshly ground
   pepper to taste

Shell and blanch the fava beans using the directions in the sidebar. Drain and remove the inner skin. Blanch the green beans in boiling water in a saucepan until bright green. Plunge the green beans into a bowl of ice water immediately to stop the cooking process; drain.

Combine the fava beans and green beans in a bowl. Add the onion and mix well. Drizzle with the olive oil and balsamic vinegar and toss to coat. Season with kosher salt and pepper.

Note: This salad can also be used to top pasta. For variety, add shaved pecorino Romano cheese or prosciutto, substituting lemon juice for the balsamic vinegar.

Serves 8

Fava Beans

Fava beans, also known as broad beans, are easy to grow and increasingly found in produce markets during the spring and early summer. Mature fava beans have glossy green pods that are six to eight inches long. To prepare them, the beans need to be removed from the pods and shelled—a two-step process. After stripping the beans from the pods, place them in boiling water for three to four minutes, then quickly plunge them in an ice water bath. Pierce the top of the skin with the thumbnail and pop the tender bean out of its shell. Fava beans are a favorite ingredient in rustic Italian and Mediterranean cooking. Dried fava beans, found in Middle Eastern markets, make a superb purée when simmered in salted water with garlic cloves, bacon rind, and thyme or rosemary. Purée in a food processor or a food mill and add extra virgin olive oil for a rich texture. Serve the puréed mixture as a spread on crostini topped with shaved Parmesan or Romano cheese.

Albertson's

In each Albertson's store, farm-fresh, high quality fruits and vegetables are in-stock all year long with each season's best varieties harvested at their peak. A fresh, wholesome selection of organically grown fruits and vegetables is also readily available. With so many types of produce to choose from, incorporating five servings of fresh fruits and vegetables in meals throughout the day is easy, and they provide all the natural vitamins a body needs.

Albertson's understands the importance of mealtime with family and friends. Cooks will find a wealth of specialty and international foods in addition to top quality fish, poultry, and meats. Busy shoppers will find quick and easy recipes and excellent selections of heat-and-serve deli entrées prepared and ready for today's lifestyles. Fine quality, extensive variety, and low prices, plus thousands of Bonus Buy savings are available in every department throughout the store.

GARDEN SPINACH SALAD

The fresh produce in this salad is available year-round.

1 bunch fresh spinach, stems removed
1 bunch fresh watercress, broken into small sprigs
2 navel oranges, peeled, cut into bite-size pieces
1 ripe avocado, cut into bite-size pieces
4 ounces fresh mushrooms, sliced
4 ounces blue cheese, crumbled
1/4 cup chopped red onion
Cider Vinegar Dressing

Combine the spinach, watercress, oranges, avocado, mushrooms, blue cheese, and onion in a large salad bowl. Add 1/3 to 1/2 cup of the Cider Vinegar Dressing, to taste, and toss to coat. Serve immediately.

Serves 8

CIDER VINEGAR DRESSING

This sweet-tart dressing is excellent on salads containing fresh fruit.

1/2 cup extra virgin olive oil
1/4 cup sugar
1/4 cup cider vinegar
1 teaspoon celery seed
1/2 teaspoon salt
1/2 teaspoon dry mustard
1/2 teaspoon oregano

Combine all ingredients in a jar with a tight-fitting lid. With the lid tight on the jar, shake to mix. Store, covered, in the refrigerator for up to two weeks.

Makes 1 cup

Dungeness Crab & Asparagus Salad

This spectacular starter or luncheon salad is easy to prepare and will impress your guests.

Lemon Dressing
2/3 cup mayonnaise
Finely chopped zest and juice of
   2 Meyer lemons, or 1 regular
   lemon
1/4 cup snipped fresh chives
1 1/2 tablespoons minced shallots
1 tablespoon Dijon mustard

Salad
40 asparagus spears (about
   2 pounds)
Salt to taste
2/3 pound Dungeness crabmeat,
   plus 4 legs for garnish
12 fresh chive spears

Combine the Lemon Dressing ingredients in a bowl and mix well.

   Snap off the woody ends of the asparagus spears and discard. Blanch the asparagus in a saucepan of boiling salted water for 1 minute or just until tender. Plunge the asparagus into a bowl of ice water to stop the cooking process and set the bright green color. Drain on a tea towel.

   Arrange the asparagus on four plates. Top each serving with a mound of crabmeat. Drizzle with the dressing. Garnish each salad with a crab leg and 3 chive spears.

Note: Two-thirds pound crabmeat is equivalent to 1 cracked and cleaned crab.

Serves 4

In April, Bodega Bay holds its annual Fisherman's Festival. Historically, the people of the town gather for the blessing of the fleet of fishing boats as it leaves the harbor at the start of the spring season. For the past twenty-five years, Bodega Bay has invited the public to join in the celebration. The festival has grown to incorporate arts and crafts and all the wonderful food and wine of the area. Visitors are welcome to sample gourmet fare and listen to live music while watching the decorated boats parade. The highlight of the festival is the bathtub races, in which brave competitors ride through the streets of town in homemade bathtub vehicles.

Table Grapes

Vineyards are one of the most popular images of Northern California. Everyone knows that California produces outstanding grapes for winemaking, but the state also produces over fifty varieties of table grapes. These varieties are grouped into color categories—green, red, and blue-black. While the growing season of all of these varieties begins in May and ends in December or January, green grapes peak from June to August, red grapes peak from October to December, and blue-black grapes peak from August to October.

Store table grapes, unwashed, in a plastic bag in the refrigerator for up to one week. Wash grapes thoroughly just before eating.

BUTTER LETTUCE WITH GRAPES & GOAT CHEESE

Blue cheese and toasted walnuts may be substituted for the goat cheese and pecans.

Salad
1 small head butter lettuce
1 small bunch red leaf lettuce
1 1/2 cups seedless red grapes, cut into halves
2 ounces pecan halves, lightly toasted
4 ounces goat cheese, crumbled

Dressing
3 tablespoons red wine vinegar
1 green onion, chopped
1 tablespoon sugar
Salt and freshly ground pepper to taste
6 to 8 tablespoons vegetable oil

Wash the lettuce and tear into bite-size pieces. Combine the lettuce, grapes, and pecans in a salad bowl. Combine the wine vinegar, green onion, sugar, salt, and pepper in a separate bowl and mix well. Whisk in the oil to taste. Add the desired amount of dressing to the salad and toss to mix. Arrange the salad on plates and top with the goat cheese.

Serves 6 to 8

LINGUINE WITH ASPARAGUS & PROSCIUTTO

*Serve with a loaf of crusty sourdough bread and a green
salad for a quick, delicious dinner.*

1¹/2 pounds fresh asparagus
8 ounces linguine
4 green onions, sliced
2 tablespoons butter
3/4 cup chicken stock

4 ounces goat cheese, crumbled
2 ounces prosciutto, chopped
Freshly ground pepper
Freshly grated Parmesan cheese

Snap off the woody ends of the asparagus spears and discard. Cut the spears into 1-inch pieces.
Cook the pasta in boiling salted water according to package instructions.

While the pasta is cooking, sauté the green onions in the butter in a large skillet for 1 minute
or until tender. Add the asparagus and stock. Cook over medium heat for 2 to 4 minutes or
until the asparagus is tender, stirring frequently. Add the goat cheese and prosciutto and stir
until the cheese is melted.

Drain the pasta, add it to the skillet, and toss to mix. Transfer to pasta bowls. Serve
immediately with freshly ground pepper and Parmesan cheese.

Serves 4

Sourdough Bread

Sourdough bread is identified
with the Bay Area, but in reality the
process of sourdough baking has
existed for centuries. During the gold
rush years, baker Isidore Boudin
brought the unique flavor to San
Francisco by combining the sourdough
process with the art of French baking.
In 1849 he created the Bay Area's
version of sourdough: a bread with a
hard crust, soft interior, tangy flavor,
and chewy texture. In short, a delicious,
unique taste that is hard to resist! To
this day, the Boudin Bakery of San
Francisco begins each loaf using the
yeast culture, called starter, that dates
back over 150 years.

Fresh sourdough bread is readily
available at the market, but it can be
made at home. Sourdough starter is
the most important ingredient, and it
must contain San Francisco yeast
culture to be authentic. Dried San
Francisco yeast starters may be
purchased in specialty food stores,
larger health food stores, and by mail
order. It is said that during the seventy-
two-hour fermentation process, the
mild climate and fog surrounding San
Francisco give sourdough its unique
taste. Nonresidents may want to
challenge that claim.

Asparagus

Asparagus was first cultivated over two thousand years ago by the Greeks and Romans in the Eastern Mediterranean region. Ever since that time, this member of the lily family has been grown and savored in such diverse locales as England, Russia, Poland, Syria, and Spain. Asparagus is often called the "Food of Kings" because King Louis XIV of France was so fond of it that he ordered special green houses built so he could enjoy asparagus year-round. Asparagus was brought to America by the early Colonists and was first planted in California during the 1860s. The moderate climate, together with a variety of fertile soils, contributes to the outstanding quality of asparagus grown here. The state produces over fifty thousand metric tons of asparagus every year, the most in the nation.

In California, the asparagus growing season peaks in the spring, although the season lasts from January to June. Asparagus is a fragile plant and needs to be kept above fifty-two degrees Fahrenheit. The range of microclimates in California enables growers to reap produce throughout the first six months of the year, even though the actual harvest season for each crop of asparagus lasts only sixty to ninety days.

Asparagus is literally the growing shoot of a perennial plant. The plants take two or more years to become established and require significant hand labor in all phases of growing and harvesting. To harvest the spears, workers walk the furrowed fields and select the choicest spears each day, cutting them individually by hand with long-handled knives. They look for those spears ten to twelve inches long with compact, tight heads and good green color. Asparagus is shipped within hours of cutting to markets around the world in specially designed crates. A moist, absorbent fiber pad is placed on the bottom of the crate to prevent drying during transit; space is left at the top to allow for elongation of spears, which continue to grow for a time after being cut.

Asparagus is not only an elegant and tasty vegetable, this delicacy is also an excellent source of vitamin C, vitamin B6, folacin, thiamine, potassium, and dietary fiber. When shopping for asparagus, choose bright green stalks with closed, compact, firm tips. Contrary to popular opinion, thicker asparagus stalks are not older or tougher than thin stalks; some plants simply produce shoots that are thicker than others.

Photo Opposite: Asparagus, Jack London Square Farmers' Market, Oakland, California

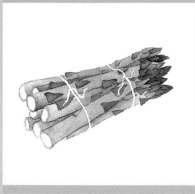

STIR-FRIED ASPARAGUS & PANCETTA

This is a favorite appetizer at Garibaldi's, a well-known neighborhood restaurant in Oakland.

12 asparagus spears
2 ounces pancetta, diced
2 tablespoons oyster sauce
1 teaspoon minced garlic
1 teaspoon hot chile oil

Snap off the woody ends of the asparagus spears and discard. Sauté the pancetta in a skillet until lightly browned. Add the asparagus and sauté over medium heat until the asparagus is al dente. Drain the fat from the pan. Stir in the oyster sauce, garlic, and chile oil. Cook just until heated through, shaking the pan to coat the spears. Arrange 6 spears on each plate and top with pancetta and remaining sauce.

Serves 2

A Spring Occasion

It must be spring when the season's hallmark, asparagus, appears in the market. Salute the season and celebrate a new beginning with a menu of asparagus salad, succulent salmon, irresistible roasted potatoes, and farm-fresh sugar snap peas. Top it off with a decadent chocolate dessert.

A Russian River Chardonnay, such as Bannister, Lynmar Winery, Sapphire Hill, or Fritz Winery

•

A Napa Valley Cabernet Sauvignon, such as Sterling Vineyards, Beringer Vineyards, or Madrigal Vineyards

California is the source of most wine made in the United States— 90 percent, in fact. Its extensive valleys, cool coastal winds and fog, and hot summer sun provide for the seemingly endless and well-dispersed microclimates that make California the national, and natural leader for quantity and quality.

Asparagus with Sun-Dried Tomatoes 39

•

Salmon with Fresh Dill Butter 45
Sautéed Sugar Snap Peas 46
Rosemary Reds 47

•

Chocolate Pound Cake with Cherries & Berries Compote 56

Asparagus with Sun-Dried Tomatoes

ASPARAGUS WITH SUN-DRIED TOMATOES

This striking dish is full of color, celebrating the arrival of spring.

Sun-Dried Tomato Vinaigrette
1/4 cup finely chopped fresh parsley
1/4 cup tarragon wine vinegar
2 tablespoons finely chopped
   shallots
2 tablespoons snipped chives
2 tablespoons minced sun-dried
   tomatoes
1 1/2 teaspoons Dijon mustard
3/4 to 1 teaspoon kosher salt
Freshly ground pepper to taste
1/2 cup extra virgin olive oil

Asparagus
2 pounds medium asparagus
   spears, woody ends removed,
   peeled
Salt to taste
1/4 cup chopped red and yellow
   bell peppers (optional)

Combine the vinaigrette ingredients in a bowl and mix well. Let stand at room temperature for 30 minutes to allow the flavors to marry. Add the olive oil and mix well. Taste and adjust the seasonings, if necessary.

Blanch the asparagus in a large skillet of boiling salted water for 1 minute or just until tender. Plunge the asparagus into a bowl of ice water to stop the cooking process and set the bright green color. Drain on a tea towel.

Arrange the asparagus on a serving platter. Drizzle with the desired amount of vinaigrette. Sprinkle with the bell peppers. Serve immediately with the remaining vinaigrette on the side.

Serves 6

Stockton Asparagus
FESTIVAL

Stockton is the center of Northern California's premier region for asparagus growing. Each spring, some eighty thousand people make their way to Stockton to celebrate this dainty but delectable vegetable. At the Stockton Asparagus Festival, nine tons of asparagus are cooked and eaten during the three-day event. The focal point of the event, Asparagus Alley, is a food pavilion offering deep-fried asparagus, asparagus bisque, asparagus salsa, and asparaberry shortcake. Festival-goers can also enjoy a nationally acclaimed arts and crafts show, the annual Asparagus Celebrity Kitchen, the AsparaZone for kids, a 5K AsparaRun, a one hundred thousand dollar Hole-In-One Contest, a classic car show, and three stages with live entertainment. Self-proclaimed as one of the best festivals in the country, the nonprofit Asparagus Festival has returned more than three million dollars over the past two decades to local community nonprofit organizations. Each year, forty-five hundred volunteers, representing nearly one hundred charities, earn two hundred thousand dollars for their causes by working as volunteer vendors selling food and merchandise or as employees of the festival, fondly called the Spear-It Staff.

Jumping Frog
JUBILEE

The short story, "The Celebrated Jumping Frog of Calaveras County," written by Mark Twain, was first published in *The Saturday Press* in 1865. Twain overheard the story told in a local tavern, and his version put Calaveras County on the map. For fun, the folks there created an annual event to celebrate the leaping amphibians. Three hours east of San Francisco, the Calaveras County Jumping Frog Jubilee is held each May in conjunction with the county fair. Contestants from around the world compete for the title of world record holder, still held by Rosie the Ribiter, who hopped an amazing twenty-one feet, five and three-quarter inches back in 1986. The Jolly Green Jumpers, a parade, and a carnival make this a hoppin' event for the whole family.

ROASTED CHICKEN WITH RICOTTA & HERBS

This rich variation of the traditional roasted chicken
will be a new family favorite.

1 whole frying chicken
1/2 cup ricotta cheese
3 tablespoons unsalted butter, softened
1/4 cup freshly grated Parmigiano-Reggiano cheese (aged Parmesan)
1 egg, lightly beaten

3 tablespoons chopped fresh herbs, such as thyme, chives, basil, tarragon, or parsley
1 garlic clove, minced
Kosher salt and freshly ground pepper
Olive oil

Using kitchen shears, cut the chicken down both sides of the backbone the entire length of the bird. Remove the backbone and tuck the wing tips under the body. Place the chicken skin side up on a work surface and firmly press the breast down. This pops the bones and flattens the breast so that it is easily stuffed and cooks evenly. Loosen the breast skin carefully, leaving the skin attached along the breastbone. Continue down both sides of the breast loosening the skin along the thighs and legs making every effort not to pierce the skin. The chicken may be prepared up to this point a day in advance and stored, covered, in the refrigerator.

Preheat the oven to 450 degrees. Mash the ricotta cheese and butter in a bowl until blended. Stir in the Parmesan cheese, egg, fresh herbs, and garlic. Season with kosher salt and pepper. Push the cheese mixture gently under the skin and spread evenly over the legs, thighs, and breast. Pierce the skin on each side of the breast tip and insert the end of a leg into each slit to keep the legs in place. Brush the surface of the chicken with olive oil and sprinkle liberally with kosher salt and pepper.

Arrange the chicken skin side up in a roasting pan so it fits snugly. Roast for 10 minutes. Decrease the oven temperature to 375 degrees. Roast for 40 minutes longer, basting occasionally with the pan juices; tent with foil if needed to prevent excessive browning. Let stand for 10 minutes. Cut into quarters to serve.

Serves 4

CHICKEN WITH LEMONS & GREEN OLIVES

*This savory braised chicken takes little time to assemble,
but two hours to cook. The lemons cook down until
they are as tender as the chicken.*

3 tablespoons olive oil
1 large yellow onion, cut into
 halves, thinly sliced
1 garlic clove, minced
1½ tablespoons chopped fresh
 parsley
2 tablespoons chopped fresh
 cilantro, divided
1 teaspoon salt

½ teaspoon freshly ground pepper
⅛ teaspoon ground saffron
1 (3-pound) frying chicken, cut up
1½ lemons, seeded, cut into
 wedges
⅓ cup pitted green olives
 (Greek Ionian or French
 Picholine olives preferred),
 see sidebar, page 24

Heat the olive oil in a heavy pan with a lid. Add the onion, garlic, parsley, 1 tablespoon cilantro, salt, pepper, and saffron and mix well. Add the chicken, turning to coat. Top with the lemon wedges. Simmer, covered, over very low heat for 2 hours or until cooked through, turning occasionally. Alternatively, the chicken may be baked in a preheated 325-degree oven for 2 hours or until cooked through, turning occasionally.

 Transfer the chicken and lemon wedges to a serving platter with a slotted spoon. Cover the chicken to keep warm. Bring the pan juices and onions to a boil. Reduce until the consistency of a thick sauce, stirring frequently. Stir in the olives. Cook until heated through, stirring frequently. Pour over the chicken. Sprinkle with 1 tablespoon cilantro.

Serves 4

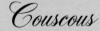

Couscous

Of Moroccan origin, couscous is tiny grains of pasta made from semolina wheat. Whether prepared plain or embellished with toasted nuts, chopped vegetables, dried fruits, fresh or dried herbs, spices, or fruit juice, couscous is a staple that can take the place of rice or pasta in many menus. Try substituting couscous for rice in casseroles and for pasta in salads, or serve with stews and kabobs.

To prepare couscous, combine two cups of water or broth with one-half teaspoon salt and one tablespoon olive oil or butter in a saucepan. Bring to a boil and stir in ten ounces of plain couscous. Remove from heat and let stand for five minutes. If desired, make any additions and fluff lightly with a fork prior to serving.

Lavender

The herb of love, lavender was a favorite of the Romans who used it in bathing; thus the name lavender comes from the Latin verb *lavare*—to wash. There are over one hundred varieties of lavender today. Its flowers are wonderfully fragrant and flavorful and historically have been an ingredient in European cuisine. The dried flowers can be found at specialty food stores and upscale markets. The Matanzas Creek Winery in Sonoma County is the largest producer of lavender in Northern California. The two million stems harvested there annually are made into soaps, bath salts, potpourri, and spice blends, and are also sold in bulk as culinary lavender. When using lavender for cooking, it is important to use it in its culinary form. Lavender that has been sprayed or enhanced for use in potpourri or sachets is not appropriate. To dry lavender, pick the blossoms from the garden just as they are beginning to open and allow them to dry.

Lavender makes a great "rub" or marinade for meats, poultry, or fish. It is also used to flavor tea, jelly, vinegar, oil, and ice or sorbet when infused into sugar syrup. As lavender's essence is quite powerful, use it sparingly. Too much will give food a soapy taste.

Lemon Lavender Rack of Lamb

Lavender adds luscious flavor to this simple lamb preparation.

1 1/2 cups fresh lemon juice
2 tablespoons dried lavender or
   rosemary
6 garlic cloves, minced
Salt and freshly ground pepper
   to taste

3/4 cup olive oil
2 racks of lamb, double cut
   (2 chops per person)

Combine the lemon juice, lavender, garlic, salt, and pepper in a bowl and mix well. Whisk in the olive oil. Pour over the lamb in two 1-gallon resealable plastic bags. Seal tightly. Marinate in the refrigerator for 6 hours, or preferably overnight, turning occasionally; drain.

   Prepare the grill. Grill the lamb over medium to medium-low coals for 16 to 18 minutes or until an instant-read thermometer registers 145 degrees for medium-rare. Transfer the lamb to a serving platter.

Serves 8

PORK TENDERLOIN WITH APRICOT GINGER SAUCE

*A combination of sweet and spicy flavors
complements this pork tenderloin.*

Spice Rub
1 1/2 tablespoons curry powder
1 1/2 tablespoons ground cumin
1 tablespoon ground ginger
1 teaspoon salt
1 teaspoon freshly ground black
   pepper
1/2 teaspoon cayenne pepper

Pork
2 (16-ounce) pork tenderloins
Olive oil
Apricot Ginger Sauce

Combine the Spice Rub ingredients in a bowl and mix well.

Prepare the grill for indirect medium heat. Brush the tenderloins with olive oil and pat approximately 2 tablespoons of the rub over the surface of each. Arrange the tenderloins on the grill rack and close the lid.

Grill, turning occasionally, for 20 to 25 minutes or until a meat thermometer registers 145 degrees. Remove the tenderloins to a platter and tent with foil. Let rest for 10 minutes. Slice the tenderloins and arrange on a serving platter. Drizzle with the Apricot Ginger Sauce.

Serves 6

APRICOT GINGER SAUCE

An excellent sauce for pork, egg rolls, and won tons.

20 California dried apricots
1 (11-ounce) can apricot nectar
3/4 cup sugar
1/2 cup white vinegar
1/2 cup water

1 1/2 tablespoons minced fresh
   ginger
1 1/2 teaspoons Asian chili sauce
   (Sriracha brand preferred)

Combine all ingredients in a saucepan and mix well. Bring just to a boil; reduce heat. Simmer, covered, for 30 minutes, stirring occasionally. Process the sauce in a blender until smooth.

Note: Avoid using Turkish dried apricots in this recipe, as they lack flavor.

Makes 3 1/2 cups

Apricots

A rose is a rose . . . or is it? The apricot, a member of the rose family, originated in Asia and made its way to California via Spanish missionaries in the 1700s. Of the two hundred thousand tons of apricots grown in the United States annually, more than 95 percent are California grown. Stanislaus is the most apricot-prolific county in the state. Fresh apricots with their dense, sweet flavor are ideal for use in desserts and preserves. An excellent source of iron when dried, they are wonderful in cookies, granola, or as a substitute for fresh apricots in many recipes. Through the use of grafting, apricot hybrids are now available, including plumcots, a cross between an apricot and a plum; pluots, a cross between an apricot and a plumcot; and apriums, a cross between a pluot and a plum. The season for apricots begins in May and runs through mid-July.

Cinco de Mayo

Cinco de Mayo, celebrated each spring on May 5, commemorates the defeat of the French Army by the Mexicans at the Battle of Puebla on May 5, 1862. It is more commonly celebrated north of the border than in Mexico, with the largest celebrations taking place in those U.S. cities with significant Mexican populations and cultural heritage. Northern California is just such a place. From San Jose to Santa Rosa, Cinco de Mayo festivities include parades, food, music, and customs unique to Mexico and its heritage. It is often the first time in spring that the grill is hot and so are the fajitas, spicy salsas, and other delectable Mexican dishes that take center stage. *¡Viva México!*

HALIBUT WITH THREE-CITRUS MARINADE

While Californians treasure their outdoor grills, this fish can be broiled in the oven as well. Garnish with sprigs of cilantro.

1/2 cup fresh lime juice
  (about 5 limes)
1/2 cup fresh lemon juice
  (about 3 lemons)
1/2 cup fresh orange juice
  (about 2 oranges)
1/2 cup olive oil

1/4 cup chopped fresh cilantro
5 garlic cloves, minced
2 teaspoons coarsely ground pepper
3 bay leaves, broken in half
Salt to taste
4 (1- to 1 1/2-inch thick) halibut
  steaks

Combine the lime juice, lemon juice, orange juice, olive oil, cilantro, garlic, pepper, bay leaves, and salt in a bowl and mix well. Let stand at room temperature for 30 minutes to allow the flavors to marry. Reserve half the marinade at room temperature, removing bay leaves.

Arrange the halibut in a dish. Pour the remaining marinade over the fish, turning to coat. Marinate, refrigerated, for up to 30 minutes, turning once; drain.

Prepare the grill. Arrange the fish on a lightly oiled grill rack over medium heat. Grill for 10 to 12 minutes or until the fish flakes easily, turning halfway through the grilling process. Serve immediately with the reserved marinade.

Serves 4

SALMON WITH FRESH DILL BUTTER

Wild spring salmon is much admired for its texture and flavor.

Fresh Dill Butter
1/2 cup (1 stick) unsalted butter,
  softened
Finely chopped zest of 1/2 lemon
1 tablespoon finely chopped fresh
  parsley
1 tablespoon chopped fresh dill
1/2 teaspoon salt
1/2 teaspoon white pepper

Salmon
4 salmon steaks or fillets
Olive oil
Salt and freshly ground pepper
  to taste
2 lemons, thinly sliced
8 sprigs of parsley

Combine the Fresh Dill Butter ingredients in a bowl and mix well. Shape into a log, 1 inch in diameter, and wrap in waxed paper. Chill until serving time.

Preheat the oven to 350 degrees or prepare the grill for medium indirect heat. Rub both sides of the fish with olive oil and sprinkle with salt and pepper. Place 2 to 3 lemon slices and 2 sprigs of parsley on the top of each piece. Wrap each loosely with foil; do not seal foil if grilling.

Bake or grill for 10 minutes per inch of thickness or until the fish flakes easily. Remove the fish from the foil and arrange on a serving platter. Immediately top each salmon steak with 1 or 2 slices of the Fresh Dill Butter. The butter will melt and spread over the top of the salmon.

Serves 4

Golden Gate
SALMON

The richest marine region on the Pacific Coast from Mexico to Alaska lies along San Francisco's coast, and salmon is king of these waters. This unique environment is created by an underwater shelf that extends about twenty-five miles out to sea before dropping off to deep trenches. In the spring, the shallow area concentrates a swell of cold, mineral-rich waters, which when combined with sunlight causes a bloom of growth of tiny aquatic organisms called plankton. Huge numbers of shrimp, herring, squid, and anchovies feed on the plankton, only to be quickly consumed by the hungry salmon. This is the only portion of the Pacific Coast where salmon can be found year-round. Deep-sea-fishing trips run regularly from several points around the Bay, and there is nothing tastier than eating freshly caught salmon.

Cut Flowers
& FOLIAGE

Fragrant bouquets of elegant pink tulips, dramatic stargazer lilies, regal purple iris, pristine white stock, and deep green foliage celebrate the arrival of spring across the country. Much of this foliage is produced in California, where more than 60 percent of all domestically grown, commercially sold cut flowers and foliage originate. Over four hundred California growers market cut flowers and foliage valued at nearly 309 million dollars annually. In Northern California, San Mateo, Monterey, and Santa Cruz Counties are the most prolific growing areas. The state's dominance is due to its favorable climate allowing for year-round production. Many cut flowers can be successfully dry-stored at near-freezing temperatures for several days, slowing down the natural maturing process and allowing flowers to be transported successfully to floral marts and homes across the country.

SAUTÉED SUGAR SNAP PEAS

Sugar snap peas, with their crunchy edible pods, are sweet and pleasing to the eye. Substitute French green beans or snow peas if sugar snap peas are not available.

1 tablespoon butter
6 ounces sugar snap peas, stems and strings removed
Juice of 1/2 lemon
Salt and freshly ground pepper to taste
Zest of 1 lemon

Melt the butter in a skillet over medium heat. Add the peas. Sauté for 3 to 5 minutes or until the peas turn bright green. Test a snap pea for desired doneness. Just before serving, stir in the lemon juice, salt, and pepper. Transfer to a serving bowl and top with the lemon zest.

Serves 4

ROSEMARY REDS

Prepare plenty of these—they are irresistible!

2 to 4 tablespoons olive oil
12 medium red potatoes, cut into quarters
6 garlic cloves, peeled
2 or 3 sprigs of rosemary, stems removed, finely chopped
Kosher salt and coarsely ground pepper to taste

Preheat the oven to 400 degrees. Pour the olive oil into a 10- × 15-inch baking dish. Add the potatoes, garlic, rosemary, kosher salt, and pepper and toss to coat. Spread the potatoes in a single layer.

Roast for 45 minutes or until brown and tender, stirring frequently. Transfer to a serving bowl. Serve immediately.

Serves 4 to 6

Morning Sun
HERB FARM

Nestled in an historic walnut orchard, Morning Sun Herb Farm is a rural oasis located just west of sprawling Vacaville. The farm features beautiful demonstration gardens perfect for a stroll, and a gift shop with herb-related products. The farm boasts over five hundred varieties of herbs, perennials, and vegetables. In the spring, choose from nearly thirty varieties of tomatoes and twelve varieties of pepper seedlings. Morning Sun also produces an extensive plant catalog and sells plants by mail, fax, and phone. Herbal gardening workshops are offered free of charge on weekends. Morning Sun offers a variety of classes on topics that include wreath making, herbal medicine, papermaking, and soap casting.

Risotto

Risotto dishes are as varied as the cook's imagination. Good wine and stock are as important to the preparation as the seafood, vegetables, or herbs added at the end. Use a wine good enough to drink, but save the best bottle for dinner. Homemade or gourmet stock will greatly enhance the flavor of the risotto, as it is much richer in flavor than the more common canned broth. Stock is added to the risotto mixture just a little at a time so the rice is never completely submerged, but always stays wet and bubbly. Risotto develops a thick, rich sauce when the rice swells and releases starch as the stock is absorbed. Take time with this process to create a rich and flavorful risotto.

ASPARAGUS & BELL PEPPER RISOTTO

This beautiful, hearty dish may be served as a side dish or as an entrée.

1 bunch asparagus, woody ends removed
4 to 5 cups chicken stock
1/2 cup dry white wine
1/4 cup (1/2 stick) unsalted butter
2 tablespoons olive oil
2 medium shallots, finely chopped
2 red bell peppers, chopped

1 orange or yellow bell pepper, chopped
1 cup arborio rice
1 cup freshly grated Parmigiano-Reggiano cheese (aged Parmesan)
1/2 teaspoon fresh thyme leaves

Cut the asparagus spears into 1/2-inch pieces. Steam until tender-crisp; cool. Bring the stock and wine to a simmer in separate saucepans or microwave in microwave-safe bowls.

Heat the butter and olive oil in a heavy 3-quart saucepan over medium-high heat. Add the shallots and sauté for 2 to 3 minutes. Stir in the bell peppers and sauté for 1 minute. Stir in the rice. Sauté for 2 minutes or until the rice begins to stick to the bottom of the pan. Add the wine gradually to the center of the saucepan, stirring constantly; an opaque sauce should form within a few seconds.

Cook until the wine is absorbed, stirring constantly. Pour 1/2 cup of the stock into the center of the saucepan. Cook until the liquid has been absorbed, stirring constantly. Continue to add the stock in the same manner in 1/2-cup increments over a period of 12 to 13 minutes, using a total of 4 to 5 cups of stock and stirring constantly. Test the rice for doneness when the stock is almost used up; the rice should be al dente. If not, continue cooking and stirring, adding stock or water. Test again in 30 seconds. At the end of the cooking process the rice should have a saucy consistency. If not, stir in additional stock or water. Remove from the heat. Stir in the asparagus, cheese, and thyme. Serve immediately.

Note: To create an entrée, add 2 ounces thinly sliced prosciutto with the shallots.

Serves 4 to 6

ARRAY OF SPRING VEGETABLES

A delicately flavored, low-calorie side dish perfect for spring.

4 quarts water
1 teaspoon salt
1/2 pound yellow squash, sliced
   diagonally
4 large carrots, peeled, sliced
   diagonally
1 bunch asparagus, woody ends
   removed, cut into 1 1/2-inch
   pieces

3 tablespoons grapeseed oil
1 pound fresh shiitake
   mushrooms, stems removed,
   caps sliced
3 shallots, minced
Kosher salt and freshly ground
   pepper to taste

Bring the water to a boil in a 6-quart pan. Stir in salt. Prepare a large bowl of ice water in which to shock the blanched vegetables and place it near the stove.

Blanch the vegetables separately in the boiling water, beginning with the lighter colored vegetables and ending with the asparagus. Blanch the yellow squash for 10 to 20 seconds. Remove with a Chinese strainer or slotted spoon and shock in the ice water. Remove from the ice water when the squash is cool to the touch. Drain and set aside. Repeat the process with the carrots and asparagus, blanching the carrots for 30 to 60 seconds depending on the thickness of the carrot slices, and blanching the asparagus for 10 seconds. Plunge each into the ice water and remove when cool to the touch; drain.

Heat a large sauté pan or wok over medium-high heat. Add 2 tablespoons of the grapeseed oil, then the mushrooms and sauté until golden brown. Transfer the mushrooms with a slotted spoon to a bowl. Add the remaining 1 tablespoon grapeseed oil and the shallots. Sauté for 1 minute. Add the squash, carrots, and asparagus. Sauté until the vegetables are heated through and tender but not soft. Stir in the mushrooms and sauté for 1 minute or until the mushrooms are heated through. Season with kosher salt and pepper to taste. Serve immediately.

Serves 8

Forni-Brown-Welsh Farms

In 1978, Lynn Brown, a ranch hand with a passion for gardening, was delivering some of his homegrown produce to a local grocer. The quality and variety caught the eye of a gourmet chef who followed Mr. Brown to his backyard garden and proclaimed, "I'll take everything you've got." Today, Forni-Brown-Welsh Farms in Calistoga is a producer of rare and exotic organic herbs and vegetables served in the finest restaurants throughout the Napa Valley and Bay Area. During three marvelous weekends in April, the farm opens to the public for its annual plant sale. Green thumbs can choose from the nearly one hundred different plant varieties the farm grows from seed. Everything from the rare *fraise des bois* (albino strawberry) to over forty different types of tomatoes is available for sale, with prices ranging from one to four dollars per plant. To further enhance the experience, partners Peter Forni, Lynn Brown, and Barney Welsh are on hand to dispense planting and growing tips.

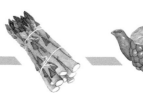

Strawberries

Poet W.B. Yeats said of strawberries, "Doubtless God could have made a better berry, but doubtless God never did." In provincial times, the French regarded strawberries as an aphrodisiac, and traditionally served a strawberry soup to newlyweds. The Victorians used the image of the strawberry to symbolize "absolute perfection." California's soil and moderate coastal climate are absolute perfection for growing this beautiful fruit, which is not really a fruit at all. In the true botanical sense, strawberries are members of the rose family and grew wild for centuries in both America and Europe. Here in the northern part of California, the chief strawberry growing regions are Watsonville and Salinas in Monterey County. Harvest in these areas begins in late February and runs through mid-November, peaking in April, May, and June. At the end of the peak harvest season each summer, the folks in Watsonville celebrate at the annual Strawberry Festival. There is a strawberry pie eating contest, gourmet food, topnotch entertainment, and lots of activities for the kids.

A strawberry's flavor is determined by the growing conditions, ripeness when harvested, and variety of fruit grown. Size does not influence the taste. Strawberries are an excellent source of vitamin C, folic acid, potassium, iron, and fiber, and contain only sixty calories per cup. Do not rinse strawberries until ready to use. These delicate fruits, green caps intact, can be refrigerated for up to four days in a large airtight container with a dry paper towel at the bottom; separate layers of berries with additional paper towels. Rinse just before using, with stems and caps attached, using a gently spray of cool water. Remove the green caps and stems after rinsing.

Pick-your-own places are very popular with locals, and Brentwood, California is the area's capital for u-pick farms. With thirty-eight farms representing nearly thirty different commodities and crops, the popularity of this pastime is evident. For those who have never picked produce from the vine, strawberries are an easy u-pick fruit for beginners. There are no prickly thorns, as with blackberry bushes, and choosing the ripest berries is as simple as seeing red. Strawberries never ripen after being picked, so choose brightly colored, plump berries without white "shoulders" and be sure to pluck the berry with its green cap attached. Strawberry picking season in Brentwood runs from mid-April through the end of July. For those less adventurous, there are plenty of flats available for purchase that have already been picked.

Photo Opposite: Strawberries, Jack London Square Farmers' Market, Oakland, California

STRAWBERRY SHORTCAKE

A classic Chez Panisse dessert.

> 2 cups flour
> 1/2 teaspoon salt
> 1 tablespoon baking powder
> 6 tablespoons sugar, divided
> 1/2 cup unsalted butter
> 3/4 cup plus 2 tablespoons heavy cream
> 4 pints fresh strawberries, washed, hulled
> Crème Chantilly (3 cups heavy cream whipped with 3 tablespoons sugar and 1 1/2 teaspoons vanilla extract)

Preheat the oven to 425 degrees. Mix the flour, salt, baking powder and 2 tablespoons sugar. Using a pastry blender, cut in the butter until the mixture looks like cornmeal with a few larger pieces of butter in it. Mix in 3/4 cup heavy cream, just until most of the dry mixture has been moistened. Turn out on a board and knead a few times until the dough just comes together. Roll 1/2-inch thick and cut into 12 squares or circles. Place on a baking sheet. Brush the tops with the remaining 2 tablespoons heavy cream and bake for 10 to 12 minutes or until the tops are lightly browned and the dough is set. Cool on a rack and serve while warm. Crush 1 pint of berries and slice the rest in with them. Toss with 4 tablespoons sugar or to taste and chill until serving time. Split the shortcakes and spoon the berries liberally over the bottom halves. Set the tops on and top with Crème Chantilly.

Serves 12

Strawberries

California is by far the nation's top producer of strawberries. In fact, nearly 84 percent of the country's strawberries are produced here—1 1/2 billion pounds per year. Statewide more than forty-eight thousand people are employed in producing and harvesting this beautiful and delicious fruit. If all the California strawberries produced in one year were laid in a row, they would circle the world fifteen times. This amount would also provide every household in the United States with twelve pints of strawberries. Strawberries are the nation's fourth most valuable fruit crop. California's strawberry harvest is worth about 785 million dollars annually.

CHOCOLATE-DIPPED STRAWBERRIES

This chocolate glaze is also wonderful on other fruits, as a topping for ice cream, or warmed for fondue.

2 pounds fresh strawberries with fresh green tops (about 30 medium berries)
8 ounces bittersweet or semisweet chocolate, cut into pieces

1/2 cup (1 stick) unsalted butter
5 teaspoons water
1 tablespoon light corn syrup

Rinse each strawberry gently under running water. Dry each strawberry thoroughly and arrange on a clean tea towel. Any moisture left on the strawberries will affect the dipping process. Chill in the refrigerator.

Fill the bottom of a double boiler or saucepan with 2 inches of water and bring to a simmer. Combine the chocolate, butter, water, and corn syrup in the top of the double boiler or in a small metal bowl that will sit above the water. Heat the chocolate mixture above the simmering water until perfectly smooth, stirring occasionally. Do not allow the water to boil. Remove the mixture and let stand to cool until an instant-read thermometer registers 90 to 92 degrees; stir occasionally.

Dip the chilled strawberries into the chocolate glaze at a slight angle. Gently shake off the excess and lightly scrape the underside of each strawberry on the edge of the bowl. Arrange on a chilled, waxed paper-lined platter. Chill until serving time.

Note: To store leftover chocolate glaze, place a piece of plastic on the surface of the glaze and refrigerate for up to two weeks. Reheat the glaze in the top of a double boiler.

Makes 30 strawberries

Garden Tea

As the pace of life moves ever more quickly, passing down a time honored tradition such as afternoon tea is even more important. Step outdoors, set the table with style and whimsy, and relax in a comfortable chair. Delight in the garden's fresh scent and share the sweets and savories of tea with a new generation.

Parmesan Poppy Seed Twists 23
Tapenade, Tomato & Basil Crostini 24
Smoked Salmon Tea Sandwiches 25

•

Orange Currant Scones 22
Lemon Curd 55

•

Chocolate-Dipped Strawberries 52
Apricot Shortbread with Almonds 159

Chocolate-Dipped Strawberries

WINE PAIRING BY
wine.com

A vibrant, crisp Riesling from the Anderson Valley, such as Nalle Winery or Greenwood Ridge Vineyards

•

Black Currant Tea
Jasmine Tea
Lemon Ginger Herb Tea

Often referred to as dessert in a glass, riesling is perhaps the world's most misunderstood white grape variety. Yet, many think it is the world's finest. Rieslings range in style from the crystalline purity of Germany's Mosel River Valley to gloriously sweet dessert wines with every conceivable stopping point in between.

Jelly Belly
JELLY BEANS

Kids are not the only ones who enjoy the Herman Goelitz Candy Company, makers of Jelly Belly Jelly Beans. The Goelitz Candy Company has been making candy since 1869. In 1976, Jelly Bellys were introduced and candy history was made. Jelly Bellys' popularity was sealed when President Ronald Reagan served red cherry, white coconut, and blueberry Jelly Bellys at his inaugural ball. The Fairfield, California, factory offers free tours where one can get a bird's-eye view of the complete Jelly Belly-making process. Visit the Jelly Belly Café for Jelly Belly-shaped pizzas and hamburgers and Jelly Belly-flavored ice cream. Browse the factory store for Jelly Belly Beanware and purchase the newest Jelly Belly rookie flavors, as well as 150 other Goelitz confections.

For kicks, try popping two lemon, a raspberry, and a strawberry cheesecake Jelly Belly to simulate the flavors found in this Caramelized Lemon Tart with Fresh Raspberry Sauce.

CARAMELIZED LEMON TART

Serve this exquisite tart with Fresh Raspberry Sauce for a truly special presentation.

Tart Shell
2 cups less 2 tablespoons flour
1/3 cup sugar
Grated zest of 1 small lemon
10 tablespoons unsalted butter, cut into 1/2-inch pieces, chilled
2 egg yolks
2 to 3 teaspoons ice water

Filling
6 eggs
1 cup plus 2 tablespoons sugar
6 tablespoons unsalted butter, cut into pieces, softened
3/4 cup fresh lemon juice (if using Meyer lemons, increase to 1 cup)
1/3 cup heavy cream

Garnish and Assembly
1/3 cup packed light brown sugar
Confectioners' sugar
Fresh Raspberry Sauce (see page 55)
Sprigs of fresh mint

For the shell, combine the flour, sugar, and lemon zest in a food processor. Pulse to blend. Add the butter and pulse until crumbly. Add the egg yolks one at a time, processing until blended. Add the water one teaspoon at a time, processing constantly until the dough forms a ball. Be careful not to over-process. Shape the pastry into a disc and wrap with plastic wrap. Chill for 30 to 60 minutes.

Preheat the oven to 325 degrees. Roll the pastry on a lightly floured surface to fit an 11-inch fluted tart pan with removable rim. Fit the pastry into the tart pan. Chill, covered, for 1 hour. Line the pastry with foil. Prick the pastry all over through the foil with a fork.

Bake in the lower third of the oven for 20 minutes. Discard the foil. Bake for 10 to 15 minutes longer or until golden brown. Cool in the pan on a wire rack. Maintain the oven temperature.

For the filling, whisk the eggs in a saucepan until blended. Whisk in the sugar. Stir in the butter. Add the lemon juice and heavy cream and mix well. Place over medium heat for 8 minutes or until thickened, whisking constantly. Whisking is essential as the mixture will curdle if allowed to get too hot. Pour the filling into the cooled tart shell. Bake for 15 to 20 minutes or until set. Cool on a wire rack.

One hour before serving, press the brown sugar through a wire mesh strainer to distribute it evenly over the tart. Broil until caramelized. Let stand until cool. Sprinkle with confectioners' sugar.

To assemble, spoon some of the Fresh Raspberry Sauce on each of twelve dessert plates. Arrange a slice of the tart on top of the sauce. Garnish with sprigs of mint.

Serves 12

FRESH RASPBERRY SAUCE

*This sauce is a delicious and beautiful addition to fruit
and chocolate desserts.*

4 cups fresh raspberries
1/2 cup pure raspberry preserves
1 tablespoon fresh lemon juice
1 tablespoon framboise (raspberry brandy)
Superfine sugar to taste

Combine the raspberries, preserves, and lemon juice in a food processor. Process until puréed. Strain into a bowl, discarding the seeds. Stir in the brandy and superfine sugar.

Makes 4 cups

LEMON CURD

*A beautiful fruit topping, tart filling, or pastry spread to
use year-round. Lemon curd is traditionally served at tea
with scones and Devonshire cream.*

4 eggs plus 4 egg yolks
1 1/2 cups sugar (reduce to 1 cup if using Meyer lemons)
1 cup fresh lemon juice
Grated zest of 6 lemons
1/2 cup (1 stick) unsalted butter, cut into pieces

Whisk the eggs and egg yolks lightly in a saucepan. Add the sugar, lemon juice, and lemon zest, whisking until mixed. Cook over medium heat until warm, stirring with a wooden spoon. Add the butter. Cook, stirring constantly, until thickened and the sauce thickly coats the back of the wooden spoon. Whisk if necessary to keep the mixture smooth.

Remove from heat and immediately strain into a bowl, discarding the zest and any curdled bits. Whisk the lemon curd lightly and carefully set the bowl in a larger bowl of ice water. Let stand until lukewarm, stirring occasionally to speed the cooling process.

Press a piece of plastic wrap onto the surface of the curd to prevent a skin from forming. Chill in the refrigerator until serving time. Do not overstir when using the curd, as it may become too thin.

Makes 4 cups

Lemon Curd

Lemon curd has many uses. Spread it between layers of a white cake. Fold it into whipped cream and use as a topping for berries, shortbread, or cake. Dip a warm scone into it. Fill a prebaked piecrust with lemon curd and top with meringue. Fill prebaked tartlet shells and top each with a raspberry. Or use it as a layer in fresh berry trifle.

If Meyer lemons are available, use them for the most delicious curd ever! Buy extra lemons and freeze the zest and juice for later use.

For those who enjoy canning, lemon curd makes an excellent hostess gift or a great pantry item for quick desserts. The recipe may be successfully doubled or tripled. And, because lemons are available year-round, the canning may be done during the cool months. Process half-pint jars in boiling water for ten minutes. The processing heat makes the curd a bit grainy, but it smoothes out when stirred.

Bing Cherries

Northern California's San Joaquin and Santa Clara Valleys have the perfect combination of rich soil, sunny days, and mild nights to enhance the production of delicious Bing cherries. These cherries are prized for their distinctive deep mahogany color, small stone, and flavorful, sweet taste. Harvest time for California Bings is just four short weeks every year, from mid-May to mid-June.

Not only are Bing cherries tasty, they are also high in potassium, vitamin C, and vitamin B complex. They contain antioxidants that can help prevent cancer and heart disease. Cherries can be enjoyed as a healthy snack by themselves, as part of a temptingly sweet dessert, or as an accompaniment to poultry, game, and meats.

CHOCOLATE POUND CAKE

This tastes like a rich, moist brownie—chocolate heaven!

3 cups sugar
2 cups flour
1 cup unsweetened cocoa
1 tablespoon baking powder
1/2 teaspoon salt
13/4 cups milk, divided

1 cup (2 sticks) butter, cut into
  pieces, softened
3 eggs
1 tablespoon vanilla extract
Cherries & Berries Compote
Confectioners' sugar (optional)

Preheat the oven to 325 degrees. Lightly butter and flour a bundt or tube pan. Combine the sugar, flour, cocoa, baking powder, and salt in a mixing bowl and mix well. Add 11/2 cups milk and butter. Beat until blended, scraping the bowl occasionally. Mix together the eggs, 1/4 cup milk, and vanilla and stir into the batter.

Pour the batter into the prepared pan. Bake for 11/4 to 11/2 hours or until a wooden pick inserted near the center comes out clean. Cool in the pan on a wire rack for 1 hour; do not invert. Remove to a cake plate. Top each serving with Cherries & Berries Compote and whipped cream, or sprinkle with confectioners' sugar.

Serves 12

CHERRIES & BERRIES COMPOTE

Beautiful when served alone or atop cake, brownies, or lemon bread.

Compote
1 pound assorted fresh or
  frozen berries (blackberries,
  raspberries, purple grapes, black
  cherries, and/or strawberry
  halves)
1/3 cup superfine sugar
Framboise (raspberry brandy)
  to taste

Whipped Cream
11/2 cups whipping cream
2 tablespoons superfine sugar

Edible flowers for garnish
  (optional)

Combine the berries, 1/3 cup sugar, and brandy in a bowl and toss gently. Chill, covered, for 2 hours or longer. Beat the whipping cream in a mixing bowl until soft peaks form. Add 2 tablespoons sugar and mix well.

Spoon the berry mixture into compote bowls or footed sherbet glasses and top with a dollop of the whipped cream. Garnish with edible flowers.

Serves 12

TOASTED ALMOND BISCOTTI

These cookies travel well, and when packaged in cellophane with a pretty bow, they make a wonderful hostess gift.

2 cups flour
1 cup sugar
1 teaspoon baking powder
1/8 teaspoon salt
3 eggs

2 tablespoons amaretto
1 teaspoon vanilla extract
1 teaspoon anise extract (optional)
1 cup whole almonds, toasted,
   chopped

Preheat the oven to 300 degrees. Position an oven rack in the middle of the oven. Grease and flour a cookie sheet or line with baking parchment.

Combine the flour, sugar, baking powder, and salt in a bowl and mix well. Whisk the eggs, amaretto, and flavorings in a large bowl until blended. Stir the flour mixture into the egg mixture. Fold in the almonds. The dough will be thick and sticky. With floured hands, shape the dough into a long, flat 5- × 10-inch loaf on the prepared cookie sheet.

Bake for 50 minutes or until firm and dry. Let cool for 10 minutes. Transfer the loaf carefully to a cutting board and cut diagonally into 1/2-inch slices with a long, serrated knife. Arrange the slices cut side down on the cookie sheet. Bake for 20 minutes; turn. Bake for 10 to 15 minutes longer or until golden brown. Cool on the cookie sheet on a wire rack. Store in an airtight container.

Makes 20 biscotti

LEMON, ANISE & WALNUT BISCOTTI

This is a delicious cookie for tea or dessert.

3 2/3 cups unbleached flour
1/2 teaspoon baking powder
1/4 teaspoon baking soda
2 eggs plus 1 egg yolk
1 1/3 cups sugar
1/2 cup (1 stick) unsalted butter,
   melted, slightly cooled

1 tablespoon anise seeds
4 teaspoons grated lemon zest
1/2 teaspoon anise extract
2 cups walnut pieces, lightly
   toasted, cooled

Preheat the oven to 375 degrees. Line a cookie sheet with baking parchment. Combine the flour, baking powder, and baking soda in a bowl and mix well.

Whisk the eggs, egg yolk, and sugar in a large bowl until smooth. Add the butter and anise seeds and mix well. Stir in the lemon zest and anise extract. Add the flour mixture and stir until a smooth dough forms. Stir in the walnuts. Shape the dough into two 14-inch logs and arrange on the prepared cookie sheet. Flatten the tops of the logs slightly.

Bake for 30 minutes or until light brown. Let cool for 20 minutes. Cut the logs diagonally into 1/2-inch slices. Arrange the slices on the cookie sheet. Reduce the oven temperature to 325 degrees. Bake for 15 minutes or until golden brown, turning the slices over halfway through the baking process. Remove to a wire rack to cool. Store in an airtight container.

Makes 4 dozen biscotti

PacBell Park

Baseball has found a home within the city limits. In an area of the city known as China Basin, the San Francisco Giants are playing ball in one of the most spectacular ballparks in the country. PacBell Park is a brick-faced, open-air stadium located on a thirteen-acre site on the shores of San Francisco Bay. The three-hundred-million-dollar project opened on April 11, 2000, just twenty-eight months after breaking ground, to a sold-out crowd of over forty thousand fans.

The retro ballpark has something for everyone. There is a play area for the kids featuring an eighty-foot Coca-Cola bottle built as a play structure and slide, a twenty-six-foot-high baseball glove, and a miniature field where children can actually run the bases. The incredible gourmet food and views of the Bay, Golden Gate Bridge, and the hills of Marin and Alameda Counties make a day at the ballpark a memory of a lifetime. Spectators may even be so lucky as to see a home run ball hit to right field drop over the wall and into the Bay!

Summer

Summer

At dawn the sprinklers sputter on to water the lawn and garden with its cheerful impatiens and petunias. Depending on the day's destination, Northern Californians layer up for a foggy morning jog in Golden Gate Park or a sizzling afternoon boating on the Delta. Summer beckons visitors to the piney shores of Lake Tahoe and to the grandeur of Yosemite. In Carmel, children play in the surf as their family enjoys a gourmet picnic on the shores of Carmel River State Beach. Closer to home, Bay Area locals enjoy hiking and biking on the golden hills of Mt. Diablo and in the redwood stands of Muir Woods. At the end of a perfect day, friends gather to grill the freshest vegetables from the farmers' market along with the catch-of-the-day, and dine poolside in flickering candlelight. The sun sets in the west casting rays in tangerine hues, and we raise a glass to another day in paradise.

SUMMER RECIPES

Honeydew Melon

Nothing tastes more like summer than sweet, juicy honeydew melons. California leads the nation in honeydew melon production with a harvest season that runs from June through November. Most melons are grown in the San Joaquin Valley, where the long, frost-free growing season, combined with plenty of sunshine and low humidity, make it ideal for melon growing.

The honeydew is a member of the Muskmelon family and has been prized for thousands of years. It was enjoyed by the ancient Egyptians and is thought to have originated in Persia. A smooth creamy-white rind and bright green flesh distinguish the oval shaped honeydew. It ranges in weight from four to eight pounds. When choosing honeydew, look for a melon that is heavy for its size. Perfectly ripe honeydew will have a creamy-white rind with yellow accents, a slight waxy feel, a sweet heady aroma and a blossom-end that yields when pressed. Under-ripe melons can be ripened at room temperature. Refrigerate ripe melons up to five days. Fresh cut honeydew melons rapidly absorb odors, so store in an airtight container.

Stanislaus County in the California Central Valley is one of the leading counties in melon production. The annual Stanislaus County Fair was originally founded as the Turlock Melon Carnival in honor of the local melon industry and shipping business. The fairs lasted until World War II when the fairgrounds were needed for wartime purposes. The fair was started up again after the war and in 1956, the name was changed to the Stanislaus County Fair.

HONEYDEW MELON SALSA

This recipe was developed for Sonoma Dried Tomatoes by Ketchum Public Relations. It is easy to prepare and refreshing with chicken and fish.

>   *1/3 cup Sonoma Dried Tomato halves, julienned*
>   *1 cup (1/3-inch cubes) honeydew melon*
>   *2 navel oranges, cut into 1/3-inch pieces*
>   *3 tablespoons finely chopped red onion*
>   *1 1/2 tablespoons fresh lime juice*
>   *1 tablespoon finely chopped jalapeño chile*
>   *Salt to taste*

Combine the tomatoes with hot water to cover in a small bowl. Let stand for 10 minutes; drain. Combine the honeydew melon, oranges, onion, lime juice, and jalapeño chile in another bowl and mix well. Add the tomatoes and toss gently. Season with salt.

Makes 2 cups

Photo Opposite: Honeydew Melon, Crow Canyon Gardens, San Ramon, California

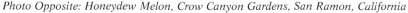

A Summer Shower

Whether the occasion is the arrival of a new baby or the upcoming wedding of dear friends, a very special get-together is in order. The centerpiece of this menu, Ahi Salad Niçoise, is sophisticated yet simple, and will create a memorable event that celebrates life's finest moments.

A California dry Rosé or blush wine, such as Bonny Doon Vineyard's Vin Gris de Cigare or Handley Cellar's Pinot Meunier Rosé

Lacy Cheese Wafers 87

•

Ahi Salad Niçoise 87
Sliced Baguettes

•

Honeydew Melon with Fresh Berries 65
Sour Cream Pound Cake 107

Why do wine buffs insist on using clear, stemmed, curvaceous glasses? Wine.com Senior Wine Merchant Jeff Prather explains: "Dozens of specialty glasses exist for all types of wine and spirits. One style, however, will suffice for almost any wine: a clear, stemmed, twelve-ounce vessel. Aside from this, the only other type of wineglass you need is a tall, slender flute to showcase the bubbles in sparkling wine. If you want to get finicky, glassware for white wine should have a tulip shape that tapers inward at the top to focus aromas, whereas red wine needs a deeper and bigger bowl to collect its bouquet."

Honeydew Melon with Fresh Berries

HONEYDEW MELON WITH FRESH BERRIES

When berries and melon are at the height of their flavor, a simple squeeze of lime is all it takes to create a beautiful and refreshing dessert.

1 large honeydew melon
3/4 cup fresh raspberries
3/4 cup fresh blackberries
3/4 cup fresh blueberries
Juice of 1 lime

Cut the honeydew melon into halves and remove the seeds. Slice each melon half into six wedges. Arrange two wedges on each serving plate.

Gently toss the raspberries, blackberries, and blueberries in a bowl. Divide the berries equally among the six plates. Drizzle with the lime juice.

Serves 6

Certified
FARMERS' MARKETS

It is a beautiful Saturday morning, the sun has barely risen, and already the local farmers' market is gearing up for the crush of eager customers. For many a family farmer, the more than 350 Certified Farmers' Markets in California represent not only a means of survival but also a chance to bask in the glow of some very appreciative customers. At these markets, only California-grown products may be sold, and no one is permitted to resell products purchased from other sources. Certified Farmers' Markets are "the real thing"—places where genuine farmers sell their own crops directly to the public. These markets typically offer the finest farm-fresh fruits and vegetables, as well as just-picked flowers, artisan breads and other baked goods, locally produced cheeses, and sometimes even freshly caught fish. In the Bay Area, some of the most popular and abundant markets on Saturdays include San Francisco Ferry Plaza, Danville, Pleasanton, and San Mateo, and on Sundays, Walnut Creek and Jack London Square in Oakland. While farmers' markets may represent a comforting return to a more relaxed, agrarian way of life, go early and bring a sturdy canvas bag—the best selections sell out quickly.

Cured Pork

Bacon is cut from the side of a pig and then cured and smoked. The fat on bacon is what provides the sweet flavor and tender crispness when it is cooked. Pancetta is an Italian bacon that is not smoked, but rather cured with salt and spices. Pancetta has a slightly salty taste. Tightly wrapped, it can be refrigerated up to three weeks or frozen for up to six months.

Ham is cut from a hog's hind leg. Fresh ham is unprocessed meat, but most hams are cured. There are three types of curing. With dry curing, the surface of the ham is salted and the meat is stored until the salt saturates it. Immersing ham in a sweet brine with seasonings is called sweet-pickle curing. When sugar is added, the ham is sugar-cured. Mass producers of ham commonly use injection curing, which involves injecting the ham with brine. Smoking takes place after the curing process to add flavor. Select a fresh ham that has a firm white layer of fat and a well-marbled lean portion. Select a cured ham that is firm and plump and finely grained. Prosciutto is an Italian ham that has been seasoned, salt-cured, and air-dried. Prosciutto has a firm, dense texture and is usually sliced very thin. Serve it as an appetizer or first course with melon or figs, or with vegetables in pasta and risotto recipes.

BREAKFAST PIZZA WITH PROSCIUTTO & EGG

Kimball Jones, Executive Chef at Wente Vineyards Restaurant, created this masterpiece.

2 tablespoons olive oil
2 small summer squash, finely diced
4 small tomatoes, peeled, seeded, diced (see note, page 99)
2 teaspoons chopped fresh chervil
1 teaspoon chopped fresh parsley
Salt and freshly ground pepper

Pizza Dough
1 1/2 tablespoons finely grated Parmesan cheese
4 ounces prosciutto, julienned
4 eggs
2 teaspoons Meyer lemon oil (optional)

Heat a sauté pan over high heat. Add the olive oil and then the squash. Remove from heat and toss the squash in the pan for 30 seconds. Transfer the squash to a bowl. Add the tomatoes, chervil, and parsley and mix well. Season with salt and pepper to taste and let stand for 5 minutes. Drain to remove any excess liquid.

Preheat the oven to 500 degrees. Roll or press each ball of Pizza Dough into a 7-inch round on a lightly floured surface. Arrange on oiled baking sheets. Spread equal amounts of the squash over the pizza rounds. Sprinkle with the cheese and top with the prosciutto. Fold and pinch the edges of the dough to form a rim. Crack one egg into the middle of each pizza.

Bake for 10 to 15 minutes or until the crust is golden brown and the eggs are set. Drizzle with the lemon oil and serve.

Serves 4

PIZZA DOUGH

Use this basic dough for all types of pizzas.

1 cup warm water
1 1/2 teaspoons dry yeast
1 1/2 teaspoons sugar

1 1/2 teaspoons salt
2 tablespoons olive oil
2 1/4 cups or more bread flour

Using a stand mixer, mix together the warm water, yeast, and sugar in the bowl with a paddle attachment. When dissolved, let stand for 10 minutes to activate the yeast. It will begin to bubble. If it does not, discard and start over with fresh yeast. Add the salt and olive oil and, mixing on low speed, add the flour in 1/2-cup increments until the dough begins to pull away from the side of the bowl. When fully incorporated, change from the paddle to the dough hook attachment and increase the speed to medium. Knead the dough for 10 minutes.

Place the dough in an oiled bowl and oil the surface of the dough. Let rise at room temperature for 1 to 1 1/2 hours, then punch down and form into rounds. Alternatively, cover with plastic and let rise slowly in the refrigerator for 2 or more hours. The dough may be frozen in individual resealable plastic bags. Defrost in the refrigerator for 3 to 4 hours before rolling out.

Makes 4 (7-inch) pizza crusts

BERRY CREAM CHEESE PUFF

When berries are not available, substitute other seasonal fruit in this breakfast treat.

1/4 cup (1/2 stick) butter
3/4 cup milk
3/4 cup flour
3 ounces cream cheese, softened
3 eggs
1 tablespoon sugar

1 1/2 cups sliced strawberries
1/2 cup blueberries
1/2 cup raspberries
1 tablespoon confectioners' sugar
1 cup sour cream (optional)
Maple syrup (optional)

Preheat the oven to 425 degrees. Select a shallow 2- or 3-quart baking pan or baking dish and add the butter. Place in the oven for 5 minutes or until the butter is melted.

Combine the milk, flour, cream cheese, eggs, and sugar in a food processor or blender. Process until smooth. Remove the baking pan from the oven and pour the batter into the baking pan. Bake for 25 to 30 minutes or until the batter puffs high and the edges are brown.

Combine the strawberries, blueberries, and raspberries in a bowl and toss gently. Top the warm puff with the berry mixture and sprinkle with confectioners' sugar. Cut into squares or wedges and serve with sour cream and warm maple syrup on the side.

Serves 4

Ahwahnee Hotel

Yosemite National Park is a favorite destination for those who appreciate nature and love the outdoors. Californians and visitors make their pilgrimage to the majestic Yosemite Valley to marvel at some of the most breathtaking scenery in the world. At day's end, for those who prefer more than a sleeping bag and a can of beans, there is the famous Ahwahnee Hotel in the heart of the valley. Built in 1927 to appeal to affluent visitors, the unique structure has twenty-five-foot ceilings in its great lounge and dining room, stained glass windows, a massive eight-foot-square fireplace with stone mantel, and, of course, exquisite service. Combining luxury and local cultural heritage, the Ahwahnee Hotel displays Native American basketry, linguistic symbols, decorative paintings, and mosaics throughout. The hotel was declared a National Monument in 1987 and is so popular that reservations are taken one year to the day in advance.

Gravenstein
APPLE FAIR

When the earliest-ripening apple varieties are ready for harvest in August each year, more than sixteen thousand people gather at Eagle Ranch Park in Sebastopol to celebrate at the Gravenstein Apple Fair. The fair began as the Sebastopol Apple Fair in the early 1900s but took a hiatus when World War II began. The fair was re-created in 1973 by the Sonoma County Farm Trails cooperative to fund the printing of its visitors' map and to promote Sebastopol apple growers.

Fair-goers look forward to sampling the "Bounty of the County" each year, including plenty of apple varieties, as well as Sonoma's world-renowned wines. Competitions in apple pie eating, applesauce eating, and apple juice drinking are highlights of the event. Visitors can observe working beehives, learn how goats are milked, watch sheepdogs at work, and see sheep being sheared. Few festival attendees leave the fair without purchasing some of Sonoma's wonderful homegrown and handcrafted products.

SANGRIA

A cool summer drink with pizzazz.

1/2 gallon red wine
1/2 cup Grand Marnier
1/2 cup brandy
1/3 cup sugar
1 unpeeled apple, thinly sliced

1 unpeeled orange, thinly sliced
1 unpeeled lemon, thinly sliced
1 quart club soda
Ice

Combine the wine, Grand Marnier, brandy, and sugar in a large pitcher and mix well. Add the apple, orange, and lemon. Chill, covered, for at least 2 hours to allow the flavors to blend. Stir in the club soda and ice just before serving.

Serves 10 to 12

PITA TRIANGLES WITH ROASTED RED PEPPER DIP

*These crisp pita wedges are a sophisticated substitute
for tortilla chips.*

1/4 cup (1/2 stick) butter
3 tablespoons chopped fresh herbs, such as oregano, basil, thyme,
    or rosemary, or 1 tablespoon dried herbs
6 pita bread rounds
Roasted Red Pepper Dip

Preheat the oven to 300 degrees. Melt the butter in a saucepan. Remove from heat and stir in the herbs.

Separate each pita into two rounds. Brush the smooth side with the butter mixture. Cut each round into six wedges and arrange them in a single layer on a baking sheet. Bake for 15 to 20 minutes or until crisp and golden brown. Thick pitas may take longer. Serve with Roasted Red Pepper Dip.

Makes 6 dozen

ROASTED RED PEPPER DIP

*This recipe uses roasted red peppers from a jar, making
it extremely easy to prepare.*

1 cup mayonnaise
1/4 cup chopped commercially prepared roasted red bell pepper
1 teaspoon chopped fresh basil
1 garlic clove, minced
1/2 cup sour cream

Combine the mayonnaise, roasted red bell pepper, basil, and garlic in a food processor or blender. Process until smooth. Stir in the sour cream. Chill, covered, in the refrigerator. May also be served with raw vegetables, on quesadillas, or as a spread for turkey sandwiches.

Makes 1 3/4 cups

Ikeda's

In Auburn, California, just off Interstate 80 before the foothills become the Sierra Mountains, Ikeda's is a traditional stop for many Bay Area families on their way to Lake Tahoe. From simple beginnings in 1970, Sally and Sam Ikeda have built a unique business around the farmers' market concept. Ikeda's is still "the place" to stop for great burgers and to pick up some excellent homegrown fruits and vegetables for the trip. In the 1980s, the Ikedas' sons expanded the business to include items such as strawberry-rhubarb pie, raspberry cobbler, and homemade tamales. Today, a wonderful assortment of fresh produce is available, along with Ikeda's Signature Family Sauces, all sorts of chips, breads, pickles, nuts, packaged pastas, olives, and mustards. Be sure to grab a made-to-order smoothie for the remaining hour-and-a-half trip to Lake Tahoe.

Tomatoes

It is believed that tomatoes were domesticated in Mexico, with the wild species originating in South America. The Spanish introduced the tomato to Europe, and it quickly became a staple of Italian and Mediterranean cuisine. However, France and Northern Europe took some time to warm to what the Italians called *pomodoro,* or golden apple. Thought to be poisonous by botanists at the time, the tomato plant was grown strictly as an ornamental until suspicion gave way to delight. The French named the fruit *pomme d'amour* (love apple) and declared it to have aphrodisiacal qualities. This fruit of summer was not widely used in the United States until the early twentieth century.

Tomatoes thrive in warm climates, making California an ideal growing environment. The state produces 90 percent of the tomatoes grown for processing and almost 50 percent of the fresh tomatoes available nationwide. Containing high amounts of water and fiber, a medium-sized raw tomato has less than thirty calories. Tomatoes are also a good source of vitamins A and C.

CALIFORNIA RANCHO BLACK BEAN SALSA

This spicy combination of ingredients travels well to picnics and backyard parties.

Dressing
1 cup vegetable oil
1/2 cup lime juice
1 canned chipotle chile or more
   to taste, minced
1 teaspoon ground cumin
3/4 teaspoon salt
1 garlic clove, minced

Salsa
2 (16-ounce) cans black beans,
   rinsed, drained
4 cups fresh corn kernels (see note)
1 red bell pepper, diced
3/4 cup diced red onion
1 large ripe tomato, diced
1 ripe avocado, diced
1/2 cup chopped fresh cilantro

Combine the dressing ingredients in a blender. Process until blended. Taste for seasonings, and adjust if necessary. The dressing should be tart and spicy.

Combine the beans, corn, bell pepper, and onion in a bowl and mix well. Add the dressing and toss to coat. Marinate, covered, at room temperature for at least 3 hours, stirring occasionally. Just before serving, stir in the tomato, avocado, and cilantro. Serve with tortilla chips.

Note: Fresh sweet corn may be used without cooking first.

Serves 16

BAJA GUACAMOLE

Try this version of guacamole with plenty of tortilla chips on hand.

3 ripe avocados, peeled, pitted
Juice of 1 lime
1 ripe medium tomato, diced
1/4 cup finely chopped fresh
   cilantro
1/4 cup finely chopped red onion

1/2 teaspoon minced garlic
2 tablespoons prepared green salsa,
   or 3 dashes of Tabasco sauce
1/2 to 1 teaspoon ground cumin
1/2 teaspoon sugar
Salt to taste

Mash the avocados in a bowl with a fork until slightly lumpy. Stir in the lime juice, tomato, cilantro, red onion, and garlic. Add the salsa or Tabasco sauce, cumin, sugar, and salt and mix well. Taste and adjust the seasonings, if necessary.

   Cover the bowl and chill or let stand at room temperature for 1 hour to allow the flavors to blend. Serve with tortilla chips.

Makes 3 cups

Mission District
MURALS

There is a unique display of art in San Francisco's Mission District. The Mission District Murals began in the 1970s as a city project and soon blossomed into a fantastic cultural display in the City's primarily Hispanic neighborhood. Fabulous murals painted on the walls of buildings by local artists are an attraction worth a special trip. Some of the murals are continually changing and growing, while others remain as pieces of San Francisco cultural art history. A virtual outdoor museum of about thirty of the incredibly colorful murals can be found on narrow Balmy Alley, located between 24th and 25th Streets, just south of Folsom Street. Maps outlining self-guided walks or guided tours are available through the Precita Eyes Mural Arts Center.

Ginger

Fresh ginger is a staple of Asian cuisine. Gingerroot, found in most markets, has a tough brown skin hiding the fresh pale meat inside. When using fresh ginger in a recipe, peel the outer skin with a paring knife or potato peeler. If mincing ginger, smash the peeled pieces with a cleaver and finely chop them with a chef's knife.

Gingerroot can be stored in the freezer and grated as needed while still frozen. It can also be peeled and stored in a jar of sherry in the refrigerator.

Ginger is a versatile plant that is easy to grow using gingerroot purchased at the local market. Buy fresh roots (rhizomes) in the early spring. Cut roots into one- to two-inch pieces, each with well-developed growth buds, and allow to dry for several days. Plant rhizomes in rich, moist soil and cover with one inch of soil. Keep plants moist but not soaked until top and root growth appear. Ginger goes dormant in winter and roots may rot in cold, wet soil. Feed plants once a month. After several months, roots should be large enough for harvest.

SATAY WITH THAI GINGER GLAZE

The versatile glaze can be used as a dipping sauce or as a sauce for grilled fish or poultry.

Thai Ginger Glaze
3/4 cup sugar
1/2 cup plus 1 tablespoon tamari (see note)
2 green onions, thinly sliced
2 tablespoons chopped fresh cilantro
1 teaspoon finely minced fresh ginger
1 teaspoon red pepper flakes
1 garlic clove, minced

Satay
64 bamboo skewers
4 boneless skinless chicken breasts
12 ounces flank steak
4 tablespoons olive oil, divided
Salt and freshly ground pepper to taste
1/2 cup sesame seeds, lightly toasted
Peanut Sauce (page 73)
Sprigs of fresh cilantro

Cover the bamboo skewers with water in a bowl. Let soak during the preparation of the satay.

Combine the glaze ingredients in a small heavy saucepan and mix well. Bring to a boil. Reduce heat and simmer for 5 minutes, stirring occasionally. Remove from heat and let stand until cool.

Starting at the breast tip end, slice the chicken diagonally into 1/4-inch-thick strips. Toss with 2 tablespoons olive oil, salt, and pepper in a bowl. Chill, covered, until ready to skewer.

Slice the flank steak against the grain into 1/4-inch-thick strips. Toss with the remaining 2 tablespoons olive oil, salt, and pepper in a bowl. Chill, covered, until ready to skewer.

Prepare the grill for medium heat. Divide the glaze into two equal portions, reserving half to use as dipping sauce. Skewer the chicken and beef on separate skewers, leaving a little room between the "loops" so that the chicken and beef will cook quickly. Grill until the chicken is firm to the touch and the beef is cooked as desired, basting with the glaze toward the end of the grilling process to avoid burning the sugar in the glaze.

Remove the skewers to a serving platter. Sprinkle with sesame seeds and scatter the cilantro over the top. Serve with the reserved Thai Ginger Glaze and Peanut Sauce in dipping bowls.

Note: Tamari, a thicker, more intensely flavored soy sauce, can be found in the International section of most large grocery stores.

Makes 64 skewers

PEANUT SAUCE

This sauce may be used for satay or over stir-fried meats and vegetables.

1/2 cup good-quality smooth
   old-fashioned peanut butter
1/3 cup soy sauce
3 tablespoons finely chopped fresh
   cilantro
3 tablespoons sugar

1 tablespoon minced garlic
1 tablespoon hot chile oil
1/2 teaspoon dry sherry
Lime juice to taste
Water or chicken stock (optional)

Combine the ingredients in a bowl and mix well. Let stand, covered, at room temperature for 1 hour to allow the flavors to develop. The sauce should have a balance of sweet, sour, salty, and hot flavors. Adjust the ingredients as needed to achieve this combination. Thin with water or stock if necessary.

Makes 11/2 cups

Snoopy's Gallery

Opened by the late, world-renowned comic strip creator Charles M. Schulz, Snoopy's Gallery & Gift Shop in Santa Rosa offers a wide variety of "Peanuts" merchandise, boasting the largest selection of Snoopy merchandise available in the world. The upstairs Gallery includes Schulz's first syndicated strip and memorabilia and awards for Charlie Brown and the gang.

Adjacent to the Gallery is the Redwood Empire Ice Arena built in 1969 by Mr. and Mrs. Schulz for their community. The Warm Puppy coffee shop, which was frequented by Schulz himself, is a great place to grab a bite to eat and watch the skaters through large picture windows.

In 2001, construction was completed on the Charles M. Schulz Museum and Research Center, the newest addition to the Peanuts complex. The museum serves to preserve, display, and interpret the art of Schulz with galleries, classrooms, an auditorium, and gardens.

PROSCIUTTO-WRAPPED FIGS WITH GOAT CHEESE

*This incredible recipe was shared by Private Chef Steven T. Smith
of Napa. The skewered figs are drizzled with Sapa,
a rich and flavorful wine sauce.*

Goat Cheese

In the past, handcrafted goat cheeses were a specialty item imported from European farms. Today, there are a number of goat cheesemakers in Northern California, including Laura Chenel, who went to France to learn cheese making in the late 1970s before returning to the Bay Area to set up shop in Sonoma. Her nationally recognized cheeses are sold in specialty food stores across the country. They are also served in the finest restaurants, including the Sonoma Mission Inn and Spa, and preferred by renowned chefs such as Bradley Ogden of the Lark Creek restaurants.

Goat cheese encompasses a wide range of styles from soft, mild, and fresh, to hard, aged types, and surface-ripened varieties. Some are specific to the cheesemaker, such as aged goat cheese wrapped in grape leaves or soft wheels decorated with flower petals. Goat cheese is very versatile and can be used in dips, salads, pizzas, pastas, and desserts.

40 to 50 small bamboo skewers	10 ounces goat cheese
25 to 30 fresh ripe figs	4 garlic cloves, minced, divided
4 shallots, minced, divided	1 pound prosciutto, thinly sliced
2 tablespoons honey	1 large bunch basil, trimmed
2 tablespoons balsamic vinegar	4 tablespoons olive oil, divided
Salt and freshly ground pepper to taste	2 cups red wine
	1 tablespoon butter

Cover the bamboo skewers with cold water in a bowl. Let soak during the preparation of the figs.

Cut the figs lengthwise into halves. Reserve ten of the ripest halves for the Sapa. Combine half of the minced shallots, honey, and balsamic vinegar in a bowl and mix well. Season with salt and pepper. Add the remaining figs and toss gently to coat. Set aside to marinate. Combine the goat cheese and half of the minced garlic in a bowl and mix well. Season with salt and pepper.

Cut the prosciutto slices in half lengthwise. Place one marinated fig half at the end of a prosciutto strip. Top with a dime-size dollop of the seasoned goat cheese and a basil leaf. Roll to enclose the filling and secure with a skewer. Arrange on a baking sheet. Repeat the process with the remaining marinated figs, prosciutto, seasoned goat cheese, and basil. Chill, covered, for at least one hour.

To prepare the Sapa, coarsely chop the reserved fig halves. Combine the chopped figs with the remaining minced shallots and garlic in a bowl and mix well. Heat 2 tablespoons olive oil in a small sauté pan. Add the fig mixture and season with salt and pepper. Cook over medium-high heat, stirring frequently, until the mixture caramelizes slightly. Stir in the wine.

Simmer until the liquid is reduced by half, stirring frequently. Stir in the butter. When the butter has melted, remove from heat. Strain through a fine sieve into a bowl, pressing with a ladle to extract all of the liquid; discard the solids. Let stand until cool.

Heat the remaining olive oil in a large sauté pan. Add the skewered figs in batches and sauté quickly until brown on both sides, adding additional olive oil as needed. Blot the figs to remove any excess oil. Arrange in a single layer on the baking sheet.

Preheat the oven to 450 degrees just before serving. Bake for 5 minutes or just until heated through; blot to remove any excess oil. Arrange the figs on a serving platter. Drizzle with the Sapa and serve immediately.

Makes 40 to 50 skewers

MANGO & BRIE QUESADILLAS

For a tasty outdoor starter, try making these on the grill.

1 yellow onion, cut into halves,
    thinly sliced
3 Anaheim chiles, finely chopped,
    or 3 cans diced mild green chiles
1/4 cup plus 2 tablespoons
    vegetable oil
10 flour tortillas
1 pound Brie cheese, rind removed,
    softened

2 ripe mangoes, chopped
    (see note, page 18)
1/4 cup (1/2 stick) butter, melted
1 cup sour cream
Grated zest of 1 lime
2 teaspoons fresh lime juice
1/4 cup chopped fresh cilantro

Sauté the onion and Anaheim chiles in 2 tablespoons of oil in a skillet over medium heat until the onion is translucent. If using canned chiles, add them to the skillet after the onion is translucent and cook for 3 minutes longer. Remove the mixture to a bowl using a slotted spoon.

Soften the tortillas by placing them in a heated nonstick skillet for about 15 seconds per side. Spread half of each tortilla with a thin layer of Brie cheese. Spread a thin layer of the onion mixture over the cheese and sprinkle lightly with the mangoes. Fold the other half of each tortilla over the top.

Combine the melted butter and 1/4 cup oil in a bowl. Heat the skillet over medium heat. Brush the quesadillas with the butter mixture and lightly brown them on both sides. Place on a baking sheet in a warm oven while browning the remaining quesadillas.

Combine the sour cream, lime zest, and lime juice in a bowl and mix well. Cut each quesadilla into wedges and arrange on a serving platter. Drizzle with the sour cream mixture and sprinkle with cilantro. Serve immediately.

Serves 8 to 10

Estimating Food
QUANTITIES

The key to estimating food quantities for a party requires consideration of several factors, including the occasion, duration, attendees, and weather. On average, 75 percent of the invited guests will be able to attend if a written invitation is issued three to four weeks before the event. Invitations issued closer to the date of the event will draw a lower percentage of guests. A "must attend" event will have higher attendance than an open house.

Common sense dictates that a party scheduled during mealtime requires more food per person. Dinner is anytime from 5P.M. to 9P.M., so count on guests arriving hungry whether or not the invitation indicated that a meal would be served. An open house from 2P.M. to 5P.M. does not require as much food per person.

People tend to eat less at a formal party or if they are not acquainted with each other. If liquor is being served, guests will tend to eat more. If the weather is hot, guests will drink more nonalcoholic beverages and eat less, so think light when selecting foods to serve.

Chiles

Chiles play an essential role in cuisine around the globe. Mexico, South America, Africa, India, Spain, China, and Thailand all depend on the heat and flavor of chiles to spice many of their traditional dishes. There are at least two hundred types of chiles in varying lengths, shapes, and sizes. Predominant colors are yellow, green, red, orange, or black. Heat varies, too, from slightly warm to eye-bugging, sinus-clearing hot. As a general rule, the larger the chile, the milder it is.

The seeds and membranes hold the potent compound that gives chiles their fiery character. Removing these seeds and veins is the only way to reduce the heat. Wear latex gloves or wash hands thoroughly to prevent painful burning of the skin or eyes. Popular fresh chiles include Anaheims, frequently stuffed or used in salsas; poblanos, commonly used in chiles rellenos; and jalapeños, those small, green, fiery-hot additions to many Asian and Mexican dishes. Two popular varieties of dried chiles are the rich, slightly fruit-flavored ancho chile (a poblano chile when fresh), used in sauces and butters; and the smoky, sweet, almost chocolaty chipotle (a dried, smoked jalapeño) used to add distinction to stews and sauces.

THAI SPRING ROLLS

Crabmeat or shrimp may be substituted for the chicken.

Thai Spring Rolls
8 ounces boneless skinless chicken breasts, cooked, diced (about 1 cup)
1/2 cup chopped fresh cilantro
1/3 cup chopped green onions
1 to 2 small red chiles, seeded, finely chopped, or 1/4 to 1/2 teaspoon red pepper flakes
6 ounces cream cheese, softened
1 tablespoon milk
Finely chopped zest of 1 lime
1 tablespoon lime juice
1/4 teaspoon salt
1 package won ton wrappers
2 cups finely shredded cabbage or iceberg lettuce

Ginger Chutney Dipping Sauce
8 ounces mango chutney (Sharwood's preferred)
1/4 cup water
2 tablespoons lime juice
2 teaspoons grated fresh ginger

Preheat the oven to 400 degrees. Combine the chicken, cilantro, green onions, and red chiles in a bowl and mix well. Mash the cream cheese with the milk in a bowl until blended. Stir in the lime zest, 1 tablespoon lime juice, and salt. Add to the chicken mixture and mix well.

Place 1 tablespoon of the chicken mixture on each won ton wrapper. Roll to enclose the filling, sealing the seam with water. Arrange the rolls seam side down on a baking sheet sprayed with nonstick cooking spray. Bake for 10 minutes and turn over. Bake for 10 minutes longer or until golden brown. Cool for several minutes.

While the spring rolls are baking, combine the sauce ingredients in a food processor or blender. Process until smooth.

Arrange the spring rolls on a bed of cabbage on a serving platter. Pour the Ginger Chutney Dipping Sauce into a small bowl and arrange in the middle of the platter.

Makes 3 dozen

Curry-Poached Prawns

Hornblower Cruises & Events' Executive Chef, Daniel B. Smith, created this Pan-Asian appetizer. The Chile Syrup and Coconut Milk Sauce may be made a day ahead.

Prawns
2 quarts water
2 ounces galangal or fresh ginger, sliced
3 garlic cloves, peeled
1 shallot, peeled
1 stalk lemongrass, cut into quarters
2 whole cloves
2 sprigs of fresh mint, plus leaves for garnish
10 fresh basil leaves
5 sprigs of fresh cilantro
2 tablespoons red curry paste (Mae Ploy preferred)
2 tablespoons salt
2 tablespoons sugar
2 tablespoons fish sauce
2 tablespoons lime juice
2 teaspoons turmeric
16 jumbo prawns, peeled, deveined

Chile Syrup
1 cup sugar
$1/2$ cup water
Juice of 1 orange
2 tablespoons fresh lime juice
2 tablespoons chile paste (Sambal Oelek preferred)
1 teaspoon fish sauce

Coconut Milk Sauce
1 (14-ounce) can coconut milk
2 teaspoons lime juice
1 teaspoon fish sauce

Cucumber Noodles
2 English (hothouse) cucumbers, peeled
2 tablespoons rice wine vinegar
2 teaspoons salt
2 teaspoons sugar

For the prawns, combine all of the ingredients except the prawns in a 4-quart pan and mix well. Bring to a boil. Reduce heat and simmer for 15 minutes. Remove from heat. Strain the broth immediately into a bowl, discarding the solids. Add the prawns and poach for 3 minutes or until cooked through. Using a slotted spoon, immediately remove the prawns to a plate and chill, covered, in the refrigerator.

Combine the Chile Syrup ingredients in a heavy saucepan and mix well. Bring to a boil over high heat. Reduce heat to maintain a slow boil. Cook for 5 minutes, stirring occasionally. Remove from heat. Let stand at room temperature.

Combine the Coconut Milk Sauce ingredients in a small saucepan. Cook over high heat until reduced by half, stirring frequently. Remove from heat. Cool slightly. Pour into a bowl. Press plastic wrap over the surface of the sauce and chill.

To make the Cucumber Noodles, cut the cucumbers into 4-inch lengths and julienne into $1/8$- × $1/8$- × 4-inch strands. Combine with the rice wine vinegar, salt, and sugar in a bowl and mix well. Let stand for 10 minutes or longer to allow the cucumbers to release liquid and become softer.

To assemble, interlock the prawns in pairs and set aside. Drain the cucumber noodles and place a small mound in the center of each of eight serving plates. Drizzle the syrup and sauce around the noodles. Place a pair of prawns on top of the noodles. Garnish with mint leaves.

Serves 8

Hornblower
CRUISES & EVENTS

For an experience unparalleled in its scenic and epicurean adventure, board one of the nine Hornblower yachts harbored on the San Francisco Bay. Bay Area residents are accustomed to seeing the yachts of Hornblower Cruises & Events on the Bay. The company that started out with two small vessels in 1980 has grown over the years to include a fleet of twenty-seven distinctive yachts, nine of which are harbored in the Bay Area. The Hornblower crew specializes in creating unique private charter events and public cruises. A Hornblower cruise is unequaled for its beautiful views of San Francisco, the hills of Oakland, the Marin Headlands, and all the sights around the Bay that can only be seen from the water. The breathtaking views and delicious food combine for a memorable occasion.

The root vegetables known today as carrots were first cultivated in central Asia for medicinal purposes before slowly spreading to the Mediterranean. The most common varieties were purple and green. The Dutch developed orange carrots, which became more widely preferred by the eighteenth century. Today California produces 60 percent of U.S. carrots mainly in Kern, Imperial, and Monterey Counties.

When they were introduced in 1989, mini-peeled and baby-cut carrots were one of the first fresh-cut vegetables available to consumers. A special variety of carrot, "caropak," is grown for mini-peeled carrots. Caropaks are grown close together resulting in smaller, more tender carrots that mature in 120 days instead of 140 to 150 days. Ninety percent of all mini-peeled carrots are grown in California's Central Valley and packaged in two large plants near Bakersfield.

Fresh carrots are firm and smooth, not cracked. If buying carrots with their green tops, the leaves should be moist and bright green. Remove the tops as soon as possible because they rob the roots of moisture and vitamins. Store carrots in a plastic bag in the refrigerator's vegetable bin away from apples, which emit ethylene gas that can give carrots a bitter taste. Carrots may be stored successfully for two to three weeks. Young carrots and tiny baby carrots need only a light rinsing, but older carrots should be peeled. If carrots become limp, re-crisp them in a bowl of ice water. If mini-peeled carrots turn white on the outside, putting them in cold water will turn them bright orange again.

In health-conscious California, carrots are valued as an excellent source of vitamin A. A single large carrot provides 220 percent of vitamin A needed by the human body on a daily basis. Carrots are also a great source of fiber, potassium, and vitamin C.

Photo Opposite: Carrots, Crow Canyon Gardens, San Ramon, California

POLENTA WITH CARROTS & GREENS

Grimmway Farms developed this colorful carrot recipe.

1/2 cup minced onion
1 tablespoon minced garlic
3 tablespoons vegetable oil, divided
1 cup polenta
3 cups vegetable stock
Salt and freshly ground pepper
1/4 cup grated fresh Parmesan cheese
1 pound Grimmway Farms baby carrots
2 tablespoons minced fresh rosemary
4 cups mixed salad greens

Preheat the oven to 400 degrees. Sauté the onion and garlic in 1 tablespoon oil over medium heat for 1 minute. Add the polenta and sauté for 30 seconds. Stir in stock. Bring to a boil. Reduce heat, season with salt and pepper to taste, and simmer, stirring constantly, for 5 minutes or until very thick and spreadable. Pour evenly into an oiled 8- × 8-inch baking dish. Sprinkle with cheese and bake for 20 minutes.

Meanwhile, cook the carrots, covered, in the remaining oil for 7 minutes over medium heat, stirring once. Add the rosemary and greens. Sauté for 1 to 2 minutes or just until the greens wilt. Cut the polenta into four squares, place on serving plates, and top with the carrots and greens.

Serves 4

CITRUS CARROT SALAD

*This gorgeous salad is perfect for a picnic or salad buffet. Prepare the
dressing the day before serving to allow the flavors to blend.*

1 pound carrots, peeled
2 ounces dried cranberries
1/2 cup finely sliced green onions
Citrus Dressing

Julienne the carrots in a food processor fitted with a 3mm × 3mm julienne disc or thinly slice
by hand into julienne pieces. Alternatively, grate the carrots using the large holes on a grater.
Combine the carrots, cranberries, and green onions in a salad bowl. Add half the Citrus
Dressing and toss to coat. Add additional dressing if the salad seems dry.

Serves 6 to 8

CITRUS DRESSING

*Serve the leftover dressing on butter lettuce or over
grilled chicken breasts or fish.*

Zest and juice of 1 orange
Zest and juice of 1/2 lemon
Zest and juice of 1/2 lime
1/4 cup vegetable oil
1/4 cup extra virgin olive oil

2 green onions, white part only,
   finely chopped
Salt and freshly ground pepper
   to taste

Combine the dressing ingredients in a blender. Process until blended. Add additional salt before
serving if desired.

Makes 1 cup

Jamba Juice

The San Francisco-based company
Jamba Juice™, juices over one million
pounds of carrots each year. During
lunch hour in San Francisco's Financial
District, the line is out the door for this
alternative to fast food. The craze that
started in California has spread across
the nation. At Jamba Juice, fresh
squeezed juices are served, as well as
blended-to-order smoothies that have
a full day's nutritional requirement of
fruit, nonfat frozen yogurt, or dairy-free
sorbet, and a dash of ice. Each twenty-
four-ounce smoothie is more that a
healthy snack—it is a nutritious,
portable meal. Jamba Juice uses only
the freshest fruits and vegetables,
sending them straight to the blender
with no added sugars, preservatives, or
artificial flavors. Jamba Juice smoothies
are low-fat and loaded with energy
from carbohydrates, protein, and other
vital nutrients.

Firecracker Picnic

A picnic following the hometown Independence Day parade is a family and social occasion combined. Pack the picnic hamper with a traditional assortment of traveling foods that are sure to be crowd pleasers. Celebrate our country's birthday in style as fireworks light up the sky.

Citrus Carrot Salad 80
New Potato Dijon Salad 84
Heirloom Tomato Platter

•

Garlic-Marinated Flank Steak 92
Grilled Garlic Bread 92

•

Chocolate Caramel Shortbread Bars 109

Citrus Carrot Salad

A crisp Napa Valley Sauvignon Blanc, such as Honig Cellars, Robert Mondavi, or Chateau Potelle

•

A fruity, red California Rhone blend, such as TVine Grenache, Edmunds St. John, or Bonny Doon Vineyard

Let a well-refrigerated wine sit out at room temperature for fifteen to thirty minutes prior to serving. Rich-tasting whites like chardonnay, pinot blanc, and pinot gris are best served near cellar temperature, around fifty to fifty-five degrees Fahrenheit. Light, crisp, bracing wines such as sauvignon blanc, semillon, dry riesling, rosé, and sparklers are best served a bit cooler, about forty to forty-five degrees Fahrenheit.

Red wine should be served at cool room temperature, preferably around sixty degrees Fahrenheit. When wine is served too warm aromas grow sharp, flavors become coarse, and the finish tastes hot from alcohol, obliterating the sense of fruit.

Foothill Traveling
FARMERS' MARKET

Everyone at Lake Tahoe looks forward to Farmers' Market Day held Thursdays at Dollar Hill, near the watermelon patch on the North Shore. While catching up on local gossip and seeing who is in town, shoppers load their baskets with the freshest produce, flowers, nuts, eggs, bread, and homemade sauces. The same group of vendors, known as the Foothill Traveling Farmers' Market, visits the West Shore on Sundays at the Homewood Ski Resort parking lot and can be found in Truckee on Tuesdays at the Truckee River Regional Park. Plan the day's menu around seasonal produce and take a trip around the lake to gather the ingredients. The vendors are on site from 8 A.M. to 1 P.M. during the summer season and into early fall.

CURRIED CARROT SOUP

This soup is easy to prepare and has spectacular flavor and color.

1 yellow onion, chopped
2 tablespoons butter
7 large carrots, peeled, cut into
 1/4-inch slices
3/4 to 1 teaspoon curry powder, or
 to taste

4 cups homemade or canned
 chicken stock (see note)
1 cup milk
1 teaspoon salt
1 teaspoon freshly ground pepper
Sour cream

Sauté the onion in the butter in a heavy saucepan until the onion is translucent. Add the carrots and curry powder and mix well. Sauté over low heat for 4 to 5 minutes or until the carrots are tender-crisp. Stir in 3 cups of the stock. Bring to a boil, reduce heat, and simmer, covered, for 20 minutes.

Warm the milk in a microwave or saucepan. Add the warm milk and remaining stock to the soup. Purée the soup in batches in a blender. Return the soup to the saucepan. Stir in the salt and pepper. Cook just until heated through, stirring frequently. Ladle into heated soup bowls and top each serving with a dollop of sour cream.

Note: If using canned chicken stock, dissolve one chicken bouillon cube in the stock.

Serves 6 to 8

CREAM OF ZUCCHINI SOUP

A tasty way to use summer's bounty of zucchini.

1 1/2 pounds zucchini, cut into
   1/2-inch slices
3/4 cup water
1 teaspoon chopped fresh basil
   or thyme
1 teaspoon salt

3/4 teaspoon sugar
2 tablespoons finely
   chopped onion
3 tablespoons butter
3 tablespoons flour
2 cups milk

Combine the zucchini, water, basil, salt, and sugar in a large saucepan. Bring to a boil; reduce heat. Simmer for 15 minutes or until the zucchini is tender, stirring occasionally. Process the zucchini and liquid in batches in a blender until smooth. Set aside.

Warm the milk in a microwave or saucepan. Sauté the onion in the butter in a large saucepan until the onion is translucent. Add the flour and cook for 1 minute, stirring constantly. Whisk in the warm milk. Cook until the mixture begins to thicken, stirring constantly. Add the zucchini purée. Cook until heated through, stirring constantly. Ladle into warm soup bowls and serve immediately.

Serves 4

Zucchini Festival

When the City of Hayward was looking to boost its morale during difficult economic times, the prolific vegetable zucchini was jokingly suggested as a possible theme for an event to raise funds for local charities. Held in mid-August, the Zucchini Festival has been drawing crowds to Kennedy Park in Hayward since 1983. Activities include arts and crafts, live entertainment, and hot rod cars and races. Children enjoy magicians, giant slides, and rides. Highlights of the two-day festival include zucchini-growing and zucchini-carving contests, as well as recipe cook-off events. Among the many food offerings, deep-fried zucchini is a crowd favorite.

Vinegar

Vinegar (sour wine) is an essential ingredient in salad dressings, sauces, marinades, and sushi. There are many wonderful varieties of vinegar on the market today. The traditional favorite, fruity apple cider vinegar, has been replaced in many pantries by the more pungent varieties made from the white or red wine preferred by the French, and the marvelous Italian balsamic vinegar made from white Trebbiano grape juice. Balsamic vinegar achieves its dark color and heady sweetness from aging over a period of years in barrels made of various woods. A properly aged bottle of balsamic vinegar may cost nearly as much as a good bottle of wine. Fruit vinegars made from raspberries or currants are also popular. They can be used with Dijon mustard to make salad dressings or in reduction sauces for wild game or pork. Herb-flavored vinegars, used in vinaigrettes, are made by steeping fresh herbs, such as dill or tarragon, in vinegar for a period of time. Mild and slightly sweet rice vinegar, made from fermented rice, is widely used in Asian cooking. Like wine, vinegar should be stored airtight in a cool, dark place. Unopened, it will keep indefinitely. Once opened, it can be kept for approximately six months.

NEW POTATO DIJON SALAD

Traditional picnic fare, updated and refined.

2 pounds unpeeled new potatoes,
   cut into quarters
1/2 cup finely chopped shallots
2 tablespoons olive oil
1/3 cup finely chopped fresh parsley
3 tablespoons white wine vinegar
3 tablespoons whole grain Dijon
   mustard (Maille preferred)

1/2 teaspoon salt
1/4 teaspoon dried tarragon,
   or 1/2 teaspoon finely minced
   fresh rosemary
3/4 cup extra virgin olive oil

Place the new potatoes in a saucepan with salted water to cover. Bring to a boil and simmer until the tip of a sharp knife easily pierces the potatoes. Drain and peel if desired. Place the potatoes in a bowl.

Sauté the shallots in the olive oil in a small skillet until the shallots are translucent but not brown. Transfer the shallots and oil to a small bowl. Add the parsley, wine vinegar, Dijon mustard, salt, tarragon, and 3/4 cup olive oil and whisk until combined.

Pour half the dressing over the warm potatoes and mix gently, adding more dressing if the potatoes seem dry. Chill, covered, until ready to use. Adjust the seasonings before serving, if necessary.

Serves 8

HERBES DE PROVENCE SUMMER SALAD

A new summer salad to add to your repertoire.

1 large head romaine lettuce, torn into bite-size pieces
1 cup cherry tomatoes (Sweet 100's preferred)
1/2 English (hothouse) cucumber, peeled, chopped
Herbes de Provence Dressing to taste
1/4 cup shelled sunflower seeds

Combine the lettuce, cherry tomatoes, and cucumber in a salad bowl. Add the Herbes de Provence Dressing and toss to coat. Sprinkle with the sunflower seeds. Serve immediately.

Serves 6

HERBES DE PROVENCE DRESSING

The entire family will love this creamy herb dressing.

1 1/3 cups mayonnaise
1/4 cup red wine vinegar
1 large garlic clove, minced
1 teaspoon Dijon mustard
1 teaspoon soy sauce

1 teaspoon salt
1 teaspoon freshly ground pepper
1 teaspoon dried herbes de
   Provence, crushed

Combine the dressing ingredients in a bowl and mix well. Chill, covered, for 2 hours to allow the flavors to blend.

Makes 1 2/3 cups

Heirloom Tomatoes

Many of the summer vegetables grown in gardens years ago and treasured for their flavor have been nearly eliminated from the marketplace. While full-flavored, many of the old varieties are not as attractive or as hardy as those now grown commercially and are thus more difficult to grow and sell to the mass market. Seeing the handwriting on the wall two decades ago, some gardeners began saving seeds from the open-pollinated varieties. These seeds are called heirloom seeds. Heirloom tomatoes, those wonderful, fragile, often misshapen fruits called by such names as Gold Nugget, Brandywine, Golden Cherry, and Sweet Orange, are a hit at local farmers' markets. They are prized for their beautiful interior color and sweet, low-acidic pulp. Just a drizzle of extra virgin olive oil and a sprinkle of kosher salt are all that is needed to bless the taste buds; with a bit of basil and some fresh mozzarella, heirlooms are almost too good to be true.

Black & White
BALL

The Black and White Ball is a San Francisco Symphony tradition dating back to 1956. The wildly successful event, held in odd-numbered years, currently raises nearly one million dollars for the Symphony. In recent years, more than twelve thousand guests have arrived dressed in their most elegant and creative black and white eveningwear ready for an unforgettable celebration. A ticket to the event entitles attendees admission to a number of venues spread over three square blocks surrounding San Francisco's Civic Center. More than fifty bands have people dancing in the streets to a dizzying array of big band, rock 'n' roll, jazz, Latin, and country music. Complimentary wine, champagne, and hors d'oeuvres are offered by some of the City's world-renowned restaurants and hotels. Tickets to the Black and White Ball must be purchased well in advance, as the event is always a sellout.

GRILLED CHICKEN & COUSCOUS SALAD

Serve this pretty combination as a main dish or eliminate the chicken and serve as a side dish to grilled meats.

1/4 cup fresh lime juice
1/4 cup mirin (sweet rice wine)
4 boneless skinless chicken breasts
1 1/2 cups no-added-salt chicken stock
4 tablespoons minced shallots, divided
3 tablespoons fresh lemon juice, divided
1 cup plain couscous
1/3 cup coarsely chopped fresh cilantro, divided

3 tablespoons olive oil, divided
12 ounces fresh mushrooms, such as cremini and shiitake, sliced
1 teaspoon fresh thyme leaves
4 ounces snow peas, trimmed, cut diagonally into 1-inch pieces
Salt and freshly ground pepper to taste
1 tablespoon red wine vinegar
Olive oil
Curly kale

Whisk the lime juice and mirin in a shallow dish. Add the chicken and turn to coat. Marinate, covered, in the refrigerator for approximately 1 hour, turning occasionally. Combine the stock, 2 tablespoons shallots, and 2 tablespoons lemon juice in a saucepan. Bring to a boil. Stir in the couscous and half the cilantro. Remove from heat. Let stand, covered, for 10 minutes or until all of the liquid has been absorbed.

Heat a wok or large skillet over medium-high heat. Add 2 tablespoons olive oil. Add the mushrooms, 2 tablespoons shallots, and thyme and stir-fry for 4 minutes or until the mushrooms begin to brown. Stir in the snow peas. Season with salt and pepper. Remove from heat.

Whisk 1 tablespoon olive oil, red wine vinegar, and 1 tablespoon lemon juice in a bowl until blended. Stir in the remaining cilantro. Transfer the couscous to a large bowl and fluff with a fork. Add just enough of the vinaigrette to moisten and fluff again with a fork. Add the mushroom mixture and toss to mix. Season with salt and pepper. Set aside.

Prepare the grill for medium heat. Pat the chicken dry with a paper towel and brush lightly with olive oil. Grill the chicken for 10 to 12 minutes or until cooked through. Remove to a cutting board and slice. Line a serving platter with kale. Mound the couscous on the kale. Top with the sliced chicken.

Serves 4 to 6

AHI SALAD NIÇOISE

A classic made even better with the addition of fresh Ahi tuna. The trick to this beautiful salad is to individually toss the lettuce, potatoes, green beans, and Ahi with a bit of the vinaigrette, then compose each plate. Serve with crusty French bread and sweet butter.

10 to 12 ounces fresh Ahi tuna steak, 1 inch thick
Salt and freshly ground pepper to taste
Olive oil
1 head butter lettuce, leaves separated
1 pound new potatoes, cut into eighths, cooked, cooled
6 ounces French green beans, trimmed, steamed, cooled
Dijon Vinaigrette
2 hard-cooked eggs, cut into quarters

3 small ripe tomatoes, cut into quarters
1 small red onion, sliced, separated into rings
1 small yellow bell pepper, cut into rings
3/4 cup niçoise olives
1 tablespoon capers, rinsed, drained
1 tablespoon chopped fresh parsley
1 1/2 teaspoons minced fresh tarragon, thyme, or basil

Sprinkle both sides of the tuna with salt and pepper and generously brush with olive oil. Sauté in a nonstick skillet or grill over medium-hot coals for 1 1/2 to 2 minutes per side, turning once. The inside of the tuna should remain rare. Transfer to a platter and chill. Cut into bite-size pieces.

In separate bowls, lightly dress the tuna, lettuce, new potatoes, and green beans with some of the Dijon Vinaigrette. Divide the lettuce between four dinner plates, then add the potatoes, green beans, and finally, the tuna. Arrange the eggs, tomatoes, onion, bell pepper, and olives among the other ingredients on the plates. Sprinkle with the capers, parsley, tarragon, and salt and pepper to taste.

Serves 4

DIJON VINAIGRETTE

The mustard in this dressing enhances the fresh flavors of the salad.

2/3 cup extra virgin olive oil
1/4 cup red wine vinegar
1 tablespoon Dijon mustard

1 tablespoon fresh lemon juice
1 teaspoon salt
Freshly ground pepper to taste

Combine the dressing ingredients in a jar with a tight-fitting lid. With the lid tight on the jar, shake to mix.

Makes 1 1/4 cups

Lacy Cheese WAFERS

Lacy cheese wafers have only one ingredient, yet they taste so good. To prepare these crisp treats, preheat the oven to 350 degrees and place the oven rack in the lower third of the oven. Line a baking sheet with baking parchment and place teaspoonfuls of finely shredded or very thinly sliced Parmigiano-Reggiano cheese (aged Parmesan) about one inch apart on the prepared sheet. Flatten the mounds of cheese lightly with a fork. Bake 4 to 8 minutes, or until the cheese is melted, bubbly, and light golden. Using a spatula, remove the wafers quickly from the baking sheet, and cool on a wire rack. The wafers become crisp as they cool. They disappear as fast as they are put out, so make plenty! Leftovers can be stored in an airtight container at room temperature for up to three days.

Prawns

Shrimp is America's favorite shellfish. In the United States, colossal shrimp (ten or less per pound) and jumbo shrimp (eleven to fifteen per pound) are commonly called "prawns," although the prawn is actually a different species. The California Spot Prawn is really a shrimp, while the Ridgeback Shrimp is truly a prawn. Four bright spots on their bodies, which reach six inches in length over their six-year life span, identify Spot Prawns. Inhabiting rocky areas at depths of 150 to 1,600 feet from San Diego to Alaska, Spot Prawns are delivered to market from California's coastal waters at a rate of over 600,000 pounds per year, accounting for over four million dollars in revenues. Monterey fishermen trap Spot Prawns year-round, while southern California trawlers fish for Spot Prawns during the summer, switching to Ridgebacks in the winter. Ridgebacks, sometimes called Santa Barbara Shrimp, are found from Monterey to Baja California. Their "ridges," or sharp spiny shells, make them difficult to peel.

The shells of prawns can be removed before or after cooking. When grilling, broiling, or boiling prawns consider cooking them in their shells to prevent them from drying out. Peeled prawns will absorb more flavors from cooking juices. Peeling involves stripping the legs and peeling off the shell, leaving the tail on or removing it, whichever is preferred.

In general, small and medium prawns do not need deveining except for cosmetic purposes. Because the intestinal vein of larger prawns contains grit, it should be removed. To devein unpeeled prawns, insert a pick or skewer between the shell segments to lift out the vein in several pieces. To devein peeled prawns, use a sharp knife or scissors to cut one-quarter inch deep along the back. Rinse out the vein under cool running water.

Featured in the sidebar is the recipe for *Almond Prawns with Papaya Butter* from Spenger's Fresh Fish Grotto. After 110 years of Spenger family management, its third-generation operator, Frank Spenger, Jr., closed the historic Berkeley seafood restaurant in the fall of 1999. Spenger's had once ranked as a national leader in customer volume and sales, grossing over ten million dollars annually. McCormick and Schmick, a growing Portland-based restaurant chain, spent nearly five million dollars to restore the gleam to Spenger's wood-paneled interior, which includes multiple dining rooms and two bars. The eclectic collection of memorabilia remains, including model boats, old ship brass, a gun collection, and jewels. The extensive menu has been updated to emphasize high-quality, fresh seafood. Since reopening, Spenger's has been successfully turning over its six hundred seats from morning until night as both new and returning customers flock to the restaurant.

Photo Opposite: Prawns, Hornblower Cruises & Events' Yacht, The Empress Hornblower, *Berkeley Marina, Berkeley, California*

ALMOND PRAWNS WITH PAPAYA BUTTER

Spenger's Fresh Fish Grotto is a well-known Berkeley landmark. Executive Chef, Steve Connolly, created this wonderful recipe.

> 2 dozen jumbo prawns, peeled, deveined
> 4 tablespoons vegetable oil, divided
> 1 cup sliced blanched almonds, very finely chopped
> 1 papaya
> 1/4 cup (1/2 stick) butter, softened
> 1 teaspoon curry powder
> 1/8 teaspoon salt

Preheat the oven to 450 degrees. Make a deep cut lengthwise along the back of each prawn so it lies flat without separating. Brush the prawns with 2 tablespoons oil and coat both sides with the almonds. Refrigerate.

Cut the papaya into halves and remove the seeds. Scoop out the pulp and discard the skin. Purée the pulp, butter, curry powder, and salt in a blender.

Brush a baking sheet with the remaining oil and heat in the oven for 2 to 3 minutes. Remove and quickly arrange the prawns on it. Bake for 5 to 6 minutes or until the almond coating is brown and the prawns are firm to the touch, turning once. Arrange the prawns on a serving platter and top them with the papaya butter.

Serves 4 to 6

Bodega Bay
SEAFOOD FESTIVAL

In late August, the Bodega Bay Seafood, Art & Wine Festival draws crowds to the seven-hundred-acre Chanslor Ranch on Highway 1, one mile north of the fishing village of Bodega Bay. Visitors traveling through Bodega Bay may recognize it as the setting for Alfred Hitchcock's film, *The Birds*. Once at the festival, attendees savor seafood specialties while enjoying a variety of musical entertainment. Wineries and microbreweries offer tastings throughout the weekend. Children enjoy the Fun Zone and horseback and pony rides. Unique features of the festival include a recycled art competition and environmental exhibits. Hosted by the Chanslor Wetlands Wildlife Project, the festival benefits the Stewards of Slavianka. These volunteers oversee trail maintenance, docent training, and seal watch and campfire programs in the California State Parks of Sonoma and Mendocino Counties.

SKEWERED CHIPOTLE SHRIMP

*These skewered delicacies of the sea make
a spicy and colorful appetizer.*

15 bamboo skewers
3 large plum tomatoes, peeled
  (see note, page 99)
6 medium garlic cloves, roasted
  (see sidebar, page 140)
1/4 cup water
2 tablespoons olive oil
1 to 2 canned chipotle chiles,
  rinsed, finely chopped

1/2 teaspoon salt
2 pounds medium-large shrimp,
  peeled, deveined
3 tablespoons chopped fresh
  cilantro
4 green onions, sliced
2 limes, cut into wedges

Soak the bamboo skewers in enough water to cover while preparing the recipe. Purée the tomatoes, garlic, and water in a food processor or blender.

Heat the olive oil in a heavy saucepan over high heat. Add the purée all at once, being careful to prevent splattering. Cook the purée for 5 to 10 minutes or until it darkens, stirring constantly. Reduce the heat and cook for 5 minutes longer or until very thick, stirring occasionally. Stir in the chipotle chiles and salt. Remove from heat. Let stand until cool.

Prepare the grill for medium-high heat. Toss the shrimp in the chipotle sauce. Thread 2 or 3 shrimp on each bamboo skewer. Grill the shrimp for 5 minutes, turning once, or until the shrimp are firm to the touch. Alternatively, the shrimp may be sautéed, without the skewers, in a non-stick skillet. Transfer the skewers to a serving platter. Top with the cilantro and green onions, and serve with the lime wedges.

Serves 8 to 10

Baja Grill

Entertaining with a Mexican theme creates a casual, fun ambience, especially when the food centers around the grill. Serve spicy skewered shrimp and vegetables, along with margaritas and sangria to cool the heat. A Mariachi band will liven the pace and lend a South-of-the-Border mood to the occasion.

Baja Guacamole & Tortilla Chips 71
Mango & Brie Quesadillas 75

•

Skewered Chipotle Shrimp 90
Grilled Vegetables with Chili Butter 98

•

Cocoa Cinnamon Wedding Cookies 108

*Sangria
(page 68)*

•

Tommy's Margaritas

*2 ounces 100%
agave tequila
1¹/₃ ounces fresh
squeezed lime juice
1 ounce Triple Sec
1 drop sweet and sour*

*Combine all the ingredients,
shake, and serve on the rocks.*

Skewered Chipotle Shrimp

Since 1965, the Bermejo family has prepared Mexican food in their restaurant on Geary Street in San Francisco's Richmond District. What sets Tommy's Mexican Restaurant apart is that son Julio Bermejo stocks the largest collection of 100 percent agave tequila outside of Mexico. Over 160 kinds of tequila are poured. Julio's mission is to educate the tequila-drinking public about the differences between 100 percent pure oak distilled agave tequila and that mass-produced, adulterated tequila immortalized in song. Currently, more than four thousand people are members of Tommy's Tequila Club. Over 90 percent of the tequila sold at Tommy's is served in margaritas.

Grilled
GARLIC BREAD

Grilled garlic bread is a treat no one can resist. While waiting for the grill to get hot, mix together the following: 3/4 cup melted unsalted butter, 1/4 cup olive oil, 4 minced garlic cloves, and 2 teaspoons kosher salt. Cut 2 large loaves of crusty French bread lengthwise into halves. Brush each cut side of bread with one-quarter of the butter mixture. Arrange butter side down on a grill rack 5 to 6 inches from the heat source. Grill for 2 to 3 minutes or until golden brown. For variety, turn the bread over during the grilling process and top with grated Parmesan cheese. Continue grilling until the cheese melts. Serve immediately or cool and wrap in foil to pack in the picnic basket.

GARLIC-MARINATED FLANK STEAK

Great on crusty bread for picnic sandwiches,
or served hot as a main course.

1 1/4 to 1 1/2 pounds flank steak
8 garlic cloves, minced
1/2 cup soy sauce
1/4 cup fresh lemon juice
1/4 cup Worcestershire sauce

2 tablespoons olive oil
1 tablespoon Dijon mustard
2 teaspoons dried oregano
1 teaspoon freshly ground pepper

Rub the surface of the steak with the garlic. Combine the soy sauce, lemon juice, Worcestershire sauce, olive oil, Dijon mustard, oregano, and pepper in a bowl and mix well. Pour over the steak in a shallow dish, turning to coat. Marinate, covered, in the refrigerator for 6 to 10 hours, turning occasionally. Drain, reserving the marinade if serving as an entrée.

Prepare the grill for medium heat. Grill the steak for 5 to 10 minutes per side or until medium rare. Use a sharp knife to make a small slice in the center of the meat to check doneness. Transfer to a cutting board. Cut the steak diagonally across the grain into thin slices. Serve on crusty bread. If serving as an entrée, strain the reserved marinade into a saucepan. Bring to a boil and simmer for 5 minutes. Drizzle over the sliced steak.

Serves 4 to 6

FETA CHICKEN WITH FRESH OREGANO

For variety, an herbed feta cheese may be substituted.

1 cup plain yogurt
2 large garlic cloves, minced
2 teaspoons chopped fresh
   oregano, or 1 teaspoon dried
   oregano

1/2 teaspoon freshly ground pepper
4 boneless skinless chicken breasts
1/2 to 3/4 cup crumbled feta cheese

Combine the yogurt, garlic, oregano, and pepper in a bowl and mix well. Add the chicken and turn to coat. Marinate, covered, in the refrigerator for 30 minutes or longer, turning occasionally.

Preheat the broiler. Arrange the chicken in a single layer on a broiler rack and place the rack in a broiler pan. Brush the chicken with any remaining marinade. Broil for 8 to 10 minutes. Turn the chicken and sprinkle with the feta cheese. Broil for 4 to 6 minutes longer or until the chicken is cooked through. Transfer the chicken to a serving platter. Serve immediately.

Serves 4

Deetjen's
BIG SUR INN

Back in the 1930s, Grandpa Helmuth Deetjen, an immigrant from Norway, built a homestead on the Big Sur Coast, south of Carmel. Nestled in the towering coastal redwoods, Deetjen's Big Sur Inn was a popular stopover for travelers, and, over the years, Helmuth and his wife added more rooms and a restaurant. The lodgings, built in the style of their caretakers' native Norway, were generally constructed of locally milled, scavenged redwood. Wood-burning stoves and fireplaces heat the rustic rooms, and the doors have no locks. Loyal visitors return year after year to escape the hubbub of city life and retreat to the simplicity of yesteryear. Days are filled with exploring the rocky coastline and hiking in shady redwood groves, while evenings are spent dining by candlelight in the intimate restaurant, reading by the fire, and listening to Grandpa's collection of classical albums.

World's Largest
SALMON BARBECUE

If a little is good and more is better, then this must be as good as it gets for salmon lovers! The World's Largest Salmon Barbecue, held the first weekend in July, boasts a bounty of nearly five thousand pounds of salmon, all locally caught when possible. Local political celebrities cook the fish over a dozen open pits in the Noya River Harbor in Fort Bragg and the town's service agencies serve it to approximately forty-five hundred hungry patrons. Started in 1971 by citizens concerned for the plight of salmon fishermen, the proceeds from this annual event benefit the Hollow Tree Fish Hatchery, dedicated to making sure each year's catch is as plentiful as the last.

SALMON WITH TOMATO BASIL SALSA

This recipe says, "Summer!" It is quick and elegant.

Tomato Basil Salsa
4 very ripe tomatoes, peeled,
   seeded, diced (see note, page 99)
2 shallots, finely diced
1/4 cup fresh basil leaves, coarsely
   chopped
2 tablespoons extra virgin olive oil
1 to 2 tablespoons balsamic vinegar
   (amount depends on the flavor
   of the tomatoes)

Salmon
4 salmon steaks or fillets
Olive oil
Salt and freshly ground pepper
   to taste

Combine the tomatoes, shallots, basil, olive oil, and balsamic vinegar in a bowl and mix well. Let stand at room temperature for 2 hours or longer to allow the flavors to blend.

   Prepare the grill for medium heat. Rub both sides of the salmon with olive oil and sprinkle with salt and pepper. Grill 5 minutes per side or until the salmon flakes easily. Top the salmon with the salsa before serving.

Serves 4

SIZZLING SHRIMP

These spicy gems are a crowd pleaser. Serve with
steamed basmati or jasmine rice.

24 bamboo skewers
1/2 cup vegetable oil
1/2 cup ketchup
1 small onion, minced
2 tablespoons Asian chili sauce
1 tablespoon fresh lemon juice, or
    2 tablespoons fresh lime juice

4 garlic cloves, minced
1 teaspoon salt
1/2 teaspoon paprika
1/4 to 1/2 teaspoon cayenne
    pepper
2 pounds large shrimp, peeled,
    deveined

Combine all of the ingredients except the shrimp in a bowl and mix well. Add the shrimp and stir to coat. Marinate, covered, in the refrigerator for 3 hours or longer. Soak the bamboo skewers in enough water to cover for the final 30 minutes of the marinating time.

    Prepare the grill for medium-high heat. Drain the shrimp, reserving the marinade. Thread three shrimp on each skewer. Grill the shrimp for 5 minutes or until firm to the touch, turning once and basting with the reserved marinade. Alternatively, broil 4 to 5 inches from the heat source until the shrimp are firm to the touch, turning once and basting with the reserved marinade.

Serves 6

Santa Cruz
BEACH BOARDWALK

The only major seaside amusement park on the entire West Coast, the Santa Cruz Beach Boardwalk is a unique attraction. In the early 1900s, promoter Fred Swanton decided to duplicate the success of New York's Coney Island on the beautiful beaches of Santa Cruz. Although his original version was destroyed by fire in 1906, the next year Swanton was able to reopen one of the most heralded attractions of its time. Today, the Beach Boardwalk has been designated as an official State Historical Landmark. Two of its rides, the 1911 Looff Carousel and the 1924 Giant Dipper Roller Coaster, are National Historical Landmarks. Both children and adults visiting the Boardwalk can enjoy amusement park rides, carnival attractions, and free concerts, all on the shores of the spectacular Pacific Ocean.

Sweet Corn

There are many classifications of corn, based mainly on kernel texture, and there are many different uses for each type of corn. Sweet corn is typically boiled on the cob to the delight of diners on warm summer evenings. What gives sweet corn its pleasant sweetness, making it ideal for fresh eating, is the natural sugar in each kernel, which has not yet converted to starch as in other corn varieties.

Columbus and other explorers introduced corn to Europe after learning of its uses and cultivation techniques from the Native Americans. Since the days of the early explorers, corn has become a major crop around the world, second only to wheat in most-planted acreage. Though corn can be cultivated in many different types of climates, California is the second-largest producer of the country's sweet corn for summertime enjoyment.

When choosing sweet corn, look for tender kernels that are milky and well developed. Kernels that are too large will be chewy and pasty, like dough. They should be just firm enough that slight pressure will puncture the kernel, releasing the milky-white juice. When buying sweet corn in the husk, look for bright green, snug husks, and golden brown silk.

FRESH CORN ENCHILADAS

An excellent vegetarian entrée from the first California Fresh *cookbook updated with goat cheese. Use Anaheim chiles for a mild dish or a poblano chile for a spicier dish.*

Goat Cheese Filling
1 medium onion, finely chopped
1 tablespoon butter
1 1/2 cups fresh corn kernels
2 fresh Anaheim chiles, or
   1 poblano chile, seeded,
   chopped, or 2 canned Anaheim
   green chiles, seeded, chopped
2 tablespoons water
1/4 teaspoon ground cumin
1/2 cup sour cream
1/2 cup crumbled mild goat cheese
1/4 teaspoon freshly ground pepper

Enchiladas
1/4 cup vegetable oil
8 corn tortillas
1 (20-ounce) can mild enchilada
   sauce (Rosarita brand preferred)
1/2 cup shredded Monterey Jack
   cheese
Sour cream
Chopped fresh cilantro

Sauté the onion in the butter in a saucepan until the onion is translucent. Stir in the corn, chiles, water, and cumin. Simmer, covered, for 5 minutes. Remove the cover and simmer until the liquid evaporates, stirring occasionally. Remove from the heat and stir in the sour cream, goat cheese, and black pepper.

Preheat the oven to 375 degrees. Heat 1/4 cup oil in a skillet. Add the tortillas one at a time. Fry for 10 seconds per side or just until limp. Blot the excess oil off the tortillas with paper towels.

Spread 1/3 cup of the enchilada sauce in the bottom of a 9- × 13-inch baking dish. Fill each tortilla with approximately 1/3 cup of the filling and roll to enclose the filling. Arrange seam side down in the baking dish. Pour the remaining enchilada sauce over the top. Sprinkle with Monterey Jack cheese. Bake, uncovered, for 20 minutes or until the cheese melts and the sauce is bubbly. Top with sour cream and sprinkle with cilantro.

Serves 4

ROASTED GREEN BEANS WITH GARLIC

Wonderful Mediterranean ingredients heighten the flavor of garden-fresh green beans in this outstanding recipe, first published in Food & Wine Magazine *in 1999.*

1 pound Blue Lake green beans,
   trimmed
1/4 cup olive oil
3 garlic cloves, minced
3 sprigs of thyme

Salt and freshly ground pepper
   to taste
3 anchovy fillets, mashed
2 to 3 teaspoons lemon juice
Finely grated zest of 1 lemon

Preheat the oven to 450 degrees. Place an oven rack in the upper third of the oven. Toss the green beans, olive oil, garlic, and thyme in a large baking dish to coat. Season with salt and pepper. Spread the beans in a single layer. Roast, stirring occasionally, for 15 minutes or until tender and lightly browned.

   Discard the thyme. Mix the anchovies and lemon juice together. Add to the beans and toss to mix. Transfer the beans to a serving bowl. Sprinkle with lemon zest. Serve warm or at room temperature.

Serves 4

Gilroy Garlic
FESTIVAL

Every year during the last full weekend in July, the town of Gilroy plays host to the Gilroy Garlic Festival. Set in the foothills of the Santa Clara Valley, it is a one-of-a-kind gourmet food and fun extravaganza. When the annual call goes out for the best garlic recipes, what comes back are some of the most original and delectable delights ever to burst forth from a garlic bulb. Gourmet Alley is the heart of the festival, where garlic lovers participate in cooking demonstrations in aromatic open-air kitchens and devour dishes such as pasta con pesto, zesty stuffed mushrooms, and even garlic ice cream. Top-notch entertainment is free to festival-goers, with three stages and strolling musicians offering blues, country, jazz, and rock 'n' roll. Plan to make the pilgrimage to Christmas Hill Park in Gilroy and become a loyal Garlic Festival fanatic.

Presentation

Presentation may not be everything when it comes to food, but it definitely matters. The eyes are the first food-samplers. Pleasing colors, textures, and arrangement on the plate set the stage for the taste buds. Good cooking deserves its moment of appreciation, that "ahhh!" before the food is consumed. Presentation begins with meal planning. When planning a menu, think not only about the complementary nutrition and flavor aspects, but also how the combination of foods will look on the plate. Mexican and Italian meals demand a bold approach; French and Asian a subtle hand. Blend textures—serve squash purée with broccoli, for example. Contrast colors—give beige foods a green or red frame with curly lettuce or kale. Think about the color of the plate and if it fits the size and shape of the meal and matches the level of refinement of the food. Just a little forethought and a few extra touches will make all the difference in capturing not only the senses of smell and taste, but the important sense of sight as well.

A cooking tip from **Sandy Sachs,** *Executive Chef, Ingredients Cooking/Lifestyle School at Andronico's Market*

GRILLED VEGETABLES WITH CHILI BUTTER

Summer's abundant vegetables are spectacular with this flavorful butter.

15 bamboo skewers
1 medium red onion, cut into
 1/2-inch-thick rounds
Olive oil
2 medium summer squash, cut
 diagonally into 1/2-inch slices
1 red bell pepper, cut into quarters
1 yellow bell pepper, cut into
 quarters

8 ounces medium-size fresh
 mushrooms
3 ears of corn, husks and silk
 removed, cut into halves
Salt and freshly ground pepper
 to taste
Chili Butter

Soak the bamboo skewers in enough water to cover for 30 minutes.

Prepare the grill for medium heat. Skewer the onion rounds like lollipops, so they do not fall apart on the grill. Thread the squash, red bell pepper, yellow bell pepper, and mushrooms on skewers, keeping one type of vegetable per skewer. Brush the vegetables, including the corn, with olive oil and sprinkle generously with salt and pepper.

Grill the vegetables over medium-hot coals until tender-crisp and brown grill marks appear, turning once. The vegetables will require different grilling times. Remove the vegetables from the skewers and arrange on a serving platter. Drizzle with melted Chili Butter.

Serves 6

CHILI BUTTER

This spicy butter is also great on grilled steak and fish.

1 cup (2 sticks) unsalted butter
11/2 tablepoons chili powder
1 tablespoon tequila
11/2 teaspoons ground cumin

1/2 teaspoon salt
1 or 2 dashes of Tabasco sauce
Freshly ground pepper to taste

Melt the butter in a small saucepan. Add the remaining ingredients and stir to combine.

Alternatively, soften the butter without melting it. Mix all of the ingredients and pack into a 1-cup ramekin. Chill, covered, in the refrigerator. Let stand at room temperature until spreadable before serving.

Makes 1 cup

ZUCCHINI, TOMATO & BASIL GRATIN

A perfect combination of summer produce that is hearty enough for a vegetarian main dish. Enjoy the delicious juices with crusty French bread.

1 pound zucchini, thinly sliced
Salt to taste
3/4 cup shredded Kasseri cheese
(Greek sheep and goat's milk cheese)
3/4 cup shredded Monterey Jack cheese

4 cups fresh basil, stems removed, coarsely chopped
1 1/2 pounds ripe tomatoes, peeled, thinly sliced, drained on paper towels (see note)
Freshly ground pepper to taste
1/4 cup olive oil

Preheat the oven to 350 degrees. Coat the bottom and sides of a 9- × 13-inch baking dish with oil. Layer the zucchini in the bottom of the prepared dish, sprinkle lightly with salt and half the Kasseri and Monterey Jack cheeses. Top with the basil and press down.

Arrange the tomato slices over the basil and sprinkle lightly with salt, pepper, and the remaining Kasseri and Monterey Jack cheeses. Drizzle with 1/4 cup olive oil. Bake for 35 minutes.

Note: To peel tomatoes, dip in boiling water for 10 to 20 seconds. Using a slotted spoon, transfer the tomatoes to a bowl of ice water to stop the cooking process. Let stand for approximately 1 minute. Peel with a sharp knife. Avoid cooking the tomatoes too long or they will fall apart. The riper the tomato, the less blanching time required.

Serves 6 to 8

Carmel
TOMATOFEST

At the peak of the summer tomato season, there is no better place to be than the Carmel TomatoFest where festival-goers can sample more than two hundred varieties of the region's plump, juicy best. The closest thing to junk food at this summer festival is fried green tomatoes served to guests as they stroll the grounds of the Quail Lodge Country Club in Carmel Valley, which is perfectly situated beyond the coastal fog.

Beneath graceful white tents, hundreds of chefs from local restaurants serve delectable tomato-inspired appetizers, from tequila-soaked sun-dried tomatoes prepared by the Pajaro Street Grill to Tarpy's gourmet BLT on herb toast points with applewood-smoked bacon, vine-ripened tomatoes, and nasturtium confetti. Wineries also provide endless tastings.

Families are welcome at this harvest celebration where children play in sand traps on the golf course and dance to live music. The price of admission supports the Boys and Girls Clubs of Monterey County.

Peaches

Over two hundred varieties of peaches, each with its own specific harvest time, flavor, and color characteristics are harvested in California from April through October. California peaches are grown mainly in the Sacramento and San Joaquin Valleys.

Peaches fall into two classifications: clingstones, where the fruit clings stubbornly to the pit, and freestone, where the flesh falls away from the pit easily. Though Georgia claims to be the "Peach State," California accounts for nearly 100 percent of the U.S. commercial production of cling peaches. The commodity ranks forty-first in California crop value at over one hundred ten million dollars at harvest, increasing to over five hundred million dollars after processing. Cling peaches are sorted and packed by hand, placed in bins, graded, and transported to processors where they are peeled, pitted, and put in cans halved, sliced, diced, or in fruit cocktail. California produces over 60 percent of U.S. freestone peaches, most of which are handpicked, packed in boxes, and shipped to market.

To ripen peaches, place them in a loosely closed paper bag away from direct sunlight for one to three days. When ripe, the fruit will be aromatic and give to gentle palm pressure. Storing unripe fruit in the refrigerator will halt the ripening process, resulting in mealy, dry, tasteless fruit. Once the fruit is ripe, it can be stored in a paper bag in the refrigerator for about a week.

In response to consumer demand for sweet fruit, California growers are increasing plantings of new varieties being marketed as Summerwhite peaches with paler skin and a light pink or whitish interior. While acid levels of traditional yellow peaches continue to decrease after harvest, making the fruit taste sweeter, the acid levels of Summerwhite peaches remain constant creating the potential for sweeter taste throughout the ripening process. In a paper bag, Summerwhite peaches ripen nearly twice as fast as yellow varieties.

Over one hundred varieties of peach and nectarine trees feature pink to red petals along the Fresno County Blossom Trail from the end of February through early March. The sixty-two-mile self-guided trail comes alive with panoramic vistas of fruit trees and wildflowers while leading bikers and drivers through the towns of Sanger, Reedley, Minkler, and Centerville southeast of Fresno, California. A highlight of the celebration comes the first weekend in March, when Sanger hosts the Blossom Days Festival with two-mile and 10K runs, food, arts and crafts, and music.

Photo Opposite: Peach Orchard, Brentwood, California

PEACH & CROISSANT BREAD PUDDING

A rich summer dessert from the California Tree Fruit Agreement.

> 1 1/2 cups coarsely chopped peeled
>   fresh peaches (2 to 3 peaches)
> 1 1/4 cups plus 2 tablespoons sugar,
>   divided
> 1 teaspoon lemon juice
> 4 to 5 cups milk
> 1/3 cup rum
> 1 teaspoon vanilla extract
> 4 eggs
> 1/2 teaspoon salt
> 3 tablespoons butter, divided
> 5 or 6 dry (day-old) croissants,
>   cut crosswise into halves

Preheat the oven to 375 degrees. Combine the peaches, 2 tablespoons sugar, and lemon juice in a bowl. Set aside. Pour the milk into a mixing bowl, using 4 cups for soft croissants, more if they are very dry. Mix in 3/4 cup sugar, rum, vanilla, eggs, and salt.

Coat a 2 1/2-quart baking dish with 1 tablespoon butter. Arrange one-fourth of the croissants in the bottom, tearing them as needed to fit. Layer with one-third of the peach mixture. Pour one-fourth of the milk mixture over the top. Let stand briefly. Repeat the process, pressing down between each layer. Sprinkle with 1/2 cup sugar and dot with the remaining butter. Bake for 45 minutes or until a knife inserted in the center comes out clean. Serve warm.

Serves 6

Enjoy summer's warm evenings with good friends by the pool. A menu of appetizers allows for easy conversation and plenty of relaxation. An Asian influence, popular in foods served on the West Coast, pulls this collection of finger foods together. Using a new variation on a traditional theme, the peach shortcake finishes off a memorable evening.

WINE PAIRINGS BY

A crisp and refreshing California Pinot Grigio, such as Pepi, Luna Vineyards, or Ivan Tamas

•

A chilled and fruity California Gewürztraminer, such as Meridian Vineyards or Stonestreet

From the French word for filling up, ullage refers to the air space in an unopened bottle between the bottom of the cork and the top of the wine. Check bottles periodically since ullage of an inch or more may indicate that wine is getting out and air is getting in. Seepage on the cork is another indication that something is wrong with the storage situation. Avoid these circumstances and minimize losses by keeping the temperature cool and constant in the cellar.

Candied Ginger Shortcakes with Peaches

CANDIED GINGER SHORTCAKES WITH PEACHES

The Point Arena Bakery originally developed this recipe for scones.
It makes a perfect shortcake with fresh peaches and cream.

Shortcakes
2 ounces candied ginger
1/4 cup sugar
2 cups cake flour
1 tablespoon baking powder
1/2 teaspoon salt
1/2 teaspoon ground ginger
1 1/4 cups heavy whipping cream
1 egg, lightly beaten
Brown sugar

Topping
6 ripe peaches, peeled, sliced
1 tablespoon sugar
1 teaspoon lemon juice
2 cups heavy whipping cream
1 tablespoon sugar

Preheat the oven to 375 degrees. Combine the candied ginger and sugar in a food processor. Process until the ginger is finely chopped. Combine the cake flour, baking powder, salt, and ground ginger in a bowl and mix well. Stir in the candied ginger mixture.

Beat 1 1/4 cups heavy whipping cream in a mixing bowl until soft peaks form. Fold half the whipped cream into the flour mixture until combined, then fold in the rest of the whipped cream. The dough will look lumpy and unblended. Knead briefly on a lightly floured surface until a soft dough forms.

Pat the dough into a 1-inch-thick rectangle and cut into eight equal rectangles or squares. Arrange the portions close together on a baking sheet lined with baking parchment. Brush with the egg and sprinkle generously with brown sugar. Bake for 20 to 25 minutes or until light brown. Remove to a wire rack to cool. Cut each shortcake horizontally into halves.

Combine the peaches, 1 tablespoon sugar, and lemon juice in a bowl and toss to mix. Beat 2 cups heavy whipping cream and 1 tablespoon sugar in a mixing bowl until soft peaks form. Place the bottom half of each shortcake on a dessert plate. Layer with the peach mixture, shortcake tops, and whipped cream. Serve immediately.

Serves 8

The Cannery

Near Fisherman's Wharf in San Francisco, visitors discover a tri-level marketplace at The Cannery, with interesting one-of-a-kind shops, art galleries, restaurants, and spectacular views. A flower-filled courtyard invites passers-by to relax under the century-old olive trees while enjoying street performers, sidewalk cafés, and vendors' stalls. The Museum of the City of San Francisco, housed on the third floor, traces the City's history with fascinating displays on the earthquakes of 1906 and 1989. The California Fruit Canners, now known as Del Monte, built the cannery in 1907 at the corner of Leavenworth and Beach Streets after the 1906 earthquake destroyed existing canneries. Peaches were shipped to the cannery by rail, pitted by hand, peeled, canned, and shipped around the world by sea. By 1909, the San Francisco Cannery was the largest fruit and vegetable cannery in the world.

Raspberries

The evolution of the red raspberry can be traced to Eastern Asia, where more than two hundred wild species are known. Propagated from suckers on the roots of the parent plant, cultivation of the berry in the United States can be traced back to the early settlers who learned propagation techniques from the Native Americans. During the months of June through October, California produces one-quarter of the total U.S. crop of raspberries in the coastal counties of Santa Cruz and Monterey.

The thorny raspberry bush comes in many varieties, including red, purple, black, and the rare yellow and white. Red raspberries are related to many other berries, including blackberries, boysenberries, and loganberries. The raspberry is unique to other berries in that its core remains on the plant when picked, leaving it hollow and consequently very fragile.

It is recommended that raspberries not be rinsed until just before eating, as moisture breaks down the delicate fruit. A one-cup serving of red raspberries has just fifty calories and is an excellent source of vitamin C, as well as a good source of folic acid and fiber.

RASPBERRY PUDDING CAKES

A beautiful dessert, easy enough for every day and special enough for dinner guests.

1 cup fresh raspberries	1/2 cup milk
2 tablespoons unsalted butter, softened	1/3 cup buttermilk
	1 tablespoon flour
1/2 cup sugar	1 teaspoon vanilla extract
2 eggs, separated	Confectioners' sugar

Preheat the oven to 350 degrees. Reserve 12 raspberries. Sprinkle equal amounts of the remaining raspberries in the bottoms of four 6-ounce ramekins.

Beat the butter in a mixing bowl until creamy. Add the sugar gradually, beating until blended. Add the egg yolks one at a time, beating well after each addition. Beat in the milk, buttermilk, flour, and vanilla until smooth.

Beat the egg whites in a separate mixing bowl until stiff peaks form. Stir 1/2 cup of the egg whites into the batter. Fold in the remaining egg whites. Spoon equal amounts of the batter into the prepared ramekins. Dot the tops with the reserved raspberries. Place the ramekins in a 9- × 13-inch baking pan. Fill the baking pan with enough boiling water to reach halfway up the sides of the ramekins. Bake for 22 to 25 minutes or until puffed and golden brown. Cool slightly. Sprinkle with confectioners' sugar. Serve warm or chilled.

Serves 4

CLASSIC CARROT CAKE

Carrot cake recipes abound, but this three-layer version
will take the blue ribbon prize every time.

2 cups flour
2 teaspoons baking soda
1 teaspoon salt
1 teaspoon nutmeg
1 teaspoon cinnamon
2 cups sugar

1 1/4 cups vegetable oil
4 eggs
2 cups peeled and grated carrots
1/2 cup raisins (optional)
2 teaspoons vanilla extract
Cream Cheese Frosting

Preheat the oven to 350 degrees. Grease and flour three 9-inch round cake pans.

Beat together all ingredients, except frosting, in a mixing bowl until smooth. Divide the batter equally between the prepared pans. Bake for 40 minutes or until a toothpick inserted in the center of the cake comes out clean. Cool completely in the pans on a wire rack. Run a sharp knife around the edges of the pans and then gently tap the bottoms of the pans to loosen the cakes. Spread the Cream Cheese Frosting between the layers and over the top and sides of the cake.

Serves 12

CREAM CHEESE FROSTING

The rich cream cheese in this frosting complements the sweetness
of many desserts, such as carrot cake and poppy seed cake.

8 ounces cream cheese, softened
1/2 cup (1 stick) butter, softened
1 teaspoon vanilla extract
1 (1-pound) package confectioners' sugar

Beat the cream cheese, butter, and vanilla in a mixing bowl until creamy. Add the confectioners' sugar gradually, beating constantly until smooth and creamy.

Makes 2 cups

Nearly one million visitors each year enjoy the California State Fair, which takes place in August at Cal Expo in Sacramento. The fair showcases exhibitors from each of the state's counties, who compete in such diverse categories as crafts, textiles, preserved foods, fine arts, cheese making, horsemanship, wine and beer making, floriculture, industrial/technical education, websites, and livestock. Beyond the exhibits, there is a lot more to see and do. The California State Fair also offers horseracing, concerts by big-name performers, rides, and carnival attractions. Most will agree that one of the main attractions is the food. Visitors will find everything from cotton candy and snow cones to fried zucchini, roasted sweet corn, and burritos. The fair's motto is "Big Fun!" and it certainly delivers on that promise.

Cobblers & Crisps

With the abundance of fresh fruit in the summer, fruit desserts are a natural. Cobblers and crisps are delicious and generally easier to prepare than pies. They speak to us of simpler days and slower lifestyles. A cobbler is a baked, deep-dish fruit dessert with a thick biscuit batter sprinkled with sugar. Cobblers can be made with one or more fruits. Many are made with a combination of berries and tree fruit, such as peaches and blackberries, nectarines and blueberries, or cherries and apricots.

Crisps are another variation on the theme of deep-dish fruit desserts. The crisp topping is usually a crumbly mixture of sugar, butter, flour, and cinnamon or another spice. Many favor the addition of rolled oats to the topping to achieve a wonderful chewy texture. The topping is spread over the sliced fruit before it is baked. Plums, apples, pears, and any of the cobbler combinations listed above will make a soul-satisfying crisp. Set calorie-counting aside; each of these treats deserves a scoop of rich vanilla ice cream on top.

BLUEBERRY NECTARINE COBBLER

The cobbler recipe from the original California Fresh *cookbook has been a hit for years. This version combines blueberries and nectarines.*

Batter
1/2 cup (1 stick) butter, melted
1 cup sugar
11/2 cups flour
1 tablespoon baking powder
1/2 teaspoon salt
1 cup milk

Fruit Filling
3 cups fresh blueberries
2 cups sliced, peeled nectarines
2 teaspoons fresh lemon juice
11/2 teaspoons cinnamon
1/4 cup sugar

Preheat the oven to 350 degrees. Pour the butter into a shallow 2-quart baking dish, tilting the dish to coat the bottom evenly. Combine 1 cup sugar, flour, baking powder, and salt in a bowl and mix well. Add the milk, stirring just until blended; the batter will be lumpy. Pour into the prepared dish; do not stir.

For the filling, toss the blueberries and nectarines with the lemon juice and cinnamon in a bowl until coated. Arrange the fruit over the batter. Sprinkle with 1/4 cup sugar; do not stir. Bake for 40 to 45 minutes or until golden brown. Serve warm with vanilla ice cream.

Serves 6 to 8

SOUR CREAM POUND CAKE

Serve with whipped cream and fresh berries
for a lovely presentation.

3 cups sifted flour
1/4 teaspoon baking soda
1 cup sour cream
1 1/2 teaspoons almond extract

1 1/2 teaspoons vanilla extract
3 cups sugar
1 cup (2 sticks) butter, softened
6 eggs, separated

Preheat the oven to 300 degrees. Grease and flour a 10-inch bundt or tube pan.

Combine the flour and baking soda in a small bowl and mix well. Mix the extracts with the sour cream and set aside. Beat the sugar and butter in a mixing bowl until creamy, scraping the bowl occasionally. Add the egg yolks one at a time, beating well after each addition. Add the flour mixture alternately with the sour cream, beating well after each addition.

Beat the egg whites in a mixing bowl until soft peaks form. Stir 1 cup of the egg whites into the batter to lighten it, then gently fold in the remaining egg whites. Pour the batter into the prepared pan. Bake for 1 1/2 hours. Cool in the pan for 15 minutes. Remove to a wire rack to cool completely.

Serves 12

Napa Valley
WINE AUCTION

For two decades, the annual Napa Valley Wine Auction has been raising millions of dollars for medical and counseling services for farm workers, low-income expectant mothers and families, domestic violence prevention, and AIDS research and treatment. With top celebrities, millionaires, and renowned restaurateurs and winemakers in attendance, the event's proceeds have totaled more than five million dollars after a four-day whirlwind of parties, wine tastings, dinners, and auctions. At the silent and live auctions, attendees bid on rare and collectible wines, along with other prizes. Gourmet tidbits are offered by acclaimed local restaurants such as The French Laundry, Napa Valley Grille, and Gordon's Café. Patrons may dine at one of the many wineries hosting lavish luncheons and dinners that include music and dancing. A complete Wine Auction package giving access to all of the events during the four days, costs one thousand dollars per person. Passes for individual events are available at lower prices. Even if only once in a lifetime, find a way to attend Napa's premier event combining great food, fine wine, and an opportunity to improve the lives of others.

It's-It

It's-It™, a delectable treat created in Northern California, is an ice cream confection made with a scoop of vanilla ice cream sandwiched between two chewy oatmeal cookies dipped in chocolate. It's-It bars first came on the scene in 1928 when San Francisco's Playland Amusement Park owner, George Whitney, concocted the treat for patrons. After devising the unique recipe, he exclaimed, "It's it!" When Playland closed in the early 1970s, the ice cream treats were so missed by their fans in the Bay Area that a San Francisco family purchased the rights and began to make It's-It bars to sell locally. Today, It's-It ice cream bars are available in fifteen western states, and in some national chain grocery stores. It's-Its are made in several flavors, including strawberry, chocolate, mint, cappuccino, and the original vanilla.

COCOA CINNAMON WEDDING COOKIES

This version of Mexican Wedding Cookies uses the classic Mexican flavorings of chocolate, almonds, and cinnamon.

1 1/4 cups flour
1/2 cup unsweetened cocoa
1/2 cup (1 stick) salted butter, softened
1/2 cup (1 stick) unsalted butter, softened

1/2 cup sugar
1 tablespoon vanilla extract
1 1/2 cups almonds, lightly toasted, finely ground
1 cup confectioners' sugar
1/4 teaspoon cinnamon

Preheat the oven to 325 degrees. Combine the flour and unsweetened cocoa in a bowl and mix well. Beat the salted butter, unsalted butter, and sugar in a mixing bowl until light and fluffy. Add the vanilla and beat until blended. Add one-third of the flour mixture at a time, mixing just until blended after each addition. Do not overmix. Fold in the almonds.

Shape the dough into 1 1/4-inch-diameter balls. Arrange the balls 2 to 3 inches apart on a cookie sheet lined with baking parchment. Bake for 22 minutes. Check for doneness by gently lifting the edge of a cookie. If the cookie lifts off the sheet fairly cleanly and the top feels medium-firm to the touch, the cookies are done. They will firm up as they cool. To prevent the cookies from crumbling, do not attempt to remove them from the cookie sheet until they are cool.

Combine the confectioners' sugar and cinnamon in a shallow bowl and mix well. Roll the cooled cookies one at a time in the confectioners' sugar mixture. Roll each cookie a second time. Store in an airtight container.

Note: To save time on this and other cookie recipes, use a 1 1/4-inch spring-release ice cream scoop to spoon the dough onto the cookie sheets. Level the scoop on the edge of the mixing bowl.

Makes 32 cookies

CHOCOLATE CARAMEL SHORTBREAD BARS

These bar cookies are sinfully rich and wonderful!

Shortbread Layer
1 cup (2 sticks) butter, softened
1/2 cup sugar
2 cups flour
1 teaspoon baking powder

Caramel Layer
1/2 cup (1 stick) butter
1/2 cup packed light brown sugar
7 ounces sweetened condensed
   milk (1/2 can)
2 tablespoons light corn syrup

Chocolate Layer
2 cups (12 ounces) semisweet
   chocolate chips
1 cup chopped pecans, lightly
   toasted (optional)

Preheat the oven to 350 degrees. For the shortbread, beat the butter and sugar in a mixing bowl until creamy. Mix the flour and baking powder together and beat into the butter mixture. Pat the dough into the bottom of a 9- × 13-inch baking pan. Bake for 20 to 25 minutes or until golden brown. Remove from oven. Let stand until cool.

For the caramel layer, combine the butter, brown sugar, sweetened condensed milk, and corn syrup in a saucepan and mix well. Bring to a boil over medium heat. Boil, stirring constantly, for 8 minutes or until a candy thermometer registers 238 degrees. Pour over the shortbread layer. Cool.

Heat the chocolate chips in a double boiler or microwave until melted. Spread over the cooled caramel layer. Sprinkle with the pecans. Let stand to cool before cutting into bars.

Makes 4 dozen

Ghirardelli Square

Ghirardelli Chocolate, with its cable car logo, has become a delicious symbol of San Francisco. Visitors to Fisherman's Wharf can walk along the San Francisco Bay past Pier 39 and reward themselves with a stop at one of the most famous chocolate shops in the world. Ghirardelli Square is a block of beautiful brick buildings that once housed a factory that made Civil War uniforms. In the late 1800s, Italian immigrant and candy maker, Domingo Ghirardelli, bought the factory and moved his chocolate-making business to the site. In the 1960s, the main operations were moved across the Bay to San Leandro. Fearing that the historic buildings would be torn down, the Roth family bought the block and began the first successful "reuse project" in the United States. Today, the square is a picturesque brick-terraced courtyard that houses elegant shops and fine restaurants. The Ghirardelli store and ice-cream parlor remains the main attraction. It houses vintage chocolate-making machinery and confections that will tempt any sweet tooth. The site also offers historic walking tours and hosts the Fourth of July Waterfront Festival (with the best views of the fireworks over the Golden Gate), the Chocolate Festival, free jazz concerts, and an annual Christmas Tree Lighting ceremony.

Fall

Fall

Three cheers for the home team! It's football season, the kids are back in school, and festive holiday celebrations are about to begin. The warm summer days are shortening into crisp evenings. Vibrant leaves in autumn tones cling to tree limbs until a chilly breeze sends them fluttering to the ground. Mums, marigolds, and asters bring a warm earthiness to flowerbeds, and baskets of cornhusks, fancy gourds, and miniature pumpkins are an inviting sign of welcome at the front door. Rain boots and slickers stand at the ready for drizzly days and kitchens are filled with the warm aroma of baking breads, slow-cooked soups, and Thanksgiving pies. In golden valleys and hillsides, plump grapes are pulled from their vines and crushed into deep crimson nectar. Children smile the toothy grins of jack-o-lanterns, beaming with pride at having chosen the perfect pumpkin from the patch. Gather together with friends and family during the months of harvest, give thanks, and partake in the bounty that Northern California bestows upon us.

FALL RECIPES

Lettuce

A member of the sunflower family and one of the oldest known vegetables, lettuce is thought to be native to the Mediterranean area. Romaine lettuce was named by the Romans who believed it had healthful properties. In fact, the Emperor Caesar Augustus erected a statue praising lettuce because he was convinced it cured him from an illness. Lettuce made its way to the Americas in the 1600s when John Winthrop, Jr., brought over packets of lettuce seed from England.

In the cool coastal valley of California's famed Monterey County lies the largest lettuce-producing region in the country. Known as "the salad bowl of the world" the Salinas Valley has a ten-month growing season with a moderate climate. Over three-quarters of all the lettuce in the U.S. is produced here on an annual basis. There are several types of lettuces grown in California, including iceberg, romaine, looseleaf lettuces like green leaf and red leaf, and butterhead varieties like Boston and Bibb lettuce. Iceberg lettuce was called "crisphead" until the 1920s when it was renamed after California began transporting large quantities of the head lettuce underneath mounds of ice to keep it cool.

Lettuce is considered one of the easier crops to grow. It starts from seed and takes about sixty to ninety days to mature. In the field, lettuce seeds are planted side-by-side in rows so that more lettuce can grow in each row. Lettuce is harvested by hand when it is mature. Almost all lettuce is packed right in the field and then transported in refrigerated trucks to help maintain its quality.

Lettuce is naturally low in calories. Darker green lettuce is higher in calcium, iron, and vitamins A and C and is more nutritious than lighter lettuce. When choosing a head of lettuce, select one that feels heavy for its size, indicating a high water content. Look for crisp, evenly colored leaves with no sign of wilting or yellowing at the edges. Lettuce should be rinsed right before use, as moisture advances decay, then dried in paper towels or spun dry in a salad spinner. To prevent bruising tender varieties, tear lettuce leaves rather than cutting them. Lettuce may be stored in the refrigerator crisper in a plastic bag lined with a paper towel to absorb excess moisture. Butterhead and leaf lettuce will last for up to one week, romaine will last for about ten days, and iceberg lettuce will last for up to two weeks.

Photo Opposite: Field of Iceberg Lettuce, Castroville, California

CAESAR SALAD

Chefs Mitchell and Steven Rosenthal of Wolfgang Puck's San Francisco restaurant, Postrio, developed this outstanding version of Caesar Salad.

> 1 egg
> 2 tablespoons lemon juice
> 1 tablespoon whole grain mustard
> 1 tablespoon sherry wine vinegar
> 2 small garlic cloves, chopped
> 2 teaspoons chopped rinsed capers
> 1 1/2 teaspoons chopped anchovy
> 1 cup olive oil
> 2 tablespoons grated Parmesan cheese
> Salt and pepper to taste
> Hearts of 2 to 3 heads romaine, chopped

Bring a small amount of water to a boil in a small saucepan. Set the egg in the boiling water gently using a slotted spoon. Boil for 2 minutes. Drain and immediately immerse the egg in a bowl of ice water. Let stand until completely cool.

Crack the egg into a bowl. Scoop out any of the remaining cooked egg from the shell into the bowl using a teaspoon. Add the lemon juice, mustard, wine vinegar, garlic, capers, and anchovy and whisk gently. Add the olive oil gradually, whisking constantly until mixed. Stir in the cheese, salt, and pepper.

Toss the romaine with the desired amount of dressing in a salad bowl until coated. Serve immediately.

Note: The egg in this recipe is not fully cooked. If you are reluctant to use raw egg, this recipe is not recommended.

Serves 6 to 8

An iced tub of beer

•

*Sonoma County
Chardonnay*

Seasoned tailgaters will not hesitate to serve this menu to friends right in the stadium parking lot. For the less adventurous, it is a menu easily prepared before heading off to the big game, as these dishes will patiently await the return of avid fans. Fall's splendor is evident in the bold spices and other flavorful ingredients. From pecans and jicama to pumpkin cheesecake, this celebratory meal will warm you through and through.

Cayenne & Chili-Spiced Pecans 118
Nachos 118

•

Leaf Lettuces with Orange-Cumin Dressing 117
Vegetarian Black Bean Chili 136
Sweet Cornbread 148

•

Praline Pumpkin Cheesecake 160

Leaf Lettuces with Orange-Cumin Dressing

LEAF LETTUCES WITH ORANGE-CUMIN DRESSING

*Crunchy jicama and southwestern flavors combine to
create this outstanding salad.*

Orange-Cumin Dressing
1/3 cup vegetable oil
1/4 cup red wine vinegar
Finely chopped zest and juice of
   1 orange
1 tablespoon honey
1/2 teaspoon chili powder
1/4 teaspoon ground cumin
1/2 teaspoon salt
Freshly ground pepper to taste

Salad
3 large oranges
3 to 4 ounces jicama, peeled,
   julienned
3 slices red onion, cut into quarters
1 head red leaf lettuce, torn into
   bite-size pieces
1/2 head green leaf lettuce, torn
   into bite-size pieces
1/2 cup shelled pumpkin seeds
   or shelled sunflower seeds,
   lightly toasted

Whisk the dressing ingredients together in a bowl.

With a sharp knife, cut the skin off the 3 oranges, then cut each section away from the membrane. Do this over a bowl to catch the juice, adding the juice to the dressing. Set aside. Combine the jicama, onion, and 2 tablespoons of dressing in a small bowl and toss to coat. Toss the lettuce with the desired amount of dressing in a salad bowl.

Divide the lettuce equally among six salad plates. Arrange the orange sections over the lettuce. Top with the jicama mixture and sprinkle with the pumpkin seeds.

Note: Shelled pumpkin seeds are available in natural foods stores and well-stocked supermarkets.

Serves 6

Berkeley Bowl
MARKETPLACE

On any given day, the produce and foodstuffs offered at the Berkeley Bowl Marketplace are the freshest around. Owner Glenn Yasuda grew up on a farm and has a passion for produce. He opened Berkeley Bowl over twenty years ago and named it for its first home, a converted bowling alley on Shattuck Avenue. It has since moved up the street to a beautiful, newly remodeled building. Everyone, from restaurateurs and students of the California Culinary Academy to health food fans and home chefs, peruses the enormous selection of fine produce, including rare and unique items like black Spanish radishes and pink honeydew. With romaine and butter lettuces, watercress, endive, and arugula, the selection of garden greens alone is impressive. And nothing at Berkeley Bowl goes to waste. To ensure that everything sells, prices fall as items ripen. It is a favorite haunt for caterers and food fanatics looking for only the best produce, or that extraordinary item that will bring their next culinary creation to life.

Nachos

Always a popular appetizer, nachos hardly require a recipe. They are easy to prepare with whatever ingredients may be on hand. For example, just pile tortilla chips on a baking sheet, cover with sliced olives, refried beans, browned ground beef, and shredded cheese. Place them under the broiler until the cheese has melted, then serve immediately with salsa and guacamole. For a more sophisticated version, spread blue and yellow corn tortilla chips in a single layer on a baking sheet. Top each chip with two teaspoons of shredded Cheddar cheese and a jalapeño chile ring. Broil until the cheese is melted and serve immediately with sour cream.

CAYENNE & CHILI-SPICED PECANS

These tasty pecans are habit-forming.

1 tablespoon vegetable oil
8 ounces pecan halves
1 1/2 teaspoons chili powder
1 1/2 teaspoons kosher salt

3/4 teaspoon cayenne pepper
1/2 teaspoon sugar
1 teaspoon fresh lemon juice

Heat a heavy skillet over medium heat. Add the oil and pecans. Cook, stirring constantly, until the pecans appear dry and begin to sizzle. Sprinkle with the chili powder, salt, cayenne pepper, and sugar and stir to coat. Drizzle with the lemon juice. Cook, stirring constantly, until the pecans are dry once again. Remove the pecans to a double thickness of paper towels to cool slightly. Serve warm. Reheat on a baking sheet in a 350-degree oven for 5 minutes if necessary.

Makes 1 1/3 cups

FOUR-CHEESE PHYLLO APPETIZERS

Rich with cheese and butter, these triangle-shaped appetizers are delicious.

1 (16-ounce) package phyllo pastry
1 pound ricotta cheese
8 ounces feta cheese, crumbled
3 ounces Monterey Jack cheese, shredded

1/4 cup grated Parmesan cheese
3 or 4 green onions, finely chopped
4 eggs, lightly beaten
1 cup (2 sticks) butter, melted

Thaw the phyllo pastry according to package instructions. Preheat the oven to 400 degrees. Place an oven rack in the upper third of the oven. Combine the cheeses, green onions, and eggs in a bowl and mix well.

Unfold the pastry and cover with waxed paper topped with a damp towel to prevent it from drying out. Remove one sheet of the pastry to a flat work surface and brush lightly with some of the melted butter. Top with another sheet. Cut in half lengthwise and cut each half crosswise into six equal portions.

Spoon 1 teaspoon of the cheese mixture on a corner of each strip. Fold that corner over to its opposite edge to cover the filling, forming a triangle. Continue folding like a flag. Arrange the triangles on a buttered baking sheet and brush with melted butter. Repeat the process with the remaining pastry, cheese mixture, and butter.

Bake for 15 to 20 minutes or until crisp and golden brown. Serve warm.

Note: These triangles may be frozen before baking. Do not thaw before baking and allow additional baking time.

Makes 120 triangles

Beach Blanket
BABYLON

An evening of live theater has never been quite as raucous as the ninety-minute production of *Beach Blanket Babylon*. This unique show, a San Francisco fixture that has run for twenty-five years, is a musical revue with a decidedly thin plot revolving around Snow White searching for love. Along the way she meets everyone from high profile movie stars to political personalities. The story line frequently changes and is often drawn from current headlines. The show is a whirlwind of song and dance numbers, one-liners, and sight gags. The talented cast not only has to keep in step, but also has to deal with elaborate costumes, many of which include extremely large, sometimes unruly hats. The *pièce de résistance* is a hat that carries the landmarks of San Francisco, from Coit Tower to the Golden Gate Bridge, and stands an amazing twelve feet tall. The show is a "must-see" for lovers of song, dance, comedy, and outrageous fun.

Mushrooms

Not long ago, only the common white or button mushroom was widely used. Today, many mushroom varieties once considered foreign and exotic—shiitakes, oysters, portobellos, cremini—are readily available at the supermarket and appear frequently in both restaurant and home cooking. With cultivation of the formerly wild varieties, the distinction between wild and domestic mushrooms has blurred.

Mushrooms have an earthy, smoky flavor and a meaty texture. To accompany meat, sauté fresh mushrooms with butter and chopped fresh parsley. Allow the mushrooms to release all of their liquid, then cook them a bit longer to evaporate the liquid and intensify the flavors. If using dried mushrooms, save the strained soaking liquid and add it back into the pan during the sauté process. For a special touch, add a little cream and/or port a few minutes before the end of cooking. Mushrooms are also a great vegetarian substitute for meat in many dishes. Instead of grilling beef, try grilling portobellos. Brush them with a little olive oil and grill them gill side up to retain their juices. Prolong the shelf life of mushrooms by storing them in a porous bag in the refrigerator. To clean mushrooms, use a soft bristled brush or damp cloth to remove any grit just before using.

MUSHROOM & GRUYÈRE TART

The dark, rich mushrooms, wonderful cheeses, and Cognac in this tart are a fabulous combination to enjoy in front of a crackling fire.

Pastry
1 1/2 cups flour
1/2 teaspoon kosher salt
1/2 cup (1 stick) unsalted butter, cut into small pieces
3 tablespoons ice water
2 tablespoons minced fresh chives

Filling
2 tablespoons olive oil
1 onion or leek, finely chopped
1 pound mixed mushrooms (shiitake, oyster, portobello, cremini), stemmed, sliced
1 cup high quality apple juice or cider
1/4 cup Cognac or brandy
1/2 teaspoon kosher salt
Freshly ground pepper to taste
1 cup heavy cream
4 eggs
1 cup grated Gruyère cheese
1/2 cup grated fresh Parmigiano-Reggiano cheese (aged Parmesan)
1/4 cup chopped fresh flat-leaf parsley
1/4 cup chopped fresh basil

To prepare the pastry, combine the flour and salt in a food processor. Pulse until blended. Add the butter and pulse until crumbly. With the motor running, add the ice water gradually until a dough begins to form. Stop the motor. Add the chives and pulse just until mixed. Shape into a disk and wrap in plastic wrap. Chill for 1 hour.

Preheat the oven to 375 degrees. Roll the pastry on a lightly floured surface. Fit the pastry into a 9- or 10-inch tart pan with a removable bottom and trim the edge. Freeze for 10 minutes. Line the pastry with foil. Bake for 20 minutes. Remove the foil and bake for 5 minutes longer or until lightly browned.

To prepare the filling, heat the olive oil in a large skillet over medium heat. Add the onion and sauté for 5 minutes. Stir in the mushrooms and sauté for 5 to 10 minutes or until the mushrooms release their liquid. Add the apple juice and Cognac and mix well. Simmer for 15 to 30 minutes or until the liquid evaporates, stirring occasionally. Season with salt and pepper. Remove from heat and let stand until cool.

Whisk the heavy cream and eggs in a bowl until blended. Stir in the Gruyère and Parmigiano-Reggiano cheeses. Add the parsley and basil. Fold in the mushroom mixture. Pour into the partially baked tart shell. Bake for 30 minutes or until a knife inserted near the center comes out clean. Cool slightly. Remove rim and cut into wedges.

Serves 6

CURRIED WALNUT CHICKEN TRIANGLES

*A unique combination of flavors creates this
outstanding phyllo hors d'oeuvre.*

1 (16-ounce) package phyllo pastry
2 tablespoons unsalted butter
2¹/₂ tablespoons flour
1 teaspoon curry powder
1 cup milk
2 boneless skinless chicken breasts,
   cooked, finely chopped (about
   2¹/₂ cups)

¹/₂ cup chopped walnuts, lightly
   toasted
¹/₂ teaspoon salt
1 cup (2 sticks) butter, melted

Thaw the pastry according to package instructions. Melt the unsalted butter in a small saucepan. Stir in the flour and curry powder. Cook over low heat for 2 minutes, stirring constantly. Whisk in the milk. Cook until thickened, stirring constantly. Remove from heat and stir in the chicken, walnuts, and salt. Let stand until cool.

   Preheat the oven to 400 degrees. Place the oven rack in the upper third of the oven. Unfold the pastry and cover with waxed paper topped with a damp towel to prevent it from drying out. Remove one sheet to a flat work surface and brush it lightly with some of the melted butter. Top with another sheet. Cut lengthwise into halves. Cut each half crosswise into six equal portions.

   Spoon 1 teaspoon of the chicken mixture on a corner of each strip. Fold that corner over to its opposite edge to cover the filling, forming a triangle. Continue folding like a flag. Arrange the triangles on a buttered baking sheet and brush with melted butter. Repeat the process with the remaining pastry, chicken mixture, and melted butter. Bake for 10 to 15 minutes or until crisp and golden brown. Serve warm.

Note: These triangles may be frozen before baking. Do not thaw before baking and allow additional baking time.

Makes 120 triangles

Organic Milk

Organic milk is produced without the use of antibiotics, pesticides, or hormones. Maintaining a certified organic dairy is difficult, but many dairy operators feel the health benefits are well worth the effort. Before producing certified organic milk, cows must be fed only 100 percent certified organic feed for at least one year. The land used to grow the feed must be pesticide-free for at least three years. Organic milk cannot come in contact with any non-organic milk during the milking, transporting, processing, or packaging stages. In California, an independent, qualified organization visits each organic farm and traces the history of all materials used on the farmland for the past three years. This organization also tests the water used on the farm and inspects the processing plants to be certain that all operations meet the requirements before organic certification is granted.

When shopping for organic milk, look for the words "certified organic" on the milk carton or bottle and expect to pay slightly more than for non-certified milk. Other organic dairy products include sour cream, half-and-half, butter, yogurt, cottage cheese, and eggs.

Stock

While stocks are now available in the freezer section of gourmet markets, making aromatic stock at home is easy. This recipe makes one gallon of chicken stock:

1 whole stewing hen
2 cups chopped onion
1 cup chopped celery
1 cup peeled, chopped carrot
4 garlic cloves
2 tablespoons vegetable oil
1 cup white wine
1 cup chopped fresh parsley
2 whole cloves
2 bay leaves
1/2 teaspoon black peppercorns

In a stockpot, combine the stewing hen with enough water to cover by 3 inches. Bring to a boil. Skim off all of the solids that rise to the surface, about 2 or 3 skimmings approximately 5 minutes apart. In a skillet, sauté the onion, celery, carrot, and garlic in the oil until light brown. Add the sautéed vegetables, white wine, parsley, cloves, bay leaves, and peppercorns to the stockpot. Gradually bring to a boil, reduce the heat, and simmer, covered, for 2 hours; strain. Let stand until cool. Store in the freezer in quart containers or resealable freezer bags for up to 3 months.

A cooking tip from **Sandy Sachs,** *Executive Chef, Ingredients Cooking/Lifestyle School at Andronico's Market*

SHERRIED WILD MUSHROOM BROTH

This is a wonderful starter for a dinner of wild game or roast beef.

1¹/2 ounces assorted dried wild mushrooms (porcini, portobello, and shiitake)
1 cup dry sherry
1/4 cup (1/2 stick) unsalted butter
1 pound fresh white or brown (cremini) mushrooms, sliced
2 medium yellow onions, finely chopped

2 ribs celery, finely chopped
1/4 cup flour
6 cups chicken stock
1 teaspoon salt
1/2 teaspoon freshly ground pepper
Crème fraîche (see note)
Chives or green onions, chopped

Rinse the dried mushrooms. Place them in the sherry and either let soak for 1 hour, or microwave on low for 2 minutes and cool for 5 minutes. Drain the mushrooms, reserving the sherry. Strain the sherry through a fine sieve and set aside. Rinse any remaining grit from the mushrooms and chop.

Melt the butter in an 8-quart pot. Add the fresh mushrooms, onions, and celery and mix well. Sauté until the onions are translucent. Stir in the flour. Cook over low heat for 2 minutes, stirring constantly. Stir in the reserved sherry and stock. Bring to a boil then reduce the heat. Stir in the wild mushrooms.

Simmer, covered, for 1 hour. Add the salt and pepper. Ladle into soup bowls. Top with a spoonful of crème fraîche and sprinkle with chives or green onions.

Note: Crème fraîche is located in the dairy case near the sour cream or in the gourmet cheese section of grocery stores.

Serves 6 to 8

BUTTERNUT SQUASH SOUP WITH SAGE

*This beautiful golden soup is garnished with spectacular,
easy-to-make, fried sage leaves.*

Soup
4 pounds butternut squash
Olive oil
4 tablespoons butter
2 large yellow onions, chopped
2 large garlic cloves, minced
3 cups chicken stock
3 cups water
2 tablespoons finely chopped
    fresh sage
1 to 1 1/2 teaspoons kosher salt
1/2 teaspoon freshly ground pepper

Garnish
12 whole sage leaves
1/4 cup olive oil
1/2 cup grated Gruyère cheese

Preheat the oven to 375 degrees. Cut the squash lengthwise into halves. Scoop out the strings and seeds and discard. Brush the cut surfaces of the squash with olive oil and place cut side down on a baking sheet. Bake for 50 minutes or until the squash is tender when pierced through the widest part of the neck with the tip of a sharp knife. Remove from the oven and turn the squash over to speed cooling. When cool enough to handle, scoop out the flesh into a bowl.

Melt the butter in a large soup pot over medium heat. Add the onions and garlic and cook, stirring occasionally, until the onions begin to brown, 12 to 15 minutes. Remove from the heat and add to the baked squash.

To prepare the garnish, heat 1/4 cup olive oil in a small skillet until nearly smoking. Working in batches, drop the whole sage leaves into the hot oil and fry until darkened, about 1 minute. Drain the leaves on a double thickness of paper towels.

To complete the soup, purée the squash mixture in batches in a blender with 1 cup chicken stock and/or water per batch. Pour the purée back into the soup pot and add any remaining chicken stock and water. Add the chopped sage, salt, and pepper and simmer, partially covered, for 25 minutes, adding more water if the soup is too thick. Serve hot, garnishing each bowl with 2 tablespoons grated cheese and 2 fried sage leaves.

Serves 6

Point Bonita
LIGHTHOUSE

The location of the Point Bonita Lighthouse in the Marin Headlands offers visitors spectacular views of the entrance to San Francisco Bay— but only to those willing to make the journey through the dark, hand-carved, 118-foot long tunnel and across the narrow, swaying footbridge leading to it. The Point Bonita Lighthouse was originally lit in 1855 after several ships ran aground and sank. At 260 feet above sea level, the original lighthouse was often obscured by fog. In 1877, it was moved to its current location at Land's End. A violent storm washed out the narrow path between the lighthouse and Point Bonita in the early 1940s, resulting in the construction of the suspension footbridge, which is a replica of the Golden Gate Bridge. The National Park Service opens the lighthouse to visitors on weekends, and twice each month by reservation for full-moon tours.

Bartlett Pears

California's three-hundred-thousand-ton pear harvest equals one-third of the total U.S. pear crop and has a cash value of more than five hundred million dollars annually. The Bartlett is the most popular pear variety grown in California and in the United States. Pears were originally cultivated by the Romans thousands of years ago. Bartletts originated in England and came to America with the early colonists. Seedlings found their way to California in the 1849 Gold Rush. California now has two main pear producing regions: the Sacramento River Delta and Upper Sacramento Valley region, called the Early Harvest District, and the region from Mendocino to Clear Lake, called the Late Harvest District. The pear harvest runs from mid-July to early October.

Pears are always picked before they fully ripen on the tree. Once picked, pears can be ripened at room temperature and then refrigerated. Bartletts are at the peak of ripeness when they have turned from green to golden yellow and have lost their firmness. To test for ripeness, press lightly near the stem; the pear should yield to gentle pressure, although the wide middle area may still feel firm. Pears are an excellent source of fiber, vitamin C, and potassium.

FENNEL & PERSIMMON SALAD

Fuyu persimmons are used in this salad. Unlike the more common Hachiya persimmon, Fuyus are firm and easy to slice when ripe and add a wonderful texture and flavor to mixed greens.

4 cups mixed salad greens, water-cress, and Belgian endive, sliced
3 firm Fuyu persimmons

1 medium fennel bulb, thinly sliced
1/2 cup pecan halves, toasted
Raspberry Pear Vinaigrette

Divide the mixed greens, watercress, and endive evenly among four chilled salad plates. Peel and thinly slice the Fuyu persimmons. Arrange the persimmons and fennel on each salad and sprinkle with the pecans. Drizzle with Raspberry Pear Vinaigrette.

Serves 4

RASPBERRY PEAR VINAIGRETTE

This flavorful vinaigrette is the perfect complement to green salads containing nuts and fresh fruit.

1 small ripe pear, peeled, cored, cut into quarters
1/2 cup mild olive oil
1/4 cup raspberry vinegar

2 teaspoons minced shallots
1 teaspoon mustard seed, toasted (optional)
Kosher salt to taste

Process the pear in a blender until puréed. Strain into a bowl. Whisk in the olive oil, raspberry vinegar, shallots, mustard seed, and salt. Taste and adjust the seasonings if desired.

Makes 1 cup

FRESH FIG, GORGONZOLA & WALNUT SALAD

*This salad is a delightful combination of the best the
season has to offer. Choose figs that are soft to the touch;
they will not ripen off the tree.*

Salad
1 3/4 cups walnut halves, toasted,
    coarsely chopped
1 pound mixed baby lettuces or
    arugula, or a combination
    of the two
12 fresh Mission figs, cut
    lengthwise into halves
2 cups crumbled Gorgonzola
    cheese

Warm Port Vinaigrette
1 cup port wine
1 tablespoon sugar
1/4 cup balsamic vinegar
3/4 cup extra virgin olive oil
Freshly ground pepper

Discard the stems from the arugula; rinse the leaves and/or the lettuce and dry thoroughly.
Divide equally among six salad plates. Top each plate with four fig halves. Sprinkle with the
walnuts and cheese.

To make the vinaigrette, cook the port in a saucepan over medium-high heat until reduced
by half. Be careful to keep the heat low enough not to ignite the port. Stir in the sugar. Cook
until dissolved, stirring constantly. Remove from heat and stir in the balsamic vinegar.
Gradually whisk in the olive oil until blended. Drizzle the warm vinaigrette over the salads.
Season with pepper. Serve immediately.

Serves 6

Monarch Butterflies

In early October, elementary school
children parade through the streets in
winged costumes of orange and black
to celebrate the return of the migrating
monarch butterflies to Pacific Grove,
California. The densest clusters of
monarchs can usually be found at the
Monarch Grove Sanctuary and George
Washington Park in Pacific Grove.
The sheltered forests of Natural Bridges
State Park north of Santa Cruz and
Montana de Oro near Morro Bay are
also prime viewing spots, with docent-
led "butterfly walks."

In March, the monarchs head north
to Western Canada and Alaska to
mate and then expire. Their offspring
metamorphose into adults that
mysteriously make their way back to
the California coast the following fall.
Visitors who miss the migrating
monarchs can explore the marvelous
year-round monarch exhibit at the
Pacific Grove Museum of Natural
History.

Bell Peppers

Bell peppers, also known as capsicums, are sweet-fleshed, bell-shaped members of the pepper family and can be enjoyed raw or cooked. Most bell peppers are green, but as they mature on the plant they turn red, yellow, orange, purple, or black. Their color can be solid or variegated.

Both sweet and hot peppers are native to tropical areas of the Western Hemisphere and were brought by Columbus to Spain where they quickly found their way into Spanish cuisine. In the United States, California is the leading producer of sweet peppers, growing nearly half of the country's annual crop. When buying sweet peppers choose those that are firm and have a richly colored shiny skin. Avoid those that are shriveled or have soft or bruised spots. Store peppers in a plastic bag in the refrigerator for up to one week. Peppers are an excellent source of vitamin C.

King City, deep in the central coast of California, holds a Salsa Fest each fall where both sweet and hot peppers are a primary ingredient in the featured food. Designed as a family event, the festival boasts local and national entertainers, a carnival, and a children's entertainment area. The festival also hosts the lucrative California Salsa Challenge where both amateur and professional cooks vie for thousands of dollars in prize money every year.

Another wonderful destination lies just west of the fertile Napa Valley in Sonoma County. Spend a Saturday traveling the country roads of Sonoma County Farm Trails in search of the freshest cut flowers, artisan cheese, meat, olive oil, wine, and the best farm produce (including peppers!). Maps are available at many Sonoma wineries.

Photo Opposite: Green Bell Peppers, Crow Canyon Gardens, San Ramon, California

TACOS VERACRUZ

El Charro Mexican Dining in Lafayette, California, serves this favorite loaded with fresh bell peppers.

1 red bell pepper, sliced
1 green bell pepper, sliced
2 medium tomatoes, diced
1/2 medium white onion, sliced
1/2 medium red onion, sliced
1/2 cup chopped fresh cilantro
1/2 cup plus 1 tablespoon vegetable
*   oil, divided*
1/2 cup red wine vinegar
Juice of 1 lime
2 tablespoons oregano
1 tablespoon garlic powder
Salt and freshly ground pepper
*   to taste*
4 boneless skinless chicken breasts
8 (6-inch) flour tortillas
1/2 cup shredded Monterey Jack
*   cheese*

Combine the vegetables and cilantro in a bowl. Whisk 1/2 cup oil, wine vinegar, lime juice, and seasonings in a small bowl. Add to the vegetables and toss to coat. Heat the remaining oil in a skillet over medium heat. Add the chicken, season with salt and pepper, cook for 15 minutes or until the chicken is cooked through, turning once. Remove the chicken to a cutting board and slice. Arrange the tortillas in a single layer on two baking sheets. Sprinkle with cheese. Broil until the cheese melts. Top each tortilla with sliced chicken and drained marinated vegetables. Serve immediately.

Serves 4

Roasted Peppers

Roasted bell peppers are delicious in salads, sandwiches, and on pizza. Roasting loosens the skin for peeling and enhances the pepper's natural sweetness. To roast a bell pepper, preheat the broiler to its highest setting. Place the pepper on a baking sheet under the broiler. Turning regularly, roast the pepper until the skin blisters and begins to blacken. Remove from the oven and place the pepper in a paper bag or cover with foil. Let it steam for 10 to 15 minutes. Peel off the skin by hand or use a knife. Remove the stem and seeds before using, but do not rinse the pepper under water.

SWORDFISH WITH ROASTED PEPPERS ON ARUGULA

Serve this gorgeous entrée in the fall when bell peppers are most abundant.

Balsamic Vinaigrette
2 unpeeled whole shallots
2 unpeeled garlic cloves
1 tablespoon olive oil
2 tablespoons balsamic vinegar
1 teaspoon kosher salt
1/4 teaspoon coarsely ground pepper
1/2 cup extra virgin olive oil

Swordfish and Assembly
2 red bell peppers, roasted, peeled, julienned (refer to sidebar)
3 yellow bell peppers, roasted, peeled, julienned
Juice of 1 lemon
8 (6-ounce) swordfish steaks
2 tablespoons olive oil
1 teaspoon kosher salt
1/2 teaspoon coarsely ground pepper
6 cups arugula, coarse stems removed
1 cup niçoise olives, pitted, coarsely chopped (refer to sidebar on page 24)

Preheat the oven to 400 degrees. Place the shallots and garlic in a small baking dish. Drizzle with 1 tablespoon olive oil. Bake, covered with foil, for 30 minutes or until tender. Remove from oven. Peel the shallots and garlic.

Combine the shallots, garlic, balsamic vinegar, 1 teaspoon salt, 1/4 teaspoon pepper, and 1/2 cup extra virgin olive oil in a blender and process until smooth. Pour into a medium glass bowl. Reserve 2 tablespoons of the vinaigrette for the arugula. Add the roasted bell peppers to the vinaigrette and toss to coat.

Prepare the grill for medium-high heat. Drizzle the lemon juice over the steaks. Brush with 2 tablespoons olive oil and sprinkle with salt and pepper. Grill the swordfish for 5 minutes per side. Do not overcook; swordfish can get very dry.

To assemble, toss the arugula with the reserved vinaigrette. Divide the arugula evenly among eight dinner plates. Arrange the swordfish steaks over the arugula. Top with the roasted peppers and olives.

Note: For quicker preparation and more intense flavor, do not roast the shallots and garlic. Peel both, finely chop the shallots, and mince the garlic. Add to the remaining vinaigrette ingredients and process in the blender.

Serves 8

Summer's End Supper

Summer's warm and relaxing pace can be difficult to relinquish as the days grow shorter. A seasonal menu that gently reminds us of the bounty of fall makes the transition easier. Share an evening with friends and celebrate the harvest. A delicious soup complements the distinctive flavors of swordfish, roasted bell peppers, and arugula. Topped off with a tart apple galette, this menu will ease you into the cozy fall season.

Butternut Squash Soup with Sage 123

·

Swordfish with Roasted Peppers on Arugula 128
Saffron Rice Pilaf 146

·

Pippin Apple Galette 154

Swordfish with Roasted Peppers on Arugula

WINE PAIRINGS BY
wine.com

·

A refreshing floral Sonoma Sauvignon Blanc, such as Kenwood, Chateau Souverain, or Dry Creek Vineyard

·

A rich, voluptuous California Viognier, such as Joseph Phelps Vineyards, Andrew Murray, or Saddleback Cellars

The rustic counterpart to Napa's allure, Sonoma County garners its own well-deserved kudos for fine wine. Sonoma's microclimates are similar to Napa's, so the county is likewise known for chardonnay, sauvignon blanc, cabernet sauvignon, merlot, pinot noir, and zinfandel. Its sparkling wines are considered admirable, too. Popular legend identifies Sonoma County as the location of the first California planting of the noble *Vitis vinifera* vine.

Healdsburg

The picturesque town of Healdsburg, located northwest of well-known Napa and Sonoma, is an increasingly popular base for exploring the wine country. The town is built around an attractive Spanish-style plaza shaded by redwood, palm, and fruit trees. The plaza houses unique clothing stores, gift shops, art galleries, antique collectives, a classic movie theater, bed and breakfast inns, and restaurants. On weekends, visitors may enjoy a free concert, a farmers' market, an art show, an antique fair, or canoeing down the nearby Russian River.

Situated where three wine-growing valleys meet, Healdsburg offers numerous wine tasting possibilities. To the south, the Russian River Valley's cool growing region is best known for pinot noir and chardonnay. The warm climate of the Dry Creek Valley to the northwest is ideal for zinfandel. The Alexander Valley to the northeast is best known for cabernet sauvignon. Throughout the region, many smaller, family-owned wineries offer a contrast to Napa's larger corporate wineries.

RACK OF LAMB WITH SPICY RED PEPPER RELISH

Roasted in the oven or grilled, this lamb dish is elegant and easy to prepare.

2 (1¹/2-pound) racks of lamb, trimmed
2 garlic cloves, slivered
Salt and freshly ground pepper to taste
6 sprigs of rosemary plus additional sprigs for garnish
Spicy Red Pepper Relish

Preheat the oven to 425 degrees. Cut each rack into halves. Make a slit between each rib with the tip of a sharp paring knife. Insert the garlic slivers into the slits. Sprinkle with salt and pepper.

Arrange the lamb in a roasting pan. Top with the sprigs of rosemary. Roast for 25 minutes or until a meat thermometer registers 140 degrees for medium-rare. Transfer the racks to a platter and tent with foil. Let rest for 15 minutes. The internal temperature will continue to rise to 150 degrees. Garnish with additional sprigs of rosemary and serve with Spicy Red Pepper Relish.

Note: To grill, prepare the grill for indirect medium heat. Grill the lamb for 30 minutes or until the internal temperature reaches 140 degrees as described above.

Serves 4

SPICY RED PEPPER RELISH

This make-ahead red pepper relish also goes well with grilled chicken breasts and sausages.

2 tablespoons olive oil
4 green bell peppers, julienned
2 yellow bell peppers, julienned
2 red bell peppers, julienned

8 red or green serrano chiles, seeded
1 cup sugar
²/3 cup tarragon wine vinegar
Salt to taste

Heat the olive oil in a large saucepan over medium heat. Add the bell peppers and serrano chiles. Cook until tender, stirring frequently. Stir in the sugar and wine vinegar. Cook for 30 minutes longer or until most of the liquid is absorbed, stirring occasionally. Let stand until cool. Add salt to taste. Transfer the relish to a nonmetallic bowl. Serve warm or chill, covered, in the refrigerator for up to one week.

Makes 1¹/2 cups

SAGE-ROASTED PORK WITH APPLE CHUTNEY

The home-spun combination of apples and pork are taken to a new level with the addition of spicy Apple Chutney.

1 (5- to 6-pound) bone-in pork loin
   roast
3 garlic cloves, slivered
3 fresh sage leaves, cut into halves
2 fresh sage leaves, finely chopped
Salt and freshly ground pepper
   to taste

1 cup chicken stock
1/2 cup apple cider
Apple Chutney
Sprigs of fresh sage

Preheat the oven to 350 degrees. Make shallow slits between the bones of the roast on the bone side. Insert the garlic slivers and sage leaf halves into the slits. Place the roast in a roasting pan. Sprinkle with finely chopped sage leaves, salt, and pepper.

Roast until a meat thermometer registers 145 degrees, basting occasionally with the pan drippings. Transfer the roast to a serving platter and tent with foil for 15 minutes. The internal temperature will continue to rise to 155 degrees.

Skim the fat from the pan drippings. Heat the remaining pan drippings over medium heat just to a sizzle. Add the stock and apple cider and stir with a wooden spoon to loosen any browned bits. Boil briefly to reduce the liquid, stirring frequently. Pour into a sauceboat.

To serve, slice the pork to the desired thickness. Top each serving with Apple Chutney and a sprig of sage. Serve with the sauce.

Serves 10 to 12

Chutney

In the Bay Area, food traditions from around the world are part of everyday cooking. Chutneys from India are a "must have" pantry item. The spicy condiment is based on four main ingredients: fruit, vinegar, sugar, and spices. It can range in texture from chunky to smooth, and in degrees of spiciness from mild to hot. Chutneys are not only a traditional accompaniment to curried dishes, but also turn grilled or poached meat and poultry into something special. Sweeter chutneys are interesting spreads on flatbread or crackers and are delicious served with cheese.

APPLE CHUTNEY

This chutney, created by Ross Browne of Absinthe Brasserie in San Francisco, is best when prepared two days in advance.

3/4 cup white wine vinegar, divided
3 tomatoes, peeled, coarsely
   chopped (see note on page 99)
13/4 cups packed dark brown sugar
11/4 cups golden raisins
1/2 large yellow onion, chopped
10 dates, pitted, coarsely chopped

1 garlic clove, finely chopped
1 teaspoon minced fresh ginger
1 teaspoon salt
1 pound Granny Smith apples
   (about 2 apples), peeled, cored,
   cut into 2-inch pieces
Bouquet garni (see note)

Combine 1/2 cup wine vinegar and all of the other ingredients in a stainless steel saucepan. Simmer over medium-low heat for 40 minutes, stirring constantly. Stir in the remaining 1/4 cup wine vinegar. Cook for 20 minutes longer or until thickened, stirring occasionally. Let stand until cool. Discard the bouquet garni. Chill, covered, in the refrigerator for up to one week.

Note: To make the bouquet garni, combine 3 black peppercorns, 2 white peppercorns, 3 coriander seeds, 1 allspice berry, 1/8 teaspoon fennel seed, 1/8 teaspoon mustard seed, and 1 bay leaf. Place in a square of cheesecloth and tie with cotton string to close.

Makes 6 cups

82, 83, 84, 92

Zacky Farms

After accidentally dropping and shattering the warm serving container she was prepared to use, Lillian Zacky created her garlic-roasted chicken recipe out of necessity. She quickly wrapped her freshly roasted Zacky Farms chicken in foil and placed it in her picnic basket, hoping it would remain warm for her outing with friends. Marinating in its own juices for about twenty minutes en route to a concert, the chicken turned out to be even more tender and juicy than her typical roasted chickens.

As a California family-owned business for over seventy years, Zacky Farms is well known for its fresh, naturally grown, hormone-free chickens and turkeys. The secret to the plump, meaty, and tender birds involves selective breeding, a diet primarily of corn and other natural grains, and efficient processing. All of this assures a consistent quality, wholesomeness, and "freshness you can taste" in every Zacky Farms product.

GARLIC-ROASTED CHICKEN

This roasted chicken recipe, created by Lillian Zacky accidentally, is easy to prepare, tender, and juicy. The trick is to wrap the chicken in foil after it has been roasted, allowing it to marinate in its own juices.

1 Zacky Farms Roasting Chicken, about 5 pounds	1 onion, cut into quarters
4 to 8 garlic cloves, to taste	Seasoned salt and freshly ground pepper to taste
1 lemon, sliced	1 cup chicken stock or water

Preheat the oven to 350 degrees or prepare the grill for indirect heat. Remove the neck and giblet pack from the body cavity of the chicken. These items can be roasted with the chicken if desired or discarded. Rinse the chicken inside and out with cool water, leaving the chicken moist to allow the seasonings to adhere to the skin.

Crush half the garlic cloves with a garlic press. Place the remaining whole garlic cloves, lemon slices, and onion quarters inside the cavity. Rub the crushed garlic over the outer surface of the chicken. Sprinkle with seasoned salt and pepper.

Pour the stock or water into a broiler pan. Arrange the chicken breast side down on a V-shaped rack in the broiler pan. Roast or grill the chicken for approximately 1 1/2 hours or until a meat thermometer registers 165 degrees. Test the temperature by piercing the area between the breast and wing portion with an instant-read thermometer. Remove the chicken from the rack and completely encase it in foil so that no steam can escape. Use caution as the chicken will be very hot. Let rest for 15 to 60 minutes before carving.

Serves 6

INDONESIAN CHICKEN ON ANGEL HAIR PASTA

This rich pasta is a complete meal. Serve fresh fruit for dessert.

Indonesian Dressing
1 1/2 cups rice vinegar
1 1/4 cups chicken stock
1/2 cup chopped fresh cilantro
5 green onions with tops, sliced
6 tablespoons soy sauce
1/4 cup peanut oil
1 1/2 tablespoons lime juice
2 teaspoons Asian sesame oil
2 teaspoons Asian chile oil
1 1/2 teaspoons ground white
    pepper
1 1/4 teaspoons red pepper flakes
1 teaspoon crushed garlic
1/2 teaspoon Tabasco sauce

Chicken and Assembly
6 boneless skinless chicken breasts
1 pound fresh sugar snap peas
16 ounces angel hair pasta
3 large carrots, peeled, grated
3/4 cup lightly salted peanuts,
    chopped

Combine the dressing ingredients in a bowl and mix well.

Arrange the chicken in a single layer in a glass dish. Pour 1 cup of the dressing over the chicken, turning to coat. Marinate the chicken, covered, in the refrigerator for 2 hours. Drain, discarding the marinade.

Preheat the broiler or grill. Broil or grill the chicken for 6 minutes per side or until cooked through. Cut the chicken into thin strips.

Blanch the sugar snap peas in boiling water in a saucepan for 1 to 2 minutes. Plunge the peas into a bowl of ice water to stop the cooking process; drain.

Cook the pasta according to package instructions; drain. Toss the pasta with the remaining dressing in a bowl for several minutes or until the pasta has absorbed some of the sauce.

To assemble, mound the pasta on eight dinner plates. Top with the sliced chicken and sugar snap peas. Arrange the grated carrots in the center of each serving and sprinkle with the chopped peanuts. Serve warm or cold.

Serves 8

Autumn Moon FESTIVAL

For over a thousand years, Asians throughout the world have celebrated the Autumn Moon Festival, also known as the Mid-Autumn Festival. The festival officially falls on the fifteenth day of the eighth moon, close to the autumnal equinox of the Western calendar, when the moon is the brightest. During ancient Autumn Moon Festivals, women made offerings of incense, candles, fruit, flowers, and mooncakes to the Moon Goddess, Chang O, who reflects the feminine principle, yin.

San Francisco's Chinatown, led by the Chinatown Merchants Association, celebrates the Autumn Moon Festival with a free street fair and mooncakes. Costumed children, giant puppets, and lion dancers parade down Grant Avenue to kick off the festivities. Their destination is the main stage on Washington Street where traditional performing arts from the Pacific Rim countries are featured. A charming cultural village with colorful lanterns, an artists' gallery, and hands-on activities are additional highlights of this annual event.

FIVE-CHEESE LASAGNA WITH CHICKEN & PESTO

For a rich and satisfying meal after a busy day, prepare this casserole ahead and bake just before serving.

Pesto

Pesto comes from the Italian verb *pestare*, which means "to pound." Pestos were traditionally made using a mortar and pestle. Despite the ease of food processors, this may still be the best method to maintain the rich flavor of basil and prevent the sometimes bitter taste caused by blending the leaves to a pulp. Pesto becomes a versatile sauce for pastas by combining it with two tablespoons of the pasta's boiling water to lighten the consistency. It is also a wonderful topping for cooked vegetables such as green beans, tomatoes, eggplant, or zucchini. It gives soups, purées, and appetizers a flavorful accent. When fresh basil is at its peak, pesto can be made in large quantities and frozen in small portions for winter soups and pastas. It can be stored in small containers with a bit of olive oil on top to prevent darkening or in airtight freezer bags. The containers or bags can be stored in the refrigerator for up to one week or in the freezer for longer storage.

Pasta
16 ounces lasagna noodles

Pesto Cream Sauce
1 bunch fresh basil (about 3 cups), stems removed
1/4 cup olive oil
2 tablespoons grated Parmesan cheese
2 tablespoons cornstarch
1/4 teaspoon salt
1/8 teaspoon white pepper
2 cups milk

Ricotta Filling
2 cups ricotta cheese
1 cup sour cream
1/4 cup grated Parmesan cheese
3 eggs, beaten
1 1/2 teaspoons ground white pepper
1/2 teaspoon salt

Cheese Mixture
8 ounces mozzarella cheese, shredded
8 ounces Parmesan cheese, grated
8 ounces fontina cheese, shredded
8 ounces Monterey Jack cheese, shredded

Assembly
1/2 cup cream, divided
2 pounds boneless skinless chicken breasts, cooked, shredded
1/4 cup chopped fresh parsley

Cook the noodles according to package instructions. Drain and set aside on clean tea towels.

For the pesto, process the basil, olive oil, and Parmesan cheese in a food processor or blender until smooth. Set aside. Combine the cornstarch, salt, and white pepper in a small saucepan and mix well. Whisk in the milk. Cook over medium heat until thickened, stirring constantly. Cool slightly. Stir in the pesto mixture.

For the ricotta filling, place all ingredients in a bowl and mix well.

For the cheese mixture, combine the cheeses in a bowl and set aside.

Preheat the oven to 350 degrees. To assemble, pour 1/4 cup of the cream into a 10- × 14-inch baking dish. Place a layer of noodles over the cream. Layer with half the pesto sauce, half the chicken, and one-third of the cheese mixture. Add another layer of noodles. Layer with half the ricotta filling. Add another layer of noodles, remaining pesto sauce, remaining chicken, and one-third of the cheese mixture. Add another layer of noodles and the remaining ricotta filling. Top with noodles. Pour the remaining 1/4 cup cream over the top and sprinkle with the remaining cheese mixture and parsley.

Bake, covered with foil, for 30 minutes. Remove the foil and bake for 30 minutes longer. Let stand for 10 to 15 minutes before serving. If assembled in advance, let stand at room temperature for 1 hour before baking.

Serves 12

CIDER-BRAISED TURKEY WITH SAUTÉED APPLES

Apple cider, white wine, and tarragon combine to make a savory sauce for braised turkey breast.

1 tablespoon butter
1 tablespoon vegetable oil
1¹/2 cups peeled, sliced carrots
1¹/2 cups chopped yellow onions
1 garlic clove, crushed
1 (5-pound) bone-in half turkey
    breast with skin
3 cups French or American hard
    apple cider

1 tablespoon salt
1 tablespoon dried tarragon
¹/4 cup dry white wine
¹/2 cup heavy cream
1 tablespoon chopped
    fresh tarragon
1 tablespoon Dijon mustard
¹/2 teaspoon ground white pepper
Sautéed Apples

Preheat the oven to 375 degrees. Select a Dutch oven or roasting pan with a tight fitting lid, large enough to hold the turkey breast. Add the butter and oil and heat over medium heat. Add the carrots, onions, and garlic and mix well. Reduce the heat to low. Cook for 10 minutes or until the vegetables are tender, stirring occasionally. Stir in the salt and dried tarragon. Add the cider. Remove from heat and place the turkey breast on top of the vegetables.

Bake, covered, for 1¹/4 to 1¹/2 hours or until a meat thermometer inserted in the thickest portion of the breast registers 160 degrees. Remove the turkey to a work surface. Let rest until cool enough to handle. Remove the skin from the turkey breast and discard. Remove the meat from the bone in one piece. Cover the meat with foil.

For the sauce, strain the liquid from the pan through a sieve into a large saucepan. Skim the fat. Stir in the wine. Bring to a boil and boil for 20 minutes or until reduced to 1 cup, stirring occasionally. Reduce the heat to a simmer and whisk in the cream, fresh tarragon, Dijon mustard, and white pepper. Cook just until heated through, stirring frequently. Pour into a sauceboat. Cover to keep warm.

To assemble, thinly slice the turkey breast across the grain and arrange on a serving platter. Serve with the sauce and Sautéed Apples.

Serves 10 to 12

SAUTÉED APPLES

A sweet and flavorful accompaniment to turkey and pork.

10 Golden Delicious apples,
    peeled, cored, cut into eighths

2 tablespoons sugar
3 to 4 tablespoons butter

Combine the sliced apples and sugar in a bowl and stir to coat. Heat the butter in a large skillet over medium heat. Sauté the apples in batches, turning to coat. With each batch, increase the heat to high and cook, undisturbed, for 3 minutes or until lightly browned. Turn the apples and cook until lightly browned. Test with a sharp knife for tenderness. Repeat until all apples have been cooked tender, adding more butter if necessary between batches.

Serves 10 to 12

Turkeys

The wild turkey is native to North America, where the early explorers first tasted it and eagerly brought it back to Europe. Its popularity quickly spread and by the 1500s, turkeys were being raised in Italy, France, and England. By the time the Pilgrims reached Plymouth Rock, they were very familiar with turkey and knew they must have it to make their Thanksgiving feast complete. Benjamin Franklin lobbied to have the turkey named the national bird of the United States. He is said to have been quite disappointed by the choice of the bald eagle instead. With turkey as the centerpiece of so many traditional feasts in America, it makes sense that when Neil Armstrong and Buzz Aldrin sat down to enjoy their first meal on the moon, their foil packets contained turkey with all the trimmings.

The average holiday turkey weighs fifteen pounds, with 70 percent of that being white meat, 30 percent dark meat. The average American consumes eighteen pounds of turkey annually, which is up more than 50 percent from twenty-five years ago. The sharp rise in consumption can be attributed to a plethora of new products using turkey, including hot dogs, burgers, and bacon. California is the fifth largest producer of turkeys in the United States.

Processed Tomatoes

While California is second in the U.S. in fresh tomato production, the state ranks first in the production of processed tomatoes (those used for canning). In fact, California grows nine out of ten tomatoes processed in the United States. The state's crop is worth 547 million dollars and covers 350 thousand acres, in all kinds of soils and climates. While tomatoes sold fresh in the stores are usually picked green, tomatoes destined for canning are picked when fully ripe and processed immediately. In fact, less than six hours pass between picking and canning. While the tomato season runs from June through November, the flavor peak is between July and September. Fresh or canned, tomatoes are an excellent source of vitamin C.

VEGETARIAN BLACK BEAN CHILI

This chili is a sure hit on a brisk night. It can be made ahead and kept on hand in the freezer.

Chili

4 cups dried, or 4 (16-ounce) cans black beans
2 tablespoons cumin seed
2 large yellow onions, finely chopped
1 1/2 cups finely chopped red bell peppers
2 garlic cloves, minced
2 tablespoons oregano
1 1/2 tablespoons paprika
1 1/2 teaspoons kosher salt
1 teaspoon coarsely ground black pepper
1/2 to 1 teaspoon cayenne pepper, or to taste
1/2 cup olive oil
3 cups canned diced tomatoes
1/2 to 1 jalapeño chile, finely chopped, or 1/2 teaspoon chopped canned jalapeño chile
1/4 cup chopped fresh cilantro

Assembly and Garnish

8 ounces Monterey Jack or Cheddar cheese, shredded
2/3 cup sour cream
1 cup chopped fresh tomatoes
1/2 cup finely chopped green onions
8 sprigs of cilantro

If using dried beans, sort and rinse them. Place the beans in a large saucepan. Add enough water to cover the beans by several inches; cover. Bring to a boil; reduce heat. Cook for 1 to 1 3/4 hours or until tender, stirring occasionally and adding more water if needed to keep the beans covered. Drain the beans, reserving 1 cup of the cooking liquid. If using canned beans, drain and reserve 1 cup of the liquid; do not simmer in water.

Preheat the oven to 325 degrees. Spread the cumin seed in a single layer on a baking sheet. Toast for 10 minutes, stirring occasionally. Heat the olive oil in an 8-quart pot and sauté the roasted cumin seed, onions, bell peppers, garlic, oregano, paprika, salt, black pepper, and cayenne pepper for 10 minutes or until the onions are translucent. Stir in the canned tomatoes, jalapeño chile, and chopped cilantro. Add the beans and reserved liquid and mix well. Cook over low heat for 20 to 30 minutes, stirring occasionally.

To assemble, place about 2 tablespoons of the cheese in eight heated chili bowls. Ladle the chili over the cheese. Top with a spoonful of sour cream. Sprinkle with the fresh tomatoes and green onions. Garnish with a sprig of cilantro.

Serves 8

DUCK WITH DRIED CHERRY PORT SAUCE

*Serve this succulent duck recipe with Roasted Garlic Thyme
Custards (page 140) for an elegant presentation. The sauce
may be made with port or a good cabernet sauvignon.*

3 tablespoons butter
6 boneless skinless duck breasts
1 tablespoon arrowroot
2 cups rich duck or chicken stock
1/3 cup minced shallots
3/4 cup port wine or cabernet
   sauvignon, divided

1 cup dried cherries, divided
1/4 teaspoon cayenne pepper
Salt and freshly ground black
   pepper to taste
6 sprigs of thyme

Preheat the oven to 200 degrees. Heat the butter in a large heavy skillet until it foams. Add the duck. Cook over medium-high heat for 8 to 10 minutes, browning both sides. Turn frequently and reduce the heat as needed to prevent the butter from burning. Transfer the duck to a baking dish, reserving the pan drippings. Cover with foil and place in the oven to keep warm.

Add the shallots to the skillet. Cook over medium heat for 3 minutes, stirring frequently. Deglaze the skillet with 1/2 cup port or cabernet sauvignon. Stir in 1 1/2 cups stock. Bring to a boil and boil until the liquid is reduced by one-third.

Chop half of the dried cherries. Add them to the sauce. Remove from heat. In a small bowl, dissolve the arrowroot in the remaining stock, mixing well. Whisk some into the sauce. Cook gently until thickened, adding more arrowroot mixture if a thicker sauce is desired; do not boil. Stir in the remaining port or cabernet sauvignon, cayenne pepper, salt, and black pepper. Cook just until heated through, stirring frequently. Pour into a sauceboat.

Remove the duck from the oven. Cut each duck breast diagonally and against the grain into 1/2-inch slices. Fan the duck slices on six dinner plates. Drizzle a small amount of the sauce over the duck and sprinkle with the remaining dried cherries. Top each serving with a sprig of thyme. Pass the remaining sauce.

Serves 6

Wild Game

With some of the most abundant wild game areas in America, many Northern California dinner menus once included venison, elk, quail, duck, goose, and pheasant. Today, as the flocks have diminished and the perception of hunting has changed, these wild game dinners at home are not as common. However, game is again featured at some of the finest restaurants and is available at some meat markets. These farm-raised animals and birds share most of the attributes of their wild counterparts with fewer drawbacks, such as a strong gamey taste or sinewy meat. Their dark, lean meat is well paired with redolent, alcohol-infused fruit sauces and savory wine sauces. Dark cherry sauce with juniper berries complements venison and elk chops. Bacon, fresh sage, and wine enhance the delicate flavor of quail and pheasant. Orange juice, currant jelly, and port form the jewel-colored Cumberland sauce that is an excellent accompaniment to wild or domestic duck.

Garlic

Garlic is a member of the lily family and is one of the earth's oldest cultivated crops. Originating in Asia, it is one of the most widely used flavorings in the world. Garlic has long been credited with promoting strength and preventing illness. It was even fed to the Egyptian slaves building the giant pyramids. Garlic's current health claims include its ability to boost blood circulation, fight viruses and bacteria, and lower cholesterol. Fresh garlic is available year-round, although the peak harvest season runs from April to mid-September. Properly stored, unbroken bulbs can be kept up to eight weeks. California is the number one producer of garlic, harvesting 88 percent of the United States' production. Fresno, Monterey, and Kern Counties lead the state in producing the crop. California's garlic harvest is worth over 145 million dollars annually, and 31,000 acres are committed to growing the pungent bulbs.

Among the lush foothills of the Santa Clara Valley, there is garlic in the air. Each July, Gilroy, also known as the Garlic Capital of the World, hosts a three-day weekend Garlic Festival with gourmet food, live entertainment, and arts and crafts.

For a fun garlic-related getaway, visit the Pizza Farm, located at the Madera District Fairgrounds in Madera, California (approximately twenty miles north of Fresno). The Pizza Farm is an educational site that demonstrates the importance of agriculture in our daily lives. Open from March through October, the one-third-acre plot is divided into eight pie-shaped wedges, like a pizza. Each "slice" contains one of the ingredients used to make a pizza, such as tomatoes, wheat, garlic, olives, peppers, cows for making cheese, and pigs for pepperoni.

The Pizza Farm's Agricultural Awareness Program teaches elementary students about California's number one industry by utilizing kids' number one food . . . pizza! The one-hour on-site presentation includes information about all of the ingredients of a pizza, as well as food safety, integrated pest management, the environment, water conservation, nutrition, urbanization, and career opportunities.

Photo Opposite: Garlic Bulbs, Garlic World, Gilroy, California

BRUSCHETTA

This recipe, contributed by Garlic Festival Foods, is the "original garlic bread."

3 ripe tomatoes, chopped
10 to 12 fresh basil leaves, chopped, plus 4 whole leaves for garnish
1 or 2 garlic cloves, minced, plus 1 whole garlic clove, peeled
Extra virgin olive oil to taste
Salt and pepper to taste
4 slices sourdough French bread

Combine the tomatoes, chopped basil, minced garlic, olive oil, salt, and pepper in a bowl and mix well. Grill the bread over hot coals or toast in the oven until brown on both sides. Rub 1 side of each bread slice with the whole garlic. Top each slice with some of the tomato mixture and 1 whole basil leaf.

Note: For variety, add crumbled feta cheese to the tomato mixture.

Serves 4

Garlic

The more garlic breaks down, the stronger its flavor becomes. Simply slicing a garlic clove will produce a mild garlic taste. A chopped or minced garlic clove will result in a more pungent flavor. Crushing garlic will yield the most intense taste.

To crush garlic, place an unpeeled clove on a chopping block. Grasp a butcher's knife by the handle, with the blade placed sideways, and give the garlic a hard press with the side of the blade. Remove the skin from the clove and add the crushed garlic to a favorite recipe for a wonderful, intense flavor.

To roast garlic, preheat the oven to 375 degrees. Cut the top off a full bulb of garlic. Cut two squares of foil large enough to wrap around the cut bulb. Stack the sheets of foil, center the garlic bulb on the foil squares, and drizzle with olive oil. Bring up the sides of the foil and twist to close. Bake for 40 minutes in the center of the oven or until the garlic is soft. To use, squeeze the soft garlic out of its peel.

ROASTED GARLIC THYME CUSTARDS

This is a great side dish for meats with sauces. Serve the individual custards alongside Duck with Dried Cherry Port Sauce (page 137).

3 eggs
1 large head garlic, roasted (refer to sidebar)
2 tablespoons fresh thyme leaves
3/4 teaspoon kosher salt
1/4 teaspoon freshly ground pepper
3/4 cup half-and-half
3/4 cup rich vegetable or chicken stock
6 sprigs of thyme

Preheat the oven to 350 degrees. Place the oven rack in the upper third of the oven. Combine the eggs, roasted garlic, 2 tablespoons thyme, salt, and pepper in a blender or food processor. Blend until smooth. Add the half-and-half and stock. Pulse until blended.

Lightly butter six 4-ounce ovenproof ramekins. Place the ramekins in a baking pan just large enough to hold them. Pour the egg mixture into the ramekins. Add enough boiling water to the baking pan to reach halfway up the sides of the ramekins.

Bake for 15 to 20 minutes or just until the center of the custard is set. Remove the ramekins from the baking pan to a wire rack. Let stand for 5 minutes. Serve warm topped with a sprig of thyme.

Serves 6

Dinner with Good Friends

An eye for detail brings elegance to the dining table. Custards of savory roasted garlic balance perfectly with the duck breast, dried cherries, and port. This menu is a special treat that calls for a sophisticated presentation to be appreciated by good friends.

Curried Walnut Chicken Triangles 121

•

Duck with Dried Cherry Port Sauce 137
Roasted Garlic Thyme Custards 140
Spinach with Pancetta & Pine Nuts 145

•

Gingerbread Cake with Caramelized Pears 158

Duck with Dried Cherry Port Sauce and Roasted Garlic Thyme Custard

WINE PAIRINGS BY
Gallo of Sonoma

Sonoma County Merlot

•

Sonoma County Chardonnay

Gallo of Sonoma is a state-of-the-art winery where traditional artisan winemaking techniques have been enhanced with the latest technologies. The result is a better way to make fine wines. For example, after carefully selecting white grapes, a "whole cluster press pad" gently extracts the juice from the grapes as if they were being squeezed by hand, and eliminates the seeds and stems. This process adds delicacy and elegance to their white wines making them fruitier and more aromatic.

With red wines, especially cabernets, zinfandels, and pinot noirs, temperature control during fermentation is absolutely critical. Rotary fermenters provide precise control over temperature. The result is red wines with greater depth of color, aroma, and flavor.

McEvoy Ranch
OLIVE OIL

In addition to producing some of the best wines in the world, Northern California is increasingly known for producing excellent olive oil, thanks in part to the McEvoy Ranch. Nan McEvoy, previously the Chairman of the Board of the Chronicle Publishing Company, is now the largest producer of estate-grown olive oil in California. In 1990, she began planting 70 acres of her 550-acre spread in Petaluma with olive trees imported from Tuscany. The first harvest was in 1995. Today, eleven thousand olive trees cover the hillsides.

The best olive oils are classified much like wines, with descriptions such as buttery, fruity, nutty, or peppery. The "extra virgin" designation means that the oil has 1 percent or less oleic acid content, and that it was extracted from the olives without using heat or chemicals. Top-quality extra virgin olive oils, like those produced by the McEvoy Ranch, are best enjoyed uncooked, as high heat destroys the delicate flavor. Drizzle the oil over grilled meats, fish, and vegetables, or use it to dress a salad or for dipping bread. Lower priced "virgin" olive oil has up to 3 percent oleic acid content and is best for cooking. Olive oil without the "virgin" designation has been refined with heat or chemicals to lower the acidity and correct the flavors. Like fine wine, olive oil should be kept in a cool, dark environment.

MEDITERRANEAN PENNE PASTA

A classic combination of flavors perfect for fall.

3 tablespoons olive oil
1 large yellow onion, chopped
1/3 cup fresh flat-leaf parsley, chopped, divided
2 garlic cloves, minced
2 pounds tomatoes, peeled, chopped (see note on page 99)
2 roasted red bell peppers, chopped (refer to sidebar on page 128)
2 roasted yellow bell peppers, chopped
1/2 cup brine-cured black olives (such as kalamata), pitted, chopped, see sidebar, page 24
1/4 cup capers, rinsed, drained
2 tablespoons chopped fresh marjoram
Salt and freshly ground pepper to taste
16 ounces penne pasta
1 cup grated Pecorino-Romano cheese, divided

Heat the olive oil in a large saucepan over medium-high heat. Add the onion, half the parsley, and the garlic. Sauté for 3 minutes. Stir in the tomatoes, roasted bell peppers, olives, capers, and marjoram. Reduce the heat and simmer, covered, for 10 minutes. Season with salt and pepper.

Cook the pasta according to package instructions; drain. Return the pasta to the saucepan. Stir in the roasted pepper mixture and 1/2 cup cheese. Season with salt and pepper. Transfer the pasta to a large serving bowl. Sprinkle with the remaining parsley and cheese.

Note: One 15-ounce jar of roasted red peppers, drained, may be substituted for the fresh roasted bell peppers.

Serves 6 to 8

PURÉE OF CARROTS & PARSNIPS

*A food processor or blender makes preparation of
this tasty purée easy.*

6 medium carrots (about 1 pound),
   peeled
3 medium parsnips, peeled
1 tablespoon salt
2 large garlic cloves, peeled
4 sprigs plus 1 tablespoon fresh
   thyme leaves

2 tablespoons butter, softened
2 green onions, chopped
1 tablespoon heavy cream
Salt and freshly ground pepper
   to taste

Slice the carrots and parsnips into 2-inch pieces. Bring a medium saucepan of water to a boil
and add the salt. Add the carrots, garlic, and 4 sprigs of thyme. Reduce the heat and simmer
for 5 minutes. Add the parsnips and cook for 15 minutes or until the vegetables are tender.
Drain, discarding the sprigs of thyme. Process the carrot mixture in small batches in a food
processor or blender until smooth.

   Return the entire mixture to the food processor or blender. Add the butter, green onions,
heavy cream, and thyme leaves. Process until puréed. Season with salt and pepper. Transfer to
a serving bowl. Garnish with additional fresh thyme if desired.

Serves 6 to 8

Napa Valley
WINE TRAIN

Rated as one of the twenty best
rail experiences in the world, the Napa
Valley Wine Train is a return to the
gracious era of elegant rail travel with
distinguished service. Since 1987, the
Napa Valley Wine Train has been
offering diners a three-hour, thirty-six-
mile round-trip excursion from the
historic town of Napa through one of
the world's most famous wine valleys
to the quaint village of St. Helena.
Travelers enjoy a relaxing journey
through the heart of Napa Valley's
picturesque vineyards and world-
renowned wineries. Champagne
brunch, a gourmet lunch, or a full-
course dinner are served in the
meticulously restored 1917 Pullman
dining car replete with etched glass,
polished brass, fine fabrics, and rich
mahogany. Guests are invited to
observe as the culinary staff prepares
menu selections from fresh regional
ingredients in the onboard professional
kitchen.

Root Vegetables

Root vegetables, such as carrots, potatoes, turnips, parsnips, rutabagas, celery root, beets, and sweet potatoes, are hearty and satisfying—the perfect food for a chilly fall evening. Over the years, the stronger tasting varieties lost favor with many cooks, yet they are wonderful additions to meaty stews and vegetable soups. Lately these old-fashioned fall vegetables have seen a resurgence as fresh seasonal cooking has taken center stage. Purées and gratins of root vegetables are again popular side dishes. Root vegetables are great complements to one another. Combine one of the stronger varieties with a milder one—parsnips and carrots, or celery root and potatoes—to soften the flavor of one and enhance the flavor of the other.

OVEN-ROASTED ROOT VEGETABLES

This is an outstanding way to prepare the earthy vegetables of fall.

Olive oil
8 ounces rutabagas, peeled, cut
   into 1¹/4-inch cubes
³/4 teaspoon kosher salt
3 small bay leaves
6 sprigs of fresh thyme
Freshly ground pepper to taste

8 ounces turnips, peeled,
   cut into 1¹/4-inch cubes
8 ounces cipolline or boiling
   onions, peeled
8 ounces parsnips, peeled,
   cut into 1¹/4-inch cubes

Preheat the oven to 375 degrees. Coat a shallow roasting pan generously with olive oil. Place the rutabagas, salt, bay leaves, thyme, and pepper in the pan and toss to mix. Roast the rutabagas for 15 minutes. Remove the pan from the oven and stir. Add the turnips and onions and toss to coat with the oil. Roast for 10 minutes. Remove the pan from the oven and stir. Add the parsnips and toss to coat with the oil. Roast, stirring every 10 minutes, for 20 minutes longer or until the vegetables are brown and tender when pierced with a sharp knife. Discard the bay leaves and thyme sprigs. Transfer to a serving bowl.

Serves 6 to 8

SPINACH WITH PANCETTA & PINE NUTS

Sautéed spinach is delicious when dressed up with pancetta and pine nuts.

1/2 cup diced pancetta
1/4 cup olive oil (optional)
2 garlic cloves, cut into halves
1 pound fresh spinach, trimmed,
   cooked, drained, chopped

1/2 cup pine nuts, lightly toasted
Salt and freshly ground pepper
   to taste

Place the pancetta in a cold skillet. Set the heat on medium-low. Cook until some of the fat has been rendered and stir. Increase the heat to medium and cook until the pancetta is well-browned, stirring frequently. Remove the pancetta with a slotted spoon to a paper towel to drain, reserving the pan drippings, if using instead of olive oil.

Sauté the garlic in the reserved pan drippings or olive oil, for 2 to 3 minutes or until golden brown. Remove from heat. Add the spinach to the pan and toss to coat. Stir in the pine nuts and pancetta. Season with salt and pepper. Transfer to a serving bowl. Serve immediately.

Serves 4

Calistoga

In his determination to create a California version of New York's famous Saratoga Spa, Sam Brannan founded the charming town of Calistoga in 1859. With money amassed by supplying miners in the Gold Rush, he purchased two thousand acres of the Wappo Indians' Hot Springs land. On the property, Old Faithful Geyser still provides evidence of the magnitude of underground geologic activity in the area. There, hot magma heats water from a river deep within the earth until intense pressure builds and is released every forty minutes or so in a stream of three-hundred-fifty-degree water spewed sixty feet into the air.

Today people continue to journey to Calistoga where more than a dozen unpretentious spas and health resorts line Old West-style streets. Visitors, anxious to relax and unwind, can sign up for "the works," which typically includes being submerged in a mud bath, led into a mineral bath, followed by a steam bath, swaddled in blankets, then given a full-body massage. The experience is the ultimate relaxation for foot-weary travelers, armchair quarterbacks, and domestic goddesses who make the trek to Calistoga.

Rice

More people in the world eat rice as a staple than any other food. In fact, more than half of the world's population eats rice daily. Second only to Arkansas in U.S. rice production, California's rice crop is worth more than five hundred million dollars per year. Rice consistently ranks in the top 10 percent of California's 250 agricultural commodities. Ninety-five percent of the state's rice is grown in the Sacramento Valley, where the claypan soil, warm, sunny days, and cool nights create the perfect growing conditions. Planting is done in late April and early May, with harvest taking place September through November. Whereas most of the world's rice is farmed using labor intensive hand techniques, California uses highly mechanized technology to farm and harvest rice, thus producing the highest yield per acre of any state or country.

Rice has an additional value to California—the thousands of acres of ricelands provide a habitat for 141 bird species, 29 mammal species, and 24 species of amphibians and reptiles. Many of these species would not survive without the wetlands the rice fields provide. In addition, the three hundred pounds of rice per acre left after harvest are a significant food source for migrating ducks and swans.

SAFFRON RICE PILAF

Saffron adds an elegant touch to this traditional side dish.

2¹/2 cups chicken stock, fish stock, or water
5 or 6 threads of saffron, or ¹/8 teaspoon ground saffron
1 teaspoon salt

¹/2 medium yellow onion, finely chopped
2 tablespoons vegetable oil
1¹/3 cups long grain white rice

Heat the stock, saffron, and salt in a small saucepan for 10 minutes or until the stock becomes infused with the saffron. Remove from heat.

Sauté the onion in the oil in a saucepan over medium heat until translucent. Add the rice and stir to coat. Sauté until the grains turn chalky white. Add the saffron liquid and bring to a boil over high heat. Stir once, cover, and reduce the heat to low.

Cook, undisturbed, for 18 minutes or until the liquid is absorbed. Remove from heat. Let stand, covered, for 5 to 10 minutes. Fluff with a fork and serve immediately.

Serves 4

HERBED MUSHROOM STUFFING

This easy variation on a traditional favorite is a wonderful side dish with Thanksgiving turkey.

1 cup (2 sticks) butter
4 ounces fresh portobello
   mushrooms, stemmed, chopped
4 ounces fresh shiitake mushrooms,
   stemmed, chopped
1 medium onion, finely chopped
4 ribs celery, chopped
1 cup water
1 egg, beaten

1 cup salt-free chicken or turkey
   stock
1 (8-ounce) package herb-seasoned
   stuffing mix (Pepperidge Farm
   preferred)
1 (8-ounce) package cubed corn
   bread stuffing mix (Pepperidge
   Farm preferred)
Madeira Gravy

Preheat the oven to 350 degrees. Heat the butter in a large saucepan over medium heat. Add the mushrooms and onion. Sauté for 1 to 2 minutes. Add the celery and sauté for 2 minutes. Stir in the water, egg, stock, and stuffing mixes and mix well. Transfer to a baking dish. Bake, covered, for 20 minutes. Remove the cover and bake for 20 minutes longer or until lightly browned. Serve with roast turkey and Madeira Gravy.

Serves 8

MADEIRA GRAVY

Madeira wine adds depth and richness to this gravy.

Pan drippings from 1 (12- to 14-pound) turkey
1¹/₄ cups Madeira wine
¹/₂ cup flour
2 to 4 cups turkey giblet stock
Salt and ground white pepper to taste

Skim the fat from the turkey drippings in the roasting pan, reserving ¹/₃ cup fat. Add the wine to the pan. Cook over medium-high heat, stirring with a wooden spoon to loosen any browned bits. Bring to a boil and remove from heat.

   Whisk the reserved fat and flour in a saucepan until blended. Cook over low heat for 3 minutes, whisking constantly and adding some of the turkey stock if the mixture starts to burn. Whisk in the wine mixture and add the stock ¹/₂ cup at a time until the desired consistency is reached. Simmer for 5 minutes, whisking occasionally as the gravy thickens. Thin with additional stock if necessary. Season with salt and white pepper. Pour into a heated sauceboat.

Serves 8

Women of Taste

Both established and up-and-coming Bay Area women chefs and restaurateurs host a spectacular evening called Women of Taste each September in Oakland. During its first nine years, the event held at the Oakland Museum of California raised more than three hundred thousand dollars for Girls Incorporated of Alameda County, an organization dedicated to providing health, education, and career programs for teenage girls. Billed as "an evening of fine cuisine prepared by leading women chefs and restaurateurs benefiting today's girls and tomorrow's women," the event typically draws as many as twelve hundred patrons. Aside from offering incredible hors d'oeuvres, pastas, artisan breads, and fabulous desserts, Women of Taste also features wine tasting, entertainment, and a silent auction.

Sweet Cornbread

Easily made from scratch, cornbread is delicious served with honey butter and chili.

1 cup stone-ground cornmeal
1 cup flour
1/2 cup sugar
2 1/2 teaspoons baking powder
1/4 teaspoon salt

1 cup milk, room temperature
1/3 cup vegetable oil or 6 tablespoons butter, melted
1 egg, lightly beaten

Preheat the oven to 400 degrees. Grease a 9- × 9-inch baking pan or 10 muffin cups. Combine the dry ingredients in a bowl and mix well. Combine the milk, oil or butter, and egg and gently stir into the cornmeal mixture.

Pour the batter into the baking pan or fill the muffin cups about two-thirds full. Bake the cornbread for approximately 25 minutes (corn muffins for approximately 20 minutes) or until the top is lightly browned.

Serves 8 to 10

POTATO FOCACCIA WITH CARAMELIZED ONIONS

*Serve this focaccia fresh out of the oven as an appetizer
or with a hearty soup.*

Focaccia

Focaccia
2 medium yellow potatoes, peeled,
   cut into quarters
1¹/2 envelopes dry yeast
   (3 teaspoons)
1¹/2 cups warm (105 degrees)
   water
3 to 3¹/2 cups flour
2 tablespoons olive oil
1 teaspoon salt

Topping and Assembly
1¹/2 cups thinly sliced yellow
   onion
1 to 2 tablespoons butter
1 tablespoon olive oil
2 teaspoons chopped fresh
   rosemary
³/4 teaspoon kosher salt
2 ounces Gorgonzola cheese,
   crumbled

Place the potatoes in a saucepan with water to cover. Simmer over medium-low heat until tender; drain. Mash the potatoes in a bowl or put through a ricer.

Combine the yeast in the warm water in a large bowl. Stir and let stand for 10 minutes. Add the mashed potatoes, 1 cup of the flour, 2 tablespoons olive oil, and salt. Mix by hand or use an electric mixer fitted with a paddle attachment until blended. Add the remaining flour 1 cup at a time, mixing until the dough comes together and is no longer sticky.

Knead the dough by hand or with a mixer fitted with a dough hook for 10 minutes. Place the dough in an oiled bowl, turning to coat the surface. Let rise, covered with a tea towel, for 1¹/2 hours or until doubled in size. Punch the dough down and press it out over the bottom of an oiled baking sheet or 10- × 15-inch baking pan. If the dough resists, allow it to rest for 10 minutes and press it out again until it fills the baking sheet. Cover with a tea towel and let rise for 1 hour.

Preheat the oven to 400 degrees. Sauté the onion in the butter in a skillet over low heat until golden. Remove from heat.

Make approximately 50 dimples in the dough with fingertips. Drizzle with 1 tablespoon olive oil. Sprinkle with the caramelized onions, rosemary, and salt. Top with the cheese. Bake on the bottom oven rack for 30 minutes or until puffed and golden brown. Serve warm or at room temperature.

Serves 6 to 9

Focaccia is a savory bread and unlike its kin, pizza, it is more dough than topping. This wonderful bread, baked by the finest local bread makers and served in many Bay Area restaurants, originated in Genoa, Italy. Deriving its name from the Latin word *focus*, meaning "hearth," focaccia evolved from unleavened hearth cake eaten during the Middle Ages. It was made by patting dough into a flat round and baking it directly on a hot stone. Whether soft or crisp, thick or thin, the dough was typically flavored with local herbs and olive oil. Today, focaccia's savory toppings vary widely and can be determined by what is on hand. Olive oil is then drizzled on top before baking.

Cheese

More than two hundred years ago, the Spanish monk, Father Junipero Serra, came to California to establish missions that to this day dot the California coast. Father Serra's teachings expanded beyond religion—he also introduced the art of cheese making. Another pioneer, David Jacks began commercially marketing his creamy white cheese in Monterey in 1882—thus Monterey Jack cheese was born. Today there are over fifty cheese producers in California making more than 120 varieties of cheeses. California is the leading dairy producer in the nation and nearly 40 percent of the milk produced is made into cheese.

Cheese is a versatile ingredient in cooking. Most cheeses are best cooked at low to medium temperatures for a short period of time, just long enough for the cheese to melt and blend into the other ingredients. Cheese will become tough and stringy if cooked at high temperatures for long periods of time.

When buying cheese, make sure it is tightly wrapped and looks appealing. Fresh unripened cheeses, such as ricotta and cottage cheese, should be treated like milk and kept sealed and refrigerated. Each package is freshness dated. Fresh cheeses can be served plain, spread on bread, or combined with pasta, potatoes, or polenta.

Semi-soft ripened cheeses such as Brie, Teleme, and Camembert can be stored longer than fresh cheeses. They will keep for several weeks in the refrigerator. Semi-soft cheeses are good eaten plain or served with crackers and fruit. They also add depth to cooked foods and sauces.

Semi-hard cheeses such as Monterey Jack, Cheddar, Gouda, and mozzarella can be refrigerated and stored, tightly wrapped in plastic, for one to two months. Most semi-hard cheeses are good eaten alone or with bread and crackers. Semi-hard cheeses are also very versatile in cooking. They are a staple in sandwiches and melt well. They can be grated and used as a topping, or melted for fondue.

Hard grating cheese such as Parmesan and Dry Jack may be held refrigerated for much longer periods of time. They are good sprinkled on soups, pastas, risotto, and vegetables. They stand up well to high heat and add abundant flavor in small quantities.

Photo Opposite: Cheese Counter, Andronico's Market, Danville, California

CHEDDAR CHEESE BUTTER BISCUITS

Straus Family Creamery produces Cheddar cheese from milk that is free of pesticides, antibiotics, or hormones. Their biscuit recipe is rich and cheesy.

2 cups flour
1 1/2 tablespoons baking powder
1 teaspoon sugar
1/4 teaspoon salt
1/2 cup (1 stick) butter
3/4 cup milk
1/2 cup shredded sharp Cheddar
*   cheese*
1 tablespoon snipped fresh chives

Preheat the oven to 400 degrees. Coat a baking sheet with butter and dust lightly with flour. Sift the flour, baking powder, sugar, and salt into a bowl and mix well. Cut in the butter with a fork or pastry cutter until crumbly. Add the milk, cheese, and chives and stir just until combined.

Knead the dough on a lightly floured surface until the ingredients are evenly mixed. Roll 1/2-inch thick. Cut with a biscuit cutter. Arrange the rounds on the prepared baking sheet. Brush with additional milk. Bake for 8 to 10 minutes or until golden brown. Serve hot with butter.

Makes 8 biscuits

Fireside Dinner

*Pull up a few comfortable chairs, sit back, relax, and savor the moment.
The warmth of the fire is the perfect backdrop to a menu of roasted pork loin
and root vegetables. A chutney of exquisitely complex flavors tries to steal the show,
only to be outdone by what follows for dessert.*

Fennel & Persimmon Salad 124

•

*Sage-Roasted Pork with Apple Chutney 131
Oven-Roasted Root Vegetables 144*

•

Goat Cheese Tart with Lavender Honey 153

*A spicy Amador County
Zinfandel, such as Sobon
Estate, Clos du Val, or
Clos LaChance*

•

*A sassy Paso Robles Syrah,
such as Ahlgren Vineyard
or Tablas Hills*

Though Americans have made their preferences for white zinfandel, chardonnay, and cabernet sauvignon resoundingly clear, many California vintners are determined to expand the national palate with a broad and evolving array of grape varieties, blends, and winemaking techniques. California produces a broad range of eloquent varietals in most of its many growing regions. The state's key wine grapes include chardonnay, sauvignon blanc, cabernet sauvignon, merlot, zinfandel, and some pinot noir. Newly basking in the California sun are venturesome varieties such as Rhone natives syrah, mourvedre, grenache, and viognier; the Italian star sangiovese; and various personal favorites of many an eclectic winemaker.

Goat Cheese Tart with Lavender Honey

GOAT CHEESE TART WITH LAVENDER HONEY

Cheese can be used in desserts quite successfully. This tart made with goat cheese is exquisite.

Pastry
10 ounces pecans
3/4 cup sugar
3 cups flour
1 cup (2 sticks) unsalted butter, cut
   into 8 pieces, softened
1 egg, lightly beaten
1 teaspoon vanilla extract

Filling and Garnish
2 eggs, lightly beaten
12 ounces goat cheese, crumbled
1 cup heavy cream
3/4 cup lavender honey or regular
   honey, divided
6 ounces pecan halves, lightly
   toasted or sautéed in butter

For the pastry, combine the pecans and sugar in a food processor. Process until the pecans are finely chopped. Add the flour and pulse until mixed. Add the butter and process until mixed. Whisk the egg and vanilla together in a bowl. Add the egg mixture to the food processor. Process until a dough forms.

Divide the dough into three equal portions. Press one portion into an 8-inch tart pan with a removable bottom. Chill for 30 minutes or longer. Flatten the remaining dough portions into 2 disks and wrap each tightly in plastic wrap and then in foil. Freeze for future use.

Preheat the oven to 350 degrees. Bake the tart for 25 minutes or until golden brown. Cool in the pan on a wire rack.

For the filling, whisk together the eggs, cheese, heavy cream, and 1/4 cup of the lavender honey. A food processor makes this step extremely easy. Pour the filling into the baked tart shell. Bake for 30 to 40 minutes or until set. Cool in the pan on a wire rack. Chill in the refrigerator for 4 to 6 hours. Remove the sides of the tart pan, slice the tart and drizzle each serving with some of the remaining lavender honey. Top with the toasted pecans.

Serves 8 to 10

Cowgirl Creamery

An hour north of San Francisco, picturesque Point Reyes Station is the home of the Cowgirl Creamery. Here, fresh batches of handmade ice cream and cheese such as fromage blanc, quark, and crème fraîche, are crafted weekly from organic milk produced at a local organic dairy. The creamery is housed in a renovated barn along with the Tomales Bay Foods Market. The airy, glassed-in site provides an opportunity for visitors to observe the process of cheese making in action. While specializing in artisan cheeses of Northern California, the market's cheese shop personnel work closely with artisan cheese makers around the United States to select, purchase, and age these delicious cheeses. In addition, the market offers farmstead cheeses from Great Britain, and handmade cheeses from France, Italy, Spain, and Greece. After a lesson in the art of cheese making, tasty picnic items can be purchased to enjoy at the nearby Point Reyes National Seashore.

The Tech
MUSEUM OF INNOVATION

The large mango box and azure dome are a stunning landmark in downtown San Jose. Inside, the Tech Museum of Innovation delivers on its mission to engage people of all ages and backgrounds in exploring technologies affecting their lives, and inspiring young people to become innovators of the technologies of the future.

With nearly 250 high-technology exhibits to explore, visitors can make movies using the latest tricks in animation and experience how the Internet, television, and other communication tools have made this a small world after all. Use inventions from the Silicon Valley to design a roller coaster, build a microchip, and make a futuristic self-portrait with a 3-D laser scanner. Experience the "how" of machines that keep people alive and explore technologies that enhance human performance.

Save time to experience the Tech's state-of-the-art Hackworth IMAX® Dome Theater, the only one of its kind in Northern California. Unlike traditional flat-screen IMAX® theaters, the Dome Theater features a giant eight-story domed screen and six-channel, digital wrap-around sound. It seats 295 people in special reclining chairs that accentuate the feeling of actually being in the movie.

PIPPIN APPLE GALETTE

This charming, roughly formed tart is mouthwatering.

Pastry
2 cups flour
1 tablespoon sugar
1/2 teaspoon salt
3/4 cup (1 1/2 sticks) unsalted butter, cut into small pieces, chilled
1/3 cup ice water

Filling and Assembly
1/2 cup (or more) sugar
1/4 teaspoon salt
1 1/2 pounds Pippin apples, peeled, cored (Golden Delicious apples may be substituted)
2 tablespoons cream
1 egg, lightly beaten
2 tablespoons coarse sugar (C&H Hawaiian Washed Raw Sugar preferred)

For the pastry, combine the flour, sugar, and salt in a food processor. Add half the butter. Process until the mixture resembles rolled oats. Add the remaining butter. Process until the mixture looks like it has pea-size bits interspersed with the original oat-like mixture.

Transfer the mixture to a bowl. Sprinkle with 2 tablespoons of the ice water and toss with a fork. Add the remaining ice water 1 tablespoon at a time until the dough is just moist enough to be shaped into a ball. Place the ball on a sheet of plastic wrap. Gather the edges of the plastic wrap over the dough and shape into a disk about 1 inch thick. Chill for 15 minutes.

For the filling, combine 1/2 cup sugar and salt in a bowl and mix well. Cut the apples into 1/2-inch wedges. Add the apples to the sugar mixture and toss to coat.

To assemble, preheat the oven to 400 degrees. Place two racks in the lower third of the oven. Place a sheet of aluminum foil on the lower rack to catch any drips.

Roll the dough out on a lightly floured surface into a 14-inch circle about 1/8-inch thick. Fold the circle gently into quarters and transfer to a baking sheet without sides. Do not use a Cushionaire-type pan as this will retard browning. Unfold the dough and spread the apples in a shallow, jumbled layer to within 2 inches of the edge. Fold the edge of the dough over the apples, overlapping them around the galette. There is no need to press the overlaps together, as they add to the rustic charm of this dessert. The apples will be almost covered by dough.

Whisk the cream and egg in a bowl until blended. Brush over the top of the galette. Sprinkle with the coarse sugar. Place the baking sheet in the oven on the rack above the foil. Bake for 35 to 40 minutes or until the top is brown and the bottom is caramel brown in color. Use a spatula to lift the edge of the galette to peek underneath. Cool slightly, carefully remove from the baking sheet, and cut into wedges. Serve warm.

Serves 6 to 8

CRÈME BRÛLÉE

*A caramelized sugar top makes this an impressive
vanilla custard dessert.*

2¹/₂ cups Berkeley Farms heavy whipping cream
1 whole vanilla bean
¹/₂ cup sugar
6 egg yolks
¹/₄ cup packed brown sugar or turbinado (raw) sugar

Preheat the oven to 300 degrees. Bring the whipping cream and vanilla bean to a boil in a medium-heavy saucepan. Remove from heat. Let stand for 10 to 60 minutes. Remove the bean and split lengthwise into halves. Scrape the seeds into the cream and discard the bean.

Whisk the sugar and egg yolks in a bowl just until combined. Add the warm cream mixture to the egg mixture gradually, whisking constantly until combined. Strain the mixture through a fine mesh sieve equally into eight 6-ounce ramekins. Place the ramekins in a baking pan. Add enough hot water to the baking pan to reach halfway up the sides of the ramekins.

Bake for 30 to 40 minutes or until when jiggled a quarter-size spot in the center of each custard still looks undercooked. Remove the ramekins from the baking pan to a wire rack to cool. The custards will continue to cook after they are removed from the water bath. Chill, covered with plastic wrap, for up to one day. Sprinkle with the brown sugar just before serving. Use a chef's blowtorch or place the ramekins briefly under the broiler to caramelize the sugar.

Serves 8

Berkeley Farms

Oreo Cookies

The Oreo cookie is simply America's favorite cookie! If every Oreo cookie ever made were stacked on top of each other (over 362 billion), the pile would reach to the moon and back more than five times. Today's most popular version of the Oreo cookie is 1³/4 inches across and can be eaten in one, two, or three bites, depending on how big the bite. Oreo cookies were introduced more than fifty years ago and over the years, there have been so many ways to enjoy them. They are a wonderful treat that can be enjoyed dunked in milk, twisted apart, eaten whole, or in the classic Oreo cookies and cream ice cream, presented here in a homemade version.

OREO™ COOKIE ICE CREAM

This rich vanilla ice cream is a hit with the addition of Oreo cookies.

2¹/4 cups sugar
4 eggs (see note)
2 quarts milk
2 cups heavy cream

4¹/2 teaspoons vanilla extract
¹/2 teaspoon salt
2 cups crushed Oreo cookies

Combine the sugar and eggs in a mixing bowl. Beat until very stiff, scraping the bowl occasionally. Add the milk, heavy cream, vanilla, and salt and stir until blended. Chill, covered, in the refrigerator for several hours.

Pour the mixture into an ice cream freezer canister. Freeze using manufacturer's instructions. Fold in the crushed cookies just before the end of the freezing process.

Note: The eggs in this recipe are not cooked. Egg substitute may be used if preferred.

Makes 5 quarts

APPLE HILL CAKE

This crowd-pleasing use of apples gets its name from well-known Apple Hill Orchards, a wonderful fall destination in Placerville in the heart of California's Gold Country.

2 cups sugar
1/2 cup vegetable oil
1/3 cup sherry
2 eggs
4 cups peeled, sliced apples
2 cups flour

2 teaspoons baking soda
2 teaspoons cinnamon
1 teaspoon salt
1 teaspoon ground nutmeg
Whipped cream or vanilla
   ice cream

Preheat the oven to 350 degrees. Combine the sugar, oil, sherry, and eggs in a bowl and mix well. Stir in the apples. Sift the flour, baking soda, cinnamon, salt, and nutmeg into a bowl and mix well. Add the flour mixture to the apple mixture and mix well.

    Pour the apple mixture into a greased 9- × 13-inch cake pan. Bake for 1 hour. Cool in the pan on a wire rack. Serve with whipped cream or vanilla ice cream.

Serves 10 to 12

Apples

Although apples have been farmed in California since the 1800s, it was not until 1980 that California became a major producer of the crop. Since then, California has become the third largest producer of apples in the country. California apple farming has been characterized as innovative in both pollination and production methods. About twenty different apple varieties are grown throughout California, from Chico in Northern California to Santa Maria on the Central Coast. Most of the farming takes place in the Central Valley and in some of the Northern Coastal regions. Today, due to cold storage, apples are available year-round, although peak harvest is in the fall.

Apples are certainly one of the most popular and versatile fruits. In addition to being eaten raw, they can be enjoyed in baked goods and salads and as a sweet accompaniment to meats. One medium apple has only eighty calories and is a significant source of fiber. Apples keep best when they are refrigerated, as they deteriorate ten times faster at room temperature. To keep cut apples fresh and prevent browning, brush them with a mixture of one part lemon juice to three parts apple juice.

Victorian Home
TOUR

Pacific Grove, California, was founded in 1875 as a Methodist summer retreat. Stately turn-of-the-century Victorian houses, inns, and churches stand where tents once were pitched. Some of the most picturesque "Grand Ladies" can be found along Ocean View Boulevard, Lighthouse Avenue, and Central Avenue, where ornate Gothic, turreted Queen Anne, and English castle-style homes can be seen. Many homes display plaques engraved with the names of the original owners and the construction dates.

Each year, usually in October, visitors have an opportunity to admire the interiors of some of the most beautiful and artfully restored homes, inns, and churches on the Victorian Home Tour. Hostesses dressed in Victorian-era clothing provide a history of each unique location. Homes on the tour change from year to year as restorations are completed around town. In recent years, some of the homes have opened to the public as quaint bed and breakfast inns ideally situated for those exploring the Monterey Peninsula.

GINGERBREAD CAKE WITH CARAMELIZED PEARS

This elegant version of gingerbread is a satisfying end to a fall meal.

3 cups flour
1 teaspoon baking soda
1 1/2 teaspoons cinnamon, divided
1 teaspoon ground ginger
1/2 teaspoon allspice
1/2 teaspoon ground cloves
1/2 teaspoon salt
3/4 cup pear purée (1 to 2 small ripe pears, peeled, cored, puréed in a blender)

1/2 cup buttermilk
1 cup (2 sticks) butter, softened
1 cup packed brown sugar
3/4 cup dark molasses
3 eggs
1 1/2 cups heavy whipping cream
1 tablespoon sugar
1 teaspoon vanilla extract
Caramelized Pears

Preheat the oven to 350 degrees. Grease and flour a 10-inch bundt pan. Combine the flour, baking soda, 1 teaspoon cinnamon, ginger, allspice, cloves, and salt in a bowl and mix well. Combine the pear purée and buttermilk in a bowl and mix well.

Beat the butter and brown sugar in a mixing bowl until creamy, scraping the bowl occasionally. Add the molasses and beat until blended. Add the eggs one at a time, beating well after each addition; the batter will appear curdled. Add the flour mixture alternately with the pear mixture, beating well after each addition and scraping the sides of the bowl frequently to make sure all of the ingredients are incorporated.

Pour the batter into the prepared pan. Bake for 40 to 50 minutes or until a wooden pick inserted in the center comes out clean and the cake begins to pull from the side of the pan. Cool in the pan for 10 minutes. Remove to a wire rack. Serve warm or at room temperature.

Beat the whipping cream, sugar, vanilla, and 1/2 teaspoon cinnamon in a mixing bowl until soft peaks form. Slice the cake and arrange the slices on individual dessert plates. Top with the whipped cream and Caramelized Pears.

Serves 12

CARAMELIZED PEARS

These sweet pears are also delicious over vanilla ice cream.

1/4 cup (1/2 stick) butter
6 ripe pears, peeled, cored, cut into 1/4-inch slices
3/4 cup sugar

Heat the butter in a large heavy skillet until sizzling. Add the pears and toss to coat. Sprinkle with the sugar and stir. Cook over medium-high heat for 10 minutes or until the pears are caramelized and tender, stirring gently. Remove from the skillet and let stand until room temperature.

Serves 12

APRICOT SHORTBREAD WITH ALMONDS

These sweet morsels are perfect with tea, coffee, or hot cocoa.

3 cups flour
1¹/2 cups sugar
³/4 cup cornstarch
³/4 teaspoon salt
1¹/4 cups (2¹/2 sticks) unsalted
   butter, melted

1 (12-ounce) jar apricot jam
1¹/3 cups sliced almonds
Confectioners' sugar

Preheat the oven to 325 degrees. Line a 10- × 15-inch baking pan with heavy-duty foil, allowing a 2-inch overhang at each end. Using a pastry brush, brush the foil with melted butter.

Combine the flour, sugar, cornstarch, and salt in a food processor. Pulse until mixed. Add the melted butter through the feed tube, processing constantly until a dough forms. Pat the dough into the prepared pan. Cover with waxed paper and roll with a rolling pin to smooth; discard the waxed paper.

Place the pan on the middle oven rack. Bake for 25 minutes or until pale gold. The bars will be too hard if allowed to brown at all. Remove from the oven. Heat the jam in a microwave-safe dish until warm and strain to remove any chunks of fruit. Spread the jam over the baked layer. Sprinkle evenly with the almonds and lightly press them into the jam.

Bake for 15 to 20 minutes longer or until the jam is bubbling and the edges of the crust are golden. Remove from the oven. Sprinkle lightly with confectioners' sugar. Cool in the pan on a wire rack for 20 minutes.

Using the foil overhang, remove the shortbread from the pan to a hard surface. Cut the warm shortbread across the width into five 3-inch-wide strips. Cut the strips again across the width into ³/4-inch bars. The cuts look best if a long, sharp knife is used and the blade is wiped clean between cuts. The knife stroke should be made straight down through the cookie, removed, wiped clean, and repositioned for the next cut. Cool on the foil until firm. Sprinkle again with confectioners' sugar if necessary. Store in an airtight container for several days or wrap in plastic wrap and then in foil to freeze for future use.

Note: The jam can be replaced with any flavor, good quality jam for variety.

Makes 65 bars

Almonds

Historians generally agree that almonds are among the earth's oldest cultivated foods. In fact, they are mentioned in the Old Testament in the story of Aaron's rod, which blossomed and bore almonds, symbolizing divine approval. Botanically, the almond is a stone fruit, related to the cherry, plum, and peach. Early explorers ate almonds while traveling the "Silk Road" between Asia and the Mediterranean. Soon the trees were found throughout Spain and Italy. Brought to California by Franciscan padres in the mid-1700s, almond trees were planted to grace their missions, but the damp, coastal climate did not provide optimal growing conditions. By the following century, almond trees had been planted inland, where they found the dry, warm sun they needed to thrive. With that, the world's almond-growing capital was born in California's Central Valley, where nearly 100 percent of the U.S. almond crop is harvested each year. Almonds are a good source of folic acid, calcium, fiber, and protein. They are naturally cholesterol-free. A 1-ounce serving contains 170 calories.

Half Moon Bay
PUMPKIN FESTIVAL

More than 250,000 people journey to the Half Moon Bay Art & Pumpkin Festival in October each year. Many stop along the way to choose a Halloween pumpkin at one of the dozens of pumpkin patches along State Highways 1 and 92 leading into this charming seaside town.

Each year, the winner of the World Championship Pumpkin Weigh-Off leads the Great Pumpkin Parade of witches, goblins, and ghosts. Highlights of the celebration include the Halloween costume, pumpkin pie eating, and pumpkin carving contests, a haunted house, harvest-inspired crafts, and the never-ending search for the Great Pumpkin. Visitors can sample tasty pancakes, pie, bread, cheesecake, ice cream, and soup all made with pumpkin. Other favorites, offered by local nonprofit groups to showcase the region's produce, include stews of artichokes and Brussels sprouts, fried calamari, and clam chowder.

PRALINE PUMPKIN CHEESECAKE

This rich dessert is a great alternative to traditional pumpkin pie.

Crust
2 cups gingersnap cookie crumbs
1/4 cup (1/2 stick) unsalted butter, melted
1 teaspoon cinnamon
1 teaspoon ground ginger

Filling
16 ounces cream cheese, softened
1 cup sour cream
1/2 cup packed brown sugar
1/2 cup sugar
4 eggs, separated
1 cup canned unsweetened pumpkin purée
3 tablespoons cornstarch
2 teaspoons vanilla extract
1 teaspoon ground ginger
1/2 teaspoon cinnamon
Pinch of nutmeg

Topping and Assembly
1/2 cup packed light brown sugar
3 tablespoons unsalted butter
3/4 cup coarsely chopped pecans
Whipped cream (optional)

Preheat the oven to 325 degrees. Combine the crust ingredients in a bowl and mix well. Press the mixture in the bottom and three-fourths of the way up the side of an 81/2-inch springform pan. Bake for 8 minutes. Cool in the pan on a wire rack.

For the filling, combine the cream cheese, sour cream, brown sugar, and sugar in a mixing bowl. Beat until smooth, scraping the bowl occasionally. Add the egg yolks and beat just until blended. Beat in the pumpkin purée, cornstarch, vanilla, ginger, cinnamon, and nutmeg until mixed. In a separate bowl, beat the egg whites until stiff peaks form. Fold the egg whites into the cream cheese mixture.

Pour the cream cheese mixture into the prepared crust. Place in the oven. Set an 8- × 8-inch baking dish, filled halfway with water, on the rack below the cheesecake. This keeps the top of the cake from cracking. Bake for 11/2 hours or until the center does not tremble when the cake is gently shaken. Cool in the pan on a wire rack until room temperature. Chill, covered, for at least 6 hours.

For the topping, preheat the oven to 325 degrees. Line a baking sheet with sides with foil. Combine the brown sugar and butter in a heavy saucepan. Cook over medium heat until the sugar dissolves and the mixture comes to a boil, stirring frequently. Boil for 1 minute without stirring. Stir in the pecans. Spread the mixture on the prepared baking sheet. Bake for 8 minutes or until the sugar syrup bubbles vigorously. Let stand until cool. Break into pieces.

To assemble, run a knife around the edge of the cheesecake and remove the rim. Place the cheesecake on a serving platter. Arrange the praline topping in a decorative pattern over the top of the cake. Slice the cheesecake and top each serving with a spoonful of whipped cream.

Note: The praline topping may be prepared up to two days ahead and stored in an airtight container.

Serves 12

CHOCOLATE GRAND MARNIER MOUSSE TART

Prepare this outrageous chocolate dessert the night before serving.

Crust
1¹/2 cups (³/4 of a 9-ounce package) chocolate wafers crumbs (Nabisco Famous Chocolate Wafers preferred)
7 tablespoons butter, melted

Filling
12 ounces high quality semisweet chocolate chips or finely chopped chocolate bar (Scharffen Berger, Guittard, or Ghirardelli preferred)
5 egg yolks (see note)
3 tablespoons strong brewed coffee
3 tablespoons Grand Marnier or 2 teaspoons orange extract
1¹/2 cups whipping cream

For the crust, combine the chocolate wafer crumbs and butter in a bowl with a fork. Press the crumb mixture in the bottom and halfway up the sides of a buttered 8¹/2-inch springform pan. Freeze for 1 hour.

For the filling, place the chocolate, egg yolks, coffee, and Grand Marnier in a blender. Place the whipping cream in a saucepan over medium-low heat. Scald the whipping cream until tiny bubbles appear at the edge of the pan, and a film has formed on the surface. Pour the scalded whipping cream into the filling ingredients with the blender running, processing constantly for 3 minutes. Pour into the prepared crust. Chill, covered, for at least 8 hours or overnight. Remove the springform sides, slice and serve chilled.

Note: The egg yolks in this recipe are not fully cooked. If you are reluctant to use raw egg, this recipe is not recommended.

Serves 12

Chocolate

Everyone has a favorite way to enjoy chocolate, whether a plain chocolate bar or an elaborate chocolate dessert. Chocolate comes in several forms and varieties: unsweetened, bittersweet, semisweet, and milk chocolate. White chocolate is not chocolate at all, but rather a combination of cocoa butter, milk solids, and flavorings. The higher the content of cocoa butter, the better the chocolate. The dark varieties of chocolate contain the highest amount of chocolate liquor, which is a combination of cocoa butter and the roasted, ground cocoa bean nibs. Unsweetened chocolate consists of about half chocolate liquor and half pure cocoa butter, while milk chocolate has only about 10 percent chocolate liquor. Bittersweet, semisweet, and milk chocolate also contain varying amounts of sugar and vanilla.

Many chocolate recipes call for melted chocolate. When melting chocolate, take care not to let the temperature rise above 115 degrees. For best results, melt the chocolate slowly at a low temperature in a double boiler. Bring the water to a boil and turn off the heat. Then set the pan containing the chocolate over the hot water. Be careful not to get any water into the melting chocolate, as even a tiny amount of water will cause the chocolate to become grainy and lumpy.

Winter

Franciscan missionaries from Mexico planted California's first olive orchards in the 1700s. During the 1800s, when olive trees were being planted by ranchers to meet an increasing demand for olive oil, Freda Ehmann and her son, Edwin, purchased an orchard in the Oroville area. The trees were barely producing when olive oil prices began to drop, leading Freda to begin experimenting with processing the 280 gallons of olives in barrels on her back porch. With her canned olives, the California ripe olive industry was born.

Despite a recent resurgence of interest in olive oil production, over 90 percent of California's olives still end up in cans. Harvest, largely done by hand, begins in mid-September and continues through the winter months primarily in the Northern California counties of Tehama, Glenn, and Butte. Olives are processed in a lye-curing solution to leach out the bitterness. During the curing process, a flow of air bubbling through the solution changes the olives' color from green to black. The state of California produces 100 percent of the olives grown in the United States.

Corning, California, the self-proclaimed "Olive City," first hosted its Olive Festival in 1947 with the belief that "there is no better way to advertise a product than with a party." A scavenger hunt for "the missing olive" kicks off the festival each year with clues in local newspapers and on the radio. One of the most popular events of the festival sends competitors wheeling through town on beds. Known as the Corning Does It 'Bedder' Bed Races, two teams compete against each other with three members pushing a bed on wheels down Solano Street. The fourth team member, who is riding on the bed, must exchange t-shirts with a pushing member halfway through the race. A street dance follows. The party continues the next day with a car show, carnival games, arts and crafts, musical entertainment, a talent show, a beauty pageant, and the annual Olive Festival Cook-Off.

The Olive Pit restaurant in Corning has been a Northern California landmark since 1967 when Pete and Ann Craig first began offering locally grown and produced olives at their hamburger and milkshake stand. When people showed an interest in purchasing the olives, a Corning tradition was born. The store has been expanded five times over the years to meet the increasing demands of customers pulling off Interstate 5 at the Corning Road exit, 110 miles north of Sacramento. Today the Craig family continues to serve tasty milkshakes and delicious olive burgers to hungry travelers. Over thirty different types of olives are available for sampling at the tasting bar to help customers choose among tempting varieties such as smoked, garlic, wine-cured, and jalapeño-stuffed olives. An expanding array of locally grown and produced products is offered for sale including olives, olive oils, mustards, vinegars, nuts, and other treats.

PICHOLINE OLIVES BRAISED WITH WHITE WINE & LEMON

Alice Waters and the cooks of Chez Panisse created this versatile olive recipe.

9 ounces picholine olives
1/4 cup water
1/4 cup dry white wine
1 (2-inch) piece lemon zest
A few sprigs thyme
1 bay leaf

Put all the ingredients in a nonreactive pan and cover tightly. Braise in the oven at 375 degrees for 1 hour. Allow the olives to cool in their juice.

Pit the olives (or not) and serve as an hors d'oeuvre or as an accompaniment to roasted new potatoes, dandelion salad, sautéed or braised fennel, or dishes that would be complemented by the olives' savory citric taste.

Serves 6

Photo Opposite: Olive Bar, Andronico's Market, Danville, California

California Olives

The most common types of olives are Manzanillo and Sevillano, accounting for 85 percent of domestic production. The others are Ascolano, Barouni, and Mission. Each type has a unique texture and flavor. Green olives and black "ripe" olives actually come off the same trees. When they are picked and how they are processed determines their color. Green olives are harvested before they ripen, while black "ripe" olives have been left on the tree until completely ripe. The taste of the ripe olive is mild and the texture softer than the saltier green olive. The California olive industry processes over 90 percent of the annual crop as canned ripe olives. In the U.S. market, 40 percent of ripe olives are used in salads, 24 percent on pizza, and 17 percent on sandwiches.

Of the 180,000 tons of olives used in the U.S. annually, 65 percent come from California, with the remainder imported from Spain and other Mediterranean countries. The California olive is characterized by a much nuttier flavor than imported varieties.

NIÇOISE OLIVE & ONION APPETIZER

Sliced into decorative strips, these tarts make an impressive hors d'oeuvre.

1 (18-ounce) package frozen
   puff pastry
3 tablespoons olive oil
2 pounds yellow onions, cut into
   1/4-inch slices
2 large garlic cloves, minced
1 tablespoon minced mixed fresh
   herbs (oregano, rosemary, thyme,
   and sage), or 1 teaspoon mixed
   dried herbs

1 teaspoon kosher salt
1 bay leaf
Freshly ground pepper to taste
12 ounces pitted niçoise or
   kalamata olives, cut into halves
   (see sidebar, page 24)
1 egg yolk
1 tablespoon water
Sprigs of fresh thyme

Thaw the puff pastry according to package instructions. Unfold the pastry and cover with plastic wrap. Store in the refrigerator while proceeding with the recipe.

Heat the olive oil in a large heavy saucepan over medium heat. Add the onions and stir until coated. Reduce the heat to the lowest setting and sweat, covered, for 15 minutes. Remove the cover and stir in the garlic, dried herbs (if using instead of fresh herbs), salt, and bay leaf. Cook, stirring occasionally, for 45 minutes or until the onions are tender, sweet, and pale in color. Remove from heat. Discard the bay leaf. Add the fresh herbs, if using. Set aside.

Preheat the oven to 425 degrees and place a rack in the lower third of the oven. Transfer one sheet of the pastry onto a lightly floured surface, leaving the remaining sheet in the refrigerator. With a rolling pin, roll the dough into a 9- × 12-inch rectangle. Using a sharp knife, cut the rectangle into four 3- × 9-inch strips; a dull knife will compress the layers of dough. Arrange these strips on a non-Cushionaire baking sheet; air-cushioned baking sheets retard the browning required for puff pastry. Prick the strips at frequent intervals with a fork to within 1/4-inch of the edges. Repeat the process with the remaining sheet of puff pastry.

Spread 2 to 3 tablespoons of the onion mixture on each strip to within 1/4-inch of the edges. Sprinkle generously with pepper. Arrange the olives cut side down in an attractive pattern over the top. Whisk the egg yolk and water in a bowl until blended. Brush the edges of the strips with the egg yolk mixture.

Bake for 15 minutes or until toasty brown. Remove to a wire rack to cool. Cut each strip diagonally into six equal portions and arrange on a serving platter. Garnish with sprigs of thyme or sprinkle thyme leaves over the strips just before serving. This appetizer may be prepared and baked a day in advance and stored at room temperature. Reheat in a 350-degree oven for 5 to 10 minutes or until crisp.

Makes 4 dozen

Holiday Open House

Gather with friends to celebrate the season! A selection of savory hors d'oeuvres and sweet confections adds to the festivities and lends itself to an evening of camaraderie and conversation. Arrange the delicacies on beautiful platters and in decorative bowls, varying the height, size, and garnish of each to create a visual masterpiece. As host, enjoy the simplicity of a buffet setting and appreciate the time spent with family and friends.

Antipasto
Niçoise Olive & Onion Appetizer 168
Italian Veal Meatballs 171
Salmon Cakes with Wasabi Cream 173

•

Sugar & Spice Walnuts 208
Caramels 209
Toffee Butter Cookies 211

Niçoise Olive & Onion Appetizer

1998 Virtual Vineyards
Zinfandel,
Shenandoah Valley

•

1999 Virtual Vineyards
Chardonnay, California

Zinfandel is a red grape variety that runs the gamut from blush to rich, dark powerhouses. With origins not entirely established by wine world scholars, zinfandel is nevertheless at home in California. The Shenandoah Valley in the Sierra foothills is among the finest appellations in California for producing zinfandel.

Simple and fruity to world class, chardonnay is the white wine darling of the wine world. Widely planted and fairly successful in many areas of the world, it varies in style from the crisp lemon-lime-mineral flavors of classic chablis to rich, oaky, buttery wines from California, Australia, and other areas of the world.

The Martini

The origin of the martini is clouded in myth. Many sources claim the drink was first named the "Martinez" by a legendary bartender named Jerry Thomas. Thomas was working at the Occidental Hotel in San Francisco when a traveler on his way to Martinez, California stopped in and asked for something special. "Very well, here is a new drink I have invented for your trip," said Thomas. "We'll call it the Martinez." It is not hard to imagine how the name could have been shortened after a few libations were consumed. While this makes a good story, the only verifiable fact is that the 1887 edition of Thomas' bartending book included a recipe for the "Martinez."

Contesting the San Francisco paternity theory, the citizens of Martinez claim that around 1870 a miner from San Francisco stopped his horse at Julio Richelieu's saloon on Ferry Street in Martinez. He plunked down a bag of gold for a bottle of whiskey. The miner was not quite satisfied, so Richelieu mixed him a small drink and dropped in an olive. The miner asked what it was, and Richelieu replied, "That is a Martinez cocktail." Although the controversial origins of this famous elixir may never be resolved, citizens of Martinez installed a plaque in 1992 attesting to the "fact" that Martinez is the true birthplace of the cocktail now known as the martini.

WILD MUSHROOM & BLUE CHEESE CROSTINI

The robust flavors of wild mushrooms and savory cheese comprise this rich appetizer.

2 tablespoons olive oil
4 ounces shiitake mushrooms, stems removed, thinly sliced
4 ounces oyster mushrooms, stems removed, thinly sliced
8 ounces cremini (brown) mushrooms, thinly sliced
2 tablespoons chopped fresh flat-leaf parsley
1 teaspoon minced fresh thyme

Salt and freshly ground pepper to taste
1/2 cup coarsely grated fontina cheese
1 cup crumbled Gorgonzola cheese
3 garlic cloves, cut into halves
12 slices coarse texture French bread, lightly toasted
Sprigs of fresh thyme

Heat the olive oil in a large skillet over medium-high heat. Add the mushrooms and mix well. Cook for 7 to 10 minutes or until the liquid evaporates and the mushrooms are golden brown, stirring occasionally. Stir in the parsley and minced thyme. Season generously with salt and pepper. Remove from heat. Let stand until cool. Stir in the cheeses.

Preheat the broiler. Rub the garlic cloves over both sides of the toasted bread slices. Spread some of the mushroom mixture on each slice. Arrange in a single layer on a baking sheet. Broil for 1 minute or until the cheese melts. Transfer the crostini to a serving platter. Garnish with sprigs of thyme. Serve immediately.

Serves 6

ITALIAN VEAL MEATBALLS

Simply baked in the oven, these meatballs are full of flavor.

1 cup good-quality marinara sauce
2/3 pound ground veal
6 tablespoons soft fresh bread
    crumbs
6 tablespoons finely chopped
    flat-leaf parsley
6 tablespoons finely grated
    Parmigiano-Reggiano cheese
    (aged Parmesan)
3 tablespoons milk

2 tablespoons pine nuts, lightly
    toasted
2 tablespoons dried currants
1 tablespoon olive oil
1 egg, lightly beaten
3/4 teaspoon salt
1/4 teaspoon freshly ground pepper
Flat-leaf parsley leaves
Collard greens for garnish
40 wooden picks

Preheat the oven to 375 degrees. Simmer the marinara sauce in a saucepan until very thick, stirring occasionally. Set aside.

Combine the ground veal, bread crumbs, chopped parsley, cheese, milk, pine nuts, currants, olive oil, egg, salt, and pepper in a bowl and mix well. Shape the mixture into 1-inch balls. Arrange the meatballs two inches apart on an oiled baking sheet with sides. Bake for 12 to 15 minutes or until cooked through.

Reheat the marinara sauce if necessary and pour into a squeeze bottle. Drizzle the sauce over the meatballs on the baking sheet. Top each meatball with a parsley leaf and skewer with a wooden pick. Arrange the meatballs on a serving platter lined with collard greens.

Makes 40 meatballs

Cocktail Food

When hosting a cocktail party, a good approach to menu planning is to estimate one-and-a-half to two pieces of every savory item per guest (based on hors d'oeuvres that are two-bite size), and twelve pieces per person total. Calculate less per person if the party is a prelude to some other event. For food selection, it is nice to start with a cheese item, then add a fruit and/or vegetable item, then seafood, and finally, meat-based hors d'oeuvres, depending on the number of guests expected.

Some examples of the rules above: at a cocktail party for thirty to fifty guests, serve five to six choices. For a larger party, seven to eight choices will be needed. Always begin with one vegetarian item, such as a cheese board, and one healthy item, such as a crudité platter. For hors d'oeuvres before a dinner party for six to ten people, serve two items, one vegetarian and one healthy. When estimating cheese, calculate about one ounce per person. Always plan on serving larger quantities of favorites like prawns or oysters on the half shell.

At cocktail parties, desserts are usually ignored in favor of foods that go with alcohol, though sweets are nice if coffee and tea are being served. Guests will serve themselves tiny portions, especially if there is more than one dessert choice.

Animal Mating
TOURS

For well over a decade, the San Francisco Zoo has been hosting an annual love-fest of sorts. On the weekend before Valentine's Day, on the day itself, and again the weekend after, lovebirds gather to watch nature at its primal best. The romantic escapade begins with a private Safari Tram tour through the main zoo led by an animal care professional, followed by exciting, up-close encounters with animals, and an array of uniquely engaging activities in the exotic aviary. Voyeurs sip champagne and indulge in savory hors d'oeuvres and chocolate truffles during the internationally acclaimed, entertaining, and educational event. Limited to adults ages eighteen and over, the two-hour affair could be the perfect start to a wild Valentine's celebration. Tickets must be purchased in advance.

BLINI WITH CAVIAR & CRÈME FRAÎCHE

These bite-sized, delicate pancakes have an elegant caviar topping. For a less expensive variation, top with smoked salmon or trout instead of caviar.

1 envelope dry yeast
1/2 cup lukewarm water
11/2 cups flour
1 cup milk
6 tablespoons butter, melted, plus additional for skillet

3 eggs, separated
1/2 teaspoon salt
1/8 teaspoon sugar
1 cup crème fraîche (see note)
1 (1-ounce) jar refrigerated fresh sevruga caviar (see note)

Stir the yeast into the lukewarm water in a bowl. Let stand for 5 minutes and stir. Combine the yeast mixture, flour, milk, butter, egg yolks, salt, and sugar in a blender or food processor. Process on high for 40 seconds; scrape down the side of the container. Process for a few more seconds. Pour the batter into a large bowl. Let rise, loosely covered, in a warm place for 11/2 to 2 hours. Do not let the batter rise much longer or the blini will taste fermented.

Beat the egg whites in a mixing bowl until stiff peaks form. Fold the egg whites into the batter. Heat a heavy skillet or griddle and brush with additional melted butter. Drop the batter by teaspoonfuls into the hot skillet, creating pancakes approximately 11/2 inches in diameter. Cook until the underside is light brown; turn. Cook briefly on the remaining side. Transfer the blini to a heated platter. Repeat the process with the remaining batter.

Arrange the warm blini on a tray lined with a linen napkin. Top each blini with 1/4 teaspoon crème fraîche and 1/8 teaspoon caviar.

The blini may be cooked, wrapped in foil, and stored in the refrigerator for use the following day. Warm the wrapped blini in a 300-degree oven for 10 minutes, adding the crème fraîche and caviar just before serving.

Note: Crème fraîche is located in the dairy case near the sour cream or in the gourmet cheese section of grocery stores.

Refrigerated fresh caviar is available at gourmet markets and fishmarkets. Vacuum-packed shelf-stable varieties are notoriously fishy tasting. Sevruga is excellent for this appetizer; the more costly beluga and osetra caviars are too delicate for this type of recipe.

Makes 5 dozen

SALMON CAKES WITH WASABI CREAM

*Wasabi cream and fresh ginger add an Asian influence
to this fresh salmon appetizer.*

4 teaspoons wasabi powder
  (see note)
1 tablespoon water
12 ounces salmon fillet, boned,
  coarsely chopped
6 green onions, thinly sliced
1 egg, lightly beaten
2 tablespoons grated fresh ginger

2 teaspoons lemon juice
1 teaspoon salt
1/4 teaspoon freshly ground pepper
1/4 cup vegetable oil
1/3 to 1/2 cup crème fraîche
  (see note)
Black sesame seeds (optional)

Combine the wasabi powder and water in a small bowl and mix well. Let stand, covered with plastic wrap, to allow the flavor to develop.

Combine the salmon, green onions, egg, ginger, lemon juice, salt, and pepper in a bowl and mix well. Shape the salmon mixture into twenty-four 1-inch cakes, 1/2-inch thick. Keep them bite-size or they will fall apart.

Preheat the oven to 200 degrees. Heat 1 tablespoon of oil in a large nonstick skillet. Sauté the salmon cakes in batches for 3 minutes or until golden brown on both sides, adding more oil as needed. Drain the cakes on paper towels and place on a baking sheet. Keep warm in the oven; the cakes will hold up for about 30 minutes. Repeat the process with the remaining oil and salmon cakes.

Combine the wasabi mixture and crème fraîche in a bowl and mix well. Transfer the wasabi cream to a squeeze bottle. Squeeze some of the wasabi cream on each salmon cake and top with a few black sesame seeds.

Note: Wasabi powder is available at most markets in the Asian food section.

Crème fraîche is located in the dairy case near the sour cream or in the gourmet cheese section of grocery stores. Do not substitute sour cream for the crème fraîche in this recipe, because the flavor of sour cream is incompatible with wasabi.

Makes 2 dozen

Fortune Cookie
FACTORY

Contrary to common belief, fortune cookies originated in San Francisco and were invented by a Japanese-American gardener. Many visitors to San Francisco's Chinatown enjoy discovering the small Golden Gate Fortune Cookie Factory, located down the narrow cobblestoned Ross Alley, a block off bustling Grant Avenue. The door is always open and the aroma of fresh baked cookies entices visitors to stop in. A peek inside reveals two women silently working; one mixes batter and places it in rotating cast-iron molds, while the other retrieves the cooked dough with a long stick and rolls each cookie around a fortune typed on a paper strip. Customers are asked whether they prefer their fortunes "regular" or "funny." Those who choose "funny" are often surprised by the racy adult fortunes they receive!

Sun-Dried
TOMATOES

For centuries, Mediterranean cooks have extended the tomato season by drying their garden tomatoes in the sun and preserving them in oil. Using ripe California Roma tomatoes, California Sun Dry Foods follows traditional sun-drying methods that give tomatoes a fresh, sweet California taste. Rushing the process by oven-drying will cause a brownish color and a slightly burnt aftertaste. This is caused by the rapid caramelization of the tomatoes' natural sugars.

California Sun Dry Foods takes juicy, vine-ripe California tomatoes, cuts them in half, and dries them in the summer sun for seven to ten days, where they are cooled by evening breezes. The moisture evaporates, the flavor intensifies, and the natural sweetness bursts forth. The slow sun-drying process allows partial rehydration at night, producing a bright red, sweet, full-bodied, dried tomato. The tomatoes, although dried, retain a sweet plumpness because of the slow drying process used.

SUN-DRIED TOMATO TORTE

This recipe created by California Sun Dry Foods is perfect for holiday parties.

24 ounces whipped cream cheese
1 (9-ounce) jar California Sun Dry Sun-Dried Tomato Spread
1 (8.5-ounce) jar California Sun Dry Sun-Dried Tomato Pesto
1 (8.5-ounce) jar California Sun Dry Julienne Cut Sun-Dried Tomatoes, drained
1/2 cup salted pistachios, coarsely chopped
Assorted crackers

Spread half the cream cheese into a rectangle 1/4-inch thick on a sheet of plastic wrap. Repeat the process with the remaining cream cheese on a separate sheet of plastic wrap, making it the same size as the first rectangle. Wrap each rectangle separately and chill until firm.

Remove the plastic wrap from one of the cream cheese rectangles. Place it on a serving platter. Cover with the sun-dried tomato spread evenly to the edges. Spoon half the sun-dried tomato pesto over the spread. Place the second cream cheese rectangle over the top. Spread with the remaining sun-dried tomato pesto. Top with the julienned sun-dried tomatoes. Chill, covered, until serving time. Press the pistachios into the sides. Serve with assorted crackers.

Serves 50

ARUGULA, SPINACH & WHITE BEAN SALAD

The distinctive flavors of arugula and hazelnuts pair nicely with cannellini beans in this winter salad.

1/2 cup dried cannellini beans, or
   1 1/2 cups canned cannellini
   beans
1 teaspoon salt
2 cups arugula leaves
2 cups baby spinach leaves

1/2 cup thinly sliced red onion
1/2 cup cherry tomato halves
Hazelnut Dressing
1/2 cup toasted hazelnuts (see
   note), or toasted walnuts,
   coarsely chopped

Soak the dried beans in water for at least 8 hours or overnight; drain. Combine the beans with enough water to cover in a heavy saucepan. Bring to a boil; reduce heat. Cook over low heat for 1 hour, stirring occasionally. Stir in the salt. Cook for 30 minutes longer or until the beans are tender; drain. Let stand until cool. If substituting canned beans for the dried beans, drain and rinse the beans but do not soak or cook.

   Toss the arugula, spinach, onion, cherry tomatoes, and beans in a bowl. Add the desired amount of Hazelnut Dressing (about 1/4 cup) and mix gently until coated. Sprinkle with the hazelnuts.

Note: To toast hazelnuts, place them on a baking sheet in a preheated 350-degree oven for 20 minutes. Remove from oven and wrap the hazelnuts in a towel. Rub the nuts in the towel until most of the skin is removed; some skin will remain. Cool briefly then chop coarsely.

Serves 4

HAZELNUT DRESSING

Walnut oil may be substituted for the hazelnut oil.

3 tablespoons hazelnut oil
3 tablespoons extra virgin olive oil
2 tablespoons white wine vinegar
1/2 teaspoon salt
1/8 teaspoon white pepper

Whisk together all of the dressing ingredients to combine.

Makes 1/2 cup

Spinach

The Spanish may have brought spinach to the United States, but its origins are in the Middle East. The leafy green vegetable, grown year-round in Northern California, prefers a cool climate like that of Monterey County, where nearly 70 percent of U.S. spinach is grown.

Spinach is fast-growing, with its leafy green foliage maturing in just seven weeks. When harvesting fresh spinach, carefully cut the leaves above the growing point and a second crop can be cultivated. When buying spinach, choose leaves that are dark green and crisp. Avoid those that are yellow or limp. Fresh market spinach may contain a lot of grit and sand. To clean it, fill a basin with water, soak the spinach leaves, and the sand will sink to the bottom. Thoroughly dry the spinach and store it in a towel-lined plastic bag in the refrigerator for up to three days.

Each February, part of San Francisco's historic Fort Mason is transformed into a warm, humid rain forest for the San Francisco Orchid Show. Orchid merchants come from all over California to display and sell their prized plants. The show offers an opportunity to see the most unusual and greatest variety of orchids, and to ask questions of the orchid experts.

Often perceived as difficult to grow, orchids are actually as hearty as wildflowers. They bloom one to three times a year, depending on the variety, and for three months at a time or longer. Most orchids available in the Bay Area originated in South America. Indoor orchids require indirect sunlight so the leaves and blossoms will not wilt and burn. Orchids do not grow in soil, but rather their roots cling to pieces of bark and sometimes moss. A nutritional substance is drizzled over the bark, which should be kept damp or the orchid will not hold its blossoms and will not rebloom. Many orchid owners find that certain orchid varieties favor a steamy bathroom setting that simulates the rain forest atmosphere of their natural habitat. Orchids that have finished blooming can be purchased for half price at the San Francisco Orchid Show. Have patience, and in a few short months the spectacular blooms will be back.

FIELD GREENS, ROASTED BEETS & ROQUEFORT

Oven-roasted beets create an irresistible and beautiful salad.

1 bunch (about 1 1/2 pounds)
   medium beets, well-scrubbed,
   green tops removed
Olive oil
3 tablespoons red wine vinegar
2 teaspoons Dijon mustard
1/2 teaspoon salt
Freshly ground pepper to taste
1/2 cup extra virgin olive oil
12 ounces mixed field greens
6 to 8 ounces Roquefort cheese,
   crumbled
1/2 cup walnuts, toasted

Preheat the oven to 350 degrees. Rub the beets with olive oil and arrange in a roasting pan. Roast for 45 to 60 minutes or until the beets are easily pierced with a knife. Let stand until cool. Peel the beets and cut into wedges or dice.

Whisk the vinegar, mustard, salt, pepper, and 1/2 cup extra virgin olive oil in a bowl to combine. Toss the beets with 2 tablespoons of the dressing and set aside. When ready to serve, gently toss the salad greens with the desired amount of dressing in a large bowl. Divide the salad evenly among six serving plates. Arrange the beets on the greens and sprinkle with the cheese and walnuts.

Serves 6

LETTUCES WITH HONEY-ORANGE DRESSING

*This refreshing citrus salad dressing is not only fat-free,
but also delightfully tasty.*

1/3 cup honey
1/3 cup orange juice
1/4 cup Dijon mustard

2 tablespoons minced fresh parsley
Freshly ground pepper
6 cups mixed baby lettuces

Whisk together all ingredients except the lettuce.

Drizzle the desired amount of dressing over the baby lettuces in a salad bowl and toss gently to coat. Serve immediately.

Serves 6

Organic Produce

The term "organic" refers to methods of growing and processing foods that rely on the earth's natural resources. Pests and weeds are managed using earth-friendly means such as beneficial insects and mechanical controls. Organic farmers work to build natural nutrients in soil that help fertilize plants without reliance on synthetic fertilizers.

Organic farming began in this country in experimental gardens in the late 1940s. In the 1970s, consumer interest in organic produce began to grow, but it was not until the California Organic Foods Act of 1990 that industry standards were developed.

There are over fifteen hundred certified organic farms in California that yield about 5 percent of the produce grown in the state. The retail food industry considers organic products to be its fastest growing segment.

Dungeness Crab

In other parts of the country, the holidays are traditionally celebrated with turkey, but in Northern California the holidays include succulent Dungeness crab. Dungeness crab is found in the waters of the Pacific Ocean from Alaska to Mexico. Crab season officially begins in mid-November and continues until June, though the peak months for Dungeness are December through February. The Dungeness crab is a ten-legged crustacean that ranges in weight from one-and-a-half to four pounds. These crabs are at their best served freshly cooked, cracked, cleaned, and iced. Dungeness crab has a firm, sweet meat that is a perfect addition to Crab Louis salad, crab cakes, gumbo, and cioppino.

San Francisco's Fisherman's Wharf is famous for Dungeness crab caught in the waters off the San Francisco Bay. It takes three to six years for a crab to reach edible size and only male crabs that are 6¼ inches or more along their carapaces may be harvested. However, there is no limit on the quantity of crab fishermen can bring in. Dungeness crab thrive in cold waters, so during El Niño years when the water in the center of the Pacific Ocean is much warmer than normal winters, crab larvae tend to be more scarce, driving up the price for mature crab in the years that follow.

Crab fishing is a difficult and dangerous job. The winter season makes the ocean waters especially treacherous and the circular crab pots or traps are made of heavy steel. Crab boats usually carry 60 to 150 traps baited with smaller crabs, clams, chopped squid, mussels, and small fish. The bait is placed in a jar with holes in the lid that allow the aroma to escape, then the jar is placed inside the trap. Traps are set in strings of about 20 in a line parallel to the shore, 300-feet deep. They are set about 150 yards apart so the watermen can raise, empty, and re-bait a trap in the time it takes to get from one trap to another. Traps are left overnight or for up to a week depending on fishing conditions. The best time to catch crabs is neither high tide nor low tide, but when currents are still, allowing the scent of the bait to be followed.

In late January on Northern California's Mendocino Coast, the focus is on crab and wine. The region offers a series of winemakers' dinners, cooking demonstrations, and educational tours that cater to crab lovers. Charter boats are available for cruises focused on crabbing. A series of educational workshops on crab is sponsored by the Noyo Women for Fisheries, a nonprofit organization that supports local fishermen and promotes the fishing industry through education and legislation.

GARLIC-STEAMED CRAB

From Joe Pucci & Sons Seafoods, this is a fantastic way to prepare Dungeness crabs for a crab feed.

1/4 cup (1/2 stick) butter
2 tablespoons minced garlic
2 fresh large Dungeness crabs, cooked, cleaned, cracked (see sidebar, page 181)
2 cups dry white wine
2 tablespoons whole grain Dijon mustard
1 tablespoon lemon juice
1 teaspoon minced lemon zest
1/2 cup minced flat-leaf parsley
Lemon wedges
2 or 3 warm baguettes, sliced

Melt the butter in a large heavy skillet or wok over medium heat. Add the garlic. Sauté about 30 seconds. Add the crabs and toss to coat. Pour in the wine and bring to a boil. Stir in the Dijon mustard, lemon juice, lemon zest, and parsley.

Simmer, covered, for 3 minutes. Serve in individual bowls with lemon wedges. Pass the baguette slices for sopping up the sauce.

Serves 6

Photo Opposite: Dungeness Crab, Swan Oyster Depot, Polk Street, San Francisco, California

Winter Solstice Supper

A bounty of fresh Dungeness crab marks the beginning of winter. A sophisticated combination of greens balances the flavorful cioppino beautifully. Soak up every last drop with San Francisco sourdough bread, then top off the meal with a warm pear crisp served with vanilla ice cream. What better meal than this to welcome the months of winter?

Arugula, Spinach & White Bean Salad 175

•

Cioppino 181
Sourdough Bread

•

Currant Pear Crisp 204

Cioppino

CIOPPINO

This traditional favorite originated in San Francisco in 1900 and is easy to make despite the long list of ingredients.

1/3 cup olive oil
1 medium carrot, peeled, finely chopped
1 red bell pepper, chopped
1/2 cup chopped onion
3 or 4 garlic cloves, minced
1/4 cup chopped celery
2 pounds fresh plum tomatoes, peeled, chopped (see note, page 99), or 1 (28-ounce) can Italian plum tomatoes, coarsely chopped
3 cups fish stock, or 2 cups water and 1 cup clam juice
1 to 2 cups zinfandel wine
1/4 cup tomato paste
2 tablespoons chopped fresh basil, or 2 teaspoons dried basil
1 tablespoon chopped fresh oregano, or 1 teaspoon dried oregano

1 teaspoon freshly ground black pepper
1 teaspoon fennel seeds
1 bay leaf
1/2 teaspoon red pepper flakes (optional)
1/8 teaspoon sugar
1/2 teaspoon kosher salt
2 dozen clams in shells, scrubbed
1 cup water or white wine
1 pound raw white fish (halibut, bass, or cod), cut into pieces
1 pound raw shrimp, peeled, deveined, or 1 pound scallops
2 large Dungeness crabs, cooked, cleaned, cracked (see sidebar)
1/4 cup chopped flat-leaf parsley

Heat the olive oil in an 8-quart stockpot. Sauté the carrot, bell pepper, onion, garlic, and celery for 5 minutes or until the vegetables begin to soften. Add the tomatoes, fish stock, zinfandel, tomato paste, basil, oregano, black pepper, fennel seeds, bay leaf, red pepper flakes, sugar, and salt. Simmer, covered, for 60 to 80 minutes, stirring occasionally. Taste and adjust seasonings, adding more salt if needed. Flavors should be mellow and rich. Discard the bay leaf.

Combine the clams and water or white wine in a saucepan. Steam, covered, over medium heat for 5 minutes or until the shells open. Remove the clams to a bowl with a slotted spoon, reserving the broth. Strain the broth through cheesecloth or a fine strainer into the tomato mixture.

Add the fish and shrimp or scallops to the stockpot and mix well. Simmer for 5 minutes or until the seafood is cooked through and the shrimp turn pink. Stir in the clams and crab and simmer for 1 minute to warm and moisten them. Ladle the cioppino into large soup bowls. Sprinkle with chopped parsley. Have bibs, napkins, shellfish forks, and pliers handy.

Serves 8

How to Crack Crab

Joe Pucci & Sons Seafoods, established in 1918 as a fish market in Oakland, recommends buying Dungeness crab fresh, not frozen, from a reputable fish market. Look for heavy, dense crabs, with no cracks or holes in the shell. Pick up the crab and give it a squeeze. A previously frozen crab will be watery and not as flavorful.

Cleaning a whole cooked crab is not as daunting as it may seem. To begin, twist off the legs at the base of the body and set aside. Turn the crab onto its back. Peel back and twist off the small triangular shell flap. Remove the crab's shell from its body and discard. At this point the yellow "crab butter," considered a delicacy by true crab fanciers, may be saved or rinsed away under cool water. Remove the spongy, finger-like gills from either side of the body and snap the body cavity in half. Carefully crack the shells of the legs with a mallet on a wood cutting board. Serve the crab with crab forks or seafood picks and be sure to include plenty of napkins. Allow about one-half to one whole crab per person, depending on the size of the crab.

Potatoes

The majority of Northern California's potato crop is farmed in Siskiyou and San Joaquin Counties. Siskiyou County harvests five thousand acres of potatoes each year, worth almost twenty million dollars. San Joaquin County's crop covers forty-four hundred acres and is worth about sixteen million dollars. California's most popular varieties include Norkotah and Centennial, both russet-style potatoes, along with Chieftain (red), Cal White (also known as White Rose), and Yukon Gold. Potatoes grow best in sandy soil with a climate of hot days and cool nights.

A "new potato" is one that has just been harvested and has not been stored, allowing the skin to remain tender. When shopping for potatoes, choose those that are firm, smooth, and of uniform size to ensure even cooking. Do not buy potatoes that have cut, wrinkled, or green skin, or soft dark areas. Green spots on the skin are caused by prolonged exposure to light and have an unpleasant bitter flavor. Potatoes should not be refrigerated. Store in a cool, dry, dark, and well-ventilated environment. Do not scrub potatoes until just before cooking. Any sprouts (sometimes called "eyes"), dark bruises, or green spots should be cut out before cooking.

SAUSAGE, POTATO, LEMON & ROSEMARY SOUP

Garlic-basil sausage adds a wonderful flavor to this soup.

1 tablespoon olive oil
4 garlic-basil sausage links, cut into
 1/2-inch slices
3 or 4 medium red potatoes,
 peeled, cut into 1-inch cubes
3 garlic cloves, minced
1 teaspoon chopped fresh rosemary,
 or 1/2 teaspoon dried rosemary

1 cup dry white wine
4 cups chicken stock
1 tablespoon finely chopped
 lemon zest
10 to 12 ounces fresh spinach,
 trimmed, shredded

Heat the olive oil in a large heavy saucepan or Dutch oven over medium heat. Add the sausage. Cook for 10 minutes or until brown on all sides, turning frequently. Reduce the heat slightly. Stir in the potatoes, garlic, and rosemary.

Cook for 5 minutes or until the potatoes are lightly browned, stirring frequently. Add the wine and stir to dislodge any browned bits. Simmer until the wine is reduced by half, stirring frequently. Add the stock and simmer, covered, for 20 minutes or until the potatoes are tender, stirring occasionally. Add half the lemon zest and the spinach. Cook until the spinach wilts, about 3 minutes, stirring frequently. Stir in the remaining lemon zest. Ladle into soup bowls. Serve immediately.

Serves 4

LAMB & FRENCH GREEN BEAN STEW

*The French green beans beautifully complement
the tender meat in this stew.*

1¹/₂ onions, chopped
3 tablespoons olive oil
1 (5- to 6-pound) leg of lamb,
 boned, cut into 1¹/₂-inch cubes
4 or 5 garlic cloves, minced
3 (14-ounce) cans stewed tomatoes
 with juice
2 (14-ounce) cans tomato sauce
1 cup dry white wine

2 teaspoons Fines Herbes
 (see note)
2 bay leaves
Salt and freshly ground pepper
 to taste
Fresh French green beans (haricots
 verts), one handful per person,
 stemmed

Sauté the onions in the olive oil in a large heavy saucepan until translucent. Add the lamb
and garlic. Sauté until the lamb is brown on all sides. Stir in the tomatoes, tomato sauce,
wine, Fines Herbes, bay leaves, salt, and pepper.

Gently simmer for 1¹/₄ to 2 hours or until the lamb is very tender. Add the green beans
during the last 15 minutes of the cooking process. Discard the bay leaves.

Serve with rice pilaf or pasta. This dish may be prepared in advance, adding the green
beans during the reheating process.

Note: A mixture of thyme, oregano, sage, rosemary, marjoram, and basil may be substituted
for the Fines Herbes.

Serves 8

Thickening Agents

Flour as a thickener is traditional for sauces and gravy. The first step in making white or brown sauce is preparing the roux. To create a white roux, butter and flour are cooked together for at least three minutes to eliminate the taste of raw flour. A brown roux cooks a bit longer as the butter and flour are browned slightly. Liquid is then whisked into the roux to create a rich velvety quality.

Because arrowroot dissolves quickly, it is often used as a thickening agent in fruit sauces, when cooking at high heat, or when boiling is undesirable. Its thickening power is about twice that of wheat flour. Arrowroot is tasteless and becomes clear when cooked. Unlike cornstarch, it does not impart a chalky taste when undercooked, nor does it require precooking like flour to eliminate its taste.

The reduction method can be used to create a quick sauce for sautéed poultry or meat. Remove the meat and deglaze the pan by adding wine or stock and cooking over medium-high heat until the liquid has reduced in volume and thickened.

A cooking tip from **Sandy Sachs,**
*Executive Chef, Ingredients
Cooking/Lifestyle School at
Andronico's Market*

Cauliflower

A member of the cabbage family, cauliflower originated over two thousand years ago in gardens of Asia Minor and the Mediterranean. Over 80 percent of the cauliflower grown in the United States today comes from the Salinas Valley in Monterey County, California.

Cauliflower, grown year-round, is difficult to detect in the fields, as the large outer leaves must be folded over the head of the cauliflower by hand to protect it from the yellowing effects of sunlight as it grows. While most of the cauliflower harvested today is white, green and purple varieties are becoming increasingly popular.

Cauliflower is fat-free, cholesterol-free, and very low in sodium and calories. Cauliflower is also a good source of folate and is high in vitamin C.

CAULIFLOWER & LEMON-PEPPER SAUSAGE SOUP

A very different and tasty way to enjoy cauliflower.

8 ounces russet potatoes, peeled, diced
1 medium yellow onion, chopped
2 tablespoons butter
Florets of 1 head cauliflower
2 cups water

2 cups whole milk
1 teaspoon salt
Freshly ground pepper to taste
1 or 2 lemon-pepper chicken sausages
3 cups packed baby arugula

Sauté the potatoes and onion in the butter in a heavy saucepan over medium heat until the onion is translucent. Reserve 1 cup of the cauliflower. Add the remaining cauliflower to the saucepan. Stir in the water. Bring to a boil; reduce heat. Simmer for 20 minutes, stirring occasionally.

Blanch the reserved 1 cup cauliflower in boiling water in a saucepan until tender-crisp. Immediately plunge the cauliflower into a bowl of ice water to stop the cooking process; drain and set aside.

Stir the milk into the soup mixture. Process the soup in batches in a blender until smooth. Return the soup to the saucepan. Add the cooked cauliflower florets, 1 teaspoon salt, and pepper. Add more water for a thinner consistency if needed. Cover the soup and keep on low heat while preparing the remainder of the ingredients.

Remove the sausage casing and break the sausage into bite-size pieces. Brown in a skillet. Drain the cooked sausage on paper towels. Blanch the arugula in boiling water until limp. Drain and coarsely chop.

Ladle the soup into soup bowls. Top with the arugula and sausage. Serve immediately.

Serves 6

SOLE PARMESAN

*Steven J. Connolly, Executive Chef at Spenger's Fresh Fish Grotto in
Berkeley, created this succulent entrée.*

1 cup flour
2 eggs
2 tablespoons milk
2 cups Panko bread crumbs
   (see note)
12 to 16 ounces freshly grated
   Parmesan cheese
6 (4-ounce) sole fillets
6 tablespoons vegetable oil

8 to 12 lemon sections (see note),
   chopped
1/4 cup (1/2 stick) butter
1/4 cup lemon juice
2 tablespoons chopped fresh
   parsley
4 teaspoons capers, rinsed, drained
2 teaspoons chopped shallots

Place the flour in a shallow dish. Whisk the eggs and milk in a separate shallow dish until
blended. Combine the bread crumbs and cheese in a third shallow dish and mix well. Coat the
fillets with the flour and shake off the excess. Dip in the egg mixture, then in the bread crumb
mixture. Take care to coat the fillets evenly and completely.

   Heat the oil in a large nonstick sauté pan. Sauté the fillets in the hot oil for 1 minute or
until brown; turn. Sauté for 1 minute longer. Transfer the fillets to a serving platter.

   Drain the skillet of any excess oil. Add the chopped lemon, butter, lemon juice, parsley,
capers, and shallots and mix well. Cook over medium heat until the butter is slightly browned,
stirring frequently. Pour over the fillets. Serve immediately.

Note: Panko bread crumbs are located in the Asian food section of most grocery stores.

   To prepare the lemon sections, cut the ends off the lemon. Cut the peel off the fruit.
Remove the fruit sections by making cuts close to the membrane. Coarsely chop the sections.

Serves 6

Mavericks
SURFING COMPETITION

Follow the coastline twenty miles south
of San Francisco to encounter one of
the world's most renowned big-wave
surf spots. Mavericks, located in Half
Moon Bay, was once a stretch of the
ocean strictly avoided by surfers. The
combination of a deep-water canyon
and precipitous drop-offs makes for an
incredibly powerful swell roaring
toward the rocky shore with the force
of an avalanche. In the 1970s, surfer
Jeff Clark challenged the big wave and
won, and surfing has not been the
same since.

During the big winter storms in the El
Niño years of the late 1990s, Clark put
together a surfing contest that drew
competitors from near and far. Now
each winter, when the word goes out
that the surf is up, big-wave riders from
all over the world come to compete in
the extreme surfing event entitled "Men
Who Ride Mountains." It has proven to
be one of the most successful surfing
contests in the history of the sport.

Mushrooms

Many so-called "wild" mushrooms, like shiitake, portobello, and oyster mushrooms, are actually cultivated. Morels, chanterelles, and porcini are truly wild and are gathered by expert foragers and sold to gourmet groceries and restaurants. Nearly 80 percent of the wild mushrooms in the United States are harvested from National Forests. Foraging in the woods for wild mushrooms may sound like fun, but it is best left to the experts. Many mushrooms resembling edible varieties can cause extreme illness or death when eaten. Though mushrooms are cultivated year-round in California, fall, winter, and spring are the peak seasons for mushrooms that are truly wild. They lie dormant during the dry summer months. As rainfall increases in the fall, the spores feed and grow into mature mushrooms. Northern California is the second largest producer of mushrooms in the nation.

FILET MIGNON WITH SAVORY MUSHROOMS

Much of this recipe for two can be prepared in advance, allowing more time to enjoy each other's company.

6 ounces fresh mushrooms
(mixture of cremini, shiitake, and oyster)
1 1/2 tablespoons minced shallots
3 to 4 tablespoons butter, divided
1 small garlic clove, minced
4 tablespoons red wine, divided
1 tablespoon chopped fresh parsley, plus additional for garnish

1 1/2 teaspoons minced fresh thyme
1/8 to 1/4 teaspoon salt
Freshly ground pepper to taste
2 tablespoons olive oil
2 (6-ounce) filet mignon steaks, 2 inches thick
1 cup homemade beef stock, or 1 cup canned reduced-sodium beef stock

Clean the cremini mushrooms and trim the stems. Remove and discard the stems from the shiitake mushrooms. Trim the tough portion of the oyster mushroom stems and discard. Chop the mushrooms coarsely.

Sauté the shallots in 2 tablespoons butter in a skillet over medium heat until tender. Stir in the garlic and cook for 1 minute. Add the mushrooms and sauté until they release their juices. Continue to sauté until the juices evaporate. Stir in 2 tablespoons wine and bring to a boil. Boil until the mushroom mixture is dry but not sticking to the skillet, stirring constantly. Stir in 1 tablespoon chopped parsley, thyme, salt, and pepper. Remove from heat. Set aside.

Preheat the oven to 425 degrees. Heat the olive oil in a skillet over medium-high heat. Season the filets generously with salt and pepper. Sear for about 2 minutes per side or until well-browned on both sides and edges. If preparing just before serving, remove the filets to an ovenproof pan (do not cover) and place in the oven for 10 minutes or until an instant-read thermometer inserted horizontally in the filets registers 125 degrees for rare or 140 degrees for medium.

Pour off and discard the oil remaining in the skillet after the steaks are seared. Add 2 tablespoons wine, scraping the bottom of the pan to release any browned bits. Add 1/2 cup of the stock and bring to a boil. Boil until most of the stock has evaporated, stirring occasionally. Add the remaining stock. Cook until reduced by half, stirring occasionally. Cool slightly. Whisk in 1 to 2 tablespoons butter to enrich the juices. Pour through a strainer into a small pitcher.

To serve, top each filet with half of the mushroom mixture and half of the sauce. Sprinkle with chopped parsley. Serve immediately.

Note: The beauty of this recipe is that the filets can be browned early in the day and stored, covered, in the refrigerator. Bake, uncovered, in a 425-degree oven for 15 minutes or until the desired degree of doneness. The sauce and mushroom mixture may also be prepared in advance, stored in the refrigerator, and reheated just before serving.

Serves 2

BRAISED SHORT RIBS OF BEEF

*Rich and savory, this is an excellent, hearty dish
to serve to guests or family.*

1/4 cup olive oil
4 pounds lean beef short ribs
Freshly ground pepper
1 cup coarsely chopped onion
1 cup coarsely chopped celery
 (optional)
1 cup sliced peeled carrots
4 garlic cloves, minced
3 tablespoons tomato paste

11/2 cups canned tomatoes
 with juice
1/2 cup cider vinegar
2 tablespoons brown sugar
11/2 teaspoons kosher salt
1 teaspoon dry mustard
1/2 teaspoon freshly ground pepper
1/4 teaspoon allspice
2 to 3 cups beef stock

Heat the olive oil in a Dutch oven or deep baking pan. Sprinkle the ribs generously with freshly ground pepper and sauté in batches in the oil until brown on all sides. Drain the ribs on paper towels. Remove all but 2 to 3 tablespoons fat from the pan, being careful to reserve the drippings.

Preheat the oven to 350 degrees. Add the onion, celery, carrots, and garlic to the reserved pan drippings. Cook for 3 minutes or until the onion is translucent and the remaining vegetables are tender, stirring frequently. Stir in the tomato paste. Cook for 2 minutes, stirring constantly. Add the tomatoes and mix well. Bring to a boil, scraping the bottom of the pan to loosen any browned bits.

Combine the vinegar, brown sugar, salt, dry mustard, 1/2 teaspoon pepper, and allspice in a bowl and mix well. Add to the vegetable mixture. Return the ribs to the Dutch oven and spoon the vegetable mixture over the ribs. Add just enough of the stock to cover. Cover the Dutch oven and bring to a simmer on the stove top.

Transfer the pan to the oven and bake for 11/2 hours; remove cover. Bake for 1 hour longer or until the ribs are fork-tender, adding more liquid if needed. Skim the fat from the sauce before serving.

Serves 6 to 8

Skiing
THE SIERRA NEVADA

There is something special about skiing in Northern California—the azure blue skies, powder white snow, and splendor of Lake Tahoe combine for scenery unlike anywhere else in the country. Avid skiers often start the season in late November and continue hitting the slopes well into April. As the debate continues as to which form of snow sport reigns supreme—downhill, snowboarding, or cross-country—the majestic mountains draw all manner of devotees trying to tame the Sierras in their own way.

The Lake Tahoe region has a variety of slopes catering to all levels of skiers and snowboarders. On the North Shore, winter sports enthusiasts can choose between world famous Squaw Valley, site of the 1960 Winter Olympics, Northstar, and many other resorts. The South Shore's Heavenly Valley offers stunning lake views, and a bustling nightlife with nearby gambling and headline shows at the local casinos.

The cross-country trails in Tahoe are some of the most beautiful and exhilarating anywhere in the United States. From Royal Gorge on the North Shore to Sorensen's Resort on the South Shore, there are many specialized centers offering equipment rentals, maintained trails, and warming huts.

Lake Tahoe

Lake Tahoe is one of the most beautiful mountain lakes in the world. It has an area of nearly 200 square miles, an altitude of approximately 6,225 feet, and with a maximum depth of 1,645 feet, it is the second deepest lake in the country. Tahoe lies in the Sierra Nevada mountain range, mostly in California, partly in Nevada. The Washoe Indians gave the lake its name: *Tahoe* means "big water in a high place." Once a remote area, Lake Tahoe is now a very popular vacation destination offering access to North America's largest concentration of ski facilities during the winter. Swimming, boating, waterskiing, river rafting, fishing, hiking, and camping draw crowds during the summer.

There are spectacular views from many points on the paved roads that circle the lake. Eagle Creek, one of the thousands of mountain streams that feed into the lake, cascades 1,500 feet over Eagle Falls into Emerald Bay at the southwestern part of the lake. Lake Tahoe's water is so clear that the human eye can see to a depth of nearly seventy feet. The area has become one of the most strictly controlled environments in the nation in hopes the crystal clear waters can be enjoyed by future generations.

VEAL SCALLOPINI

This is a perfect winter comfort meal when served over pasta, arborio rice, or soft polenta.

1/2 cup flour
1 teaspoon freshly ground pepper
2 pounds veal sirloin, cut into thin slices (see note)
2 tablespoons olive oil
2 tablespoons butter
1 pound fresh mushrooms, thinly sliced
1/3 cup chopped onion
2 garlic cloves, minced

4 cups beef broth
2 tablespoons tomato paste
1 to 2 teaspoons salt
1 teaspoon dry mustard
1 teaspoon paprika
1/2 cup chianti wine
1 1/2 pounds fresh fettuccine
2 tablespoons chopped flat-leaf parsley

Combine the flour and pepper in a resealable plastic bag. Add the veal to the bag and shake to coat. Heat the olive oil and butter in a large skillet. Brown the veal for 3 to 5 minutes per batch. Remove the veal to a platter. Scrape the browned bits from the bottom of the skillet between each batch and add to the platter of veal.

Add the mushrooms to the skillet and cook until tender, stirring frequently. Remove the mushrooms to the platter containing the veal. Add the onion to the pan and cook until caramelized, stirring frequently. Stir in the garlic. Cook for 1 minute longer. Stir in the broth, tomato paste, dry mustard, paprika, and salt.

Simmer, covered, over low heat for 8 minutes. Remove the cover and stir in the veal, mushrooms, and chianti. Simmer for 5 minutes longer, stirring occasionally.

Cook the fettuccine according to package instructions; drain. Transfer the pasta onto a serving platter. Top with the veal scallopini. Sprinkle with the parsley.

Note: Boneless, skinless chicken breasts may be substituted. Gently pound each breast between two pieces of plastic wrap until of an even thickness, then cut into thin slices.

Serves 8

Dijon Cornish Game Hens

Serve this easy-to-prepare dish with sautéed greens and rice.

3 large Cornish game hens
1 cup soy sauce
3/4 cup Dijon mustard
1 teaspoon minced fresh ginger, or 1/2 teaspoon ground ginger
2 tablespoons sesame seeds

Preheat the oven to 450 degrees. Cut each game hen into halves using poultry shears or a sharp knife. Arrange the halves breast side up in a 9- × 13-inch baking dish.

Combine the soy sauce, Dijon mustard, and ginger in a medium bowl and mix well. Pour over the game hens, making sure to coat each half thoroughly. Sprinkle with the sesame seeds.

Bake uncovered for 1 hour, basting with the pan juices occasionally. If the hens begin to overbrown, cover each half game hen individually with foil and continue baking. Serve immediately.

Serves 6

Napa Valley
MUSTARD FESTIVAL

California's rainy season is a wonderful time to visit the Wine Country, when brilliant gold mustard blossoms carpet the vineyards of Napa Valley. From late January through late March, local merchants and nonprofit organizations sponsor a variety of events to attract visitors to the Napa Valley Mustard Festival. At the festival's Marketplace, visitors sample prepared mustards along with Wine Country gourmet products, world famous wine, and hearty craft brews. Chefs compete for the title of Napa Valley Mustard Festival Chef of the Year, and mustards from around the world are judged in twelve categories. Restaurants and wineries throughout the Valley feature special mustard fare throughout the season. The festival concludes with The Photo Finish, where photographic images of blooming mustard are on display.

Broccoli

Broccoli made national news when former President George Bush, Sr., admitted to a group of schoolchildren that he did not like it. Millions of other Americans must disagree with him, because over the last twenty-five years, broccoli consumption has increased 940 percent! California grows over 90 percent of the broccoli produced in the United States. That makes it the fourteenth most valuable crop in the state, with an annual cash value of over five hundred million dollars. Though it is harvested continuously, most of the state's broccoli is grown from March through December in Monterey County.

Broccoli is a cruciferous vegetable related to cabbage, cauliflower, and Brussels sprouts. The edible florets are actually unopened flower buds. Broccoli is packed with nutrition—it is an excellent source of vitamins A and C, potassium, folic acid, iron, and fiber. Ounce for ounce, broccoli has as much calcium as milk. Plus, the American Cancer Society has determined that the phytochemicals in broccoli actually help prevent cancer.

The city of Greenfield, California is known as "The Heart of the Salinas Valley." And since the Salinas Valley is the United States' largest producer of broccoli, it makes sense that Greenfield would play host to the annual Broccoli Festival. The festival takes place every September and visitors can sample broccoli prepared in every imaginable way, including broccoli ice cream. In addition, the festival offers music, arts and crafts, a children's carnival, and a car show.

Broccoli cooks more quickly and evenly if its stems are peeled. Separate broccoli into florets, cutting them off of the main stem. Smaller florets will cook evenly without peeling the stems, but for larger florets, as well as the main stem, peel off the tough outer skin using a paring knife or vegetable peeler.

While broccoli can be eaten raw in salads or as part of a crudité tray, it is most often served cooked. To blanch broccoli, cook it in salted, boiling water, testing it after two minutes. The stem should be easily pierced with a sharp knife, and it should bend easily without being limp. Once done, immediately remove from the water, douse with cold water, and drain well. Broccoli is excellent with hollandaise or béchamel sauce, or topped with fresh buttered, toasted bread crumbs. When adding broccoli to a stir-fry or pasta dish, sauté it in a small amount of olive or sesame oil until it reaches a tender-crisp state. Care must be taken to prevent overcooking regardless of the cooking method used. Overcooked broccoli is mushy and tasteless and loses its beautiful bright green color.

Photo Opposite: Broccoli, Jack London Square Farmers' Market, Oakland, California

BROCCOLI RAAB PASTA

This Chez Panisse recipe uses broccoli raab, which resembles sprouting broccoli.

*1 large onion
6 to 8 garlic cloves
2 bunches broccoli raab
    (about 1 1/2 pounds)
Extra virgin olive oil
Red pepper flakes to taste
Salt to taste
8 to 12 ounces penne pasta
Red wine vinegar
Pecorino Romano cheese*

Peel and thinly slice the onion. Smash, peel, and thinly slice the garlic. Wash the broccoli raab, removing the heavy stems, and chop the leaves and sprouts coarsely. Put a large pot of water on to boil.

Liberally cover the bottom of a sauté pan with olive oil and sauté the onion over high heat. When the onion has begun to wilt and brown a little, add the garlic and red pepper flakes, to taste, and salt. Toss briefly, then add the broccoli raab and a splash of water. Lower the heat and cook until tender, stirring or tossing frequently. Meanwhile, cook the pasta. Taste the broccoli raab for seasoning and add a generous amount of extra virgin olive oil and a splash of red wine vinegar. Toss with the freshly cooked and drained pasta, and garnish with grated cheese.

Serves 4

WINE PAIRING BY

wine.com

A California Sangiovese in the Tuscan tradition, such as Pepi, Luna Vineyards, Atlas Peak, or Adella

Ideally, wine should be stored at fifty-five degrees Fahrenheit, although when the temperature remains constant, sixty-five degrees Fahrenheit and below will guarantee wine's comfort. Wine responds to temperature changes by expanding and contracting in the bottle. When it is expanding, wine can push against the cork and break the bottle's airtight seal. Contact with air is one of wine's worst enemies because of the threat of oxidation. Lack of humidity dries out corks, which can also break the bottle's seal. Humid air allows corks to stay plump and firm. Though it is generally better to err on the damp side, too much humidity can cause moldy labels.

Après Ski Fare

A day of shushing down the mountain through fresh powder calls for a hearty evening meal. Warm up by the stone fireplace and serve saucy braised short ribs on polenta, complemented by warm broccoli with mustard sauce. Then refuel for another day of Sierra activities with a luscious Panettone bread pudding.

Warm Broccoli with Mustard Dressing

WARM BROCCOLI WITH MUSTARD DRESSING

*The tart dressing on the broccoli will complement
a rich and savory main dish.*

Mustard Dressing
2 tablespoons red wine or sherry
  vinegar
2 tablespoons minced shallots
1/4 teaspoon minced garlic
1/4 teaspoon salt
2 teaspoons Dijon mustard
3 to 5 tablespoons extra virgin
  olive oil
3 tablespoons crème fraîche
  (see note) or sour cream
1 tablespoon chopped fresh parsley
Freshly ground pepper to taste

Broccoli
3 pounds fresh broccoli with stems
Salt to taste

For the dressing, combine the wine vinegar, shallots, garlic, and salt in a bowl and mix well.
Let stand for 15 minutes. Whisk in the Dijon mustard, olive oil, and crème fraîche until
smooth and thick. Add the parsley and pepper and mix well. Store, covered, in the
refrigerator if not using immediately. Bring to room temperature to serve.

Trim the broccoli stems to measure about 4 inches, discarding the tough ends; peel the
stems. Steam the broccoli, covered, in a steamer over boiling water for 3 minutes. Uncover
partially and steam for 8 to 10 minutes longer or until the stems are tender but firm. Transfer
the broccoli to a serving platter or individual plates. Sprinkle with salt. Drizzle with the
dressing, about 2 tablespoons per serving.

Note: Crème fraîche is located in the dairy case near the sour cream or in the gourmet cheese
section of grocery stores.

Serves 6 to 8

Edible Schoolyard
PROJECT

If Alice Waters has her way, schoolchildren all over the country will enjoy
foods made with organic, freshly picked
ingredients like those served to diners
at Waters' renowned restaurant, Chez
Panisse, in Berkeley, California. Inspired
by the Garden Project at the San
Francisco County Jail, Waters started
the Edible Schoolyard Project in 1996.
Waters' concern is that the American
culture's reliance on fast food, in
addition to the prevalence of frozen,
processed foods in school cafeteria
menus, has not only eroded family
mealtime, but led to unhealthy eating
habits for our children.

The pilot program for the Edible
Schoolyard is at Martin Luther King,
Jr., Middle School in Berkeley, where an
asphalt lot has been transformed into
organic vegetable plots rimmed with
flowers. Students take turns digging,
planting, weeding, and harvesting foods
with which they prepare meals for their
classmates. The cafeteria has been
turned into a kitchen classroom, where
educators incorporate math, social
studies, and science into the gardening
and cooking time. By all accounts, the
program is a tremendous success and
now Waters' goal is to have the Edible
Schoolyard serve as a model for school
lunch programs throughout the country.

Chinese New Year

With nearly one-third of its residents of Asian descent, San Francisco takes its Chinese New Year celebration seriously. The Chinese calendar is based on solar and lunar phases. Thus the New Year falls on a different date each year, usually at the end of January or in early February. Chinese New Year is a fifteen-day festival where tradition dictates each day's activities.

The Chinese New Year Flower Fair is held the weekend before the New Year arrives. Celebrants buy traditional plants, flowers, and fruits that symbolize the awakening of nature and represent happiness and prosperity for the year to come. While somewhat less than traditional, the City's celebration has grown to include the Miss Chinatown USA Pageant and a 10K Run. An impressive parade and fireworks display on New Year's Eve usher out the old year and herald the new. The celebration culminates in the Lantern Festival on the fifteenth night.

STIR-FRIED BROCCOLI WITH GINGER

This easy stir-fry adds color and flavor to a variety of menus.

1 tablespoon canola oil
1 1/2 teaspoons sesame oil
1 tablespoon grated fresh ginger
1 garlic clove, minced
1 pound broccoli florets

1/2 cup chicken broth
3 tablespoons soy sauce
3 tablespoons oyster sauce
1/4 cup slivered almonds, toasted

Have all of the ingredients at hand and ready to use. Heat the canola oil and sesame oil in a 10-inch skillet or wok over medium heat. Stir-fry the ginger and garlic in the oil for 30 seconds. Add the broccoli. Stir-fry for 1 to 2 minutes. Add the broth, soy sauce, and oyster sauce. Steam, covered, for 2 to 3 minutes or until the broccoli is tender-crisp. Spoon the broccoli onto a serving platter. Sprinkle with the almonds.

Serves 3 to 4

CAPER LEMON BRUSSELS SPROUTS

Even doubters will love this Brussels sprouts recipe.

1¹/2 pounds fresh Brussels sprouts
3 tablespoons olive oil
1 to 2 tablespoons capers, rinsed, drained
Juice of ¹/2 lemon
¹/4 cup grated Parmesan cheese

Trim the stems of the Brussels sprouts and remove the outer leaves until each sprout measures about 1- to 1¹/2-inches in diameter; cut into halves. Steam, covered, in a basket over simmering water for about 8 minutes or until tender-crisp. Remove from heat.

Heat the olive oil in a skillet over medium-high heat. Add the Brussels sprouts. Cook until browned on all sides. Stir in the capers and lemon juice. Spoon the Brussels sprouts into a serving bowl. Sprinkle with the Parmesan cheese.

Serves 4

Brussels Sprouts

Brussels sprouts received their name from the Belgian city of Brussels where they are thought to first have been grown. More than 90 percent of all commercial production in the United States today is from the California coastal counties of Monterey, Santa Cruz, and San Mateo. Brussels sprouts grow on long, thick stalks with eighty to one hundred sprouts per stalk. They are most readily available between August and mid-March.

Brussels sprouts have never gained the popularity here that they have in Europe. At one time, Santa Cruz hosted a Brussels sprouts festival, which waned due to lack of interest. People willing to give the newer, less bitter varieties of Brussels sprouts a try will find the sweetest flavor in small, firm, compact sprouts with bright green color. To bring out the best flavor, store Brussels sprouts in the refrigerator for no more than five days and avoid overcooking them.

Mandolines,
GRATERS & FOOD PROCESSORS

Expert cooks slice vegetables with speed and precision using a mandoline. This French tool, usually made of stainless steel, has several cutting blades that can be adjusted for slices of varying thickness, from approximately one-half inch to paper-thin. The blades can be interchanged to julienne, shred, or waffle-cut vegetables. A hand guard protects fingers and holds the vegetables in place as they slide along the blades. Mandolines are expensive; most versions will cost more than one hundred dollars.

The box grater and the plane grater are inexpensive and easy-to-find hand graters. The rotary grater, generally used for hard cheeses, is more expensive but much faster and easier to use. Specialty graters exist specifically for ginger, citrus, nuts, and chocolate and can be found through culinary retailers.

Food processors are efficient, powerful, and capable of performing a wide variety of functions in the kitchen. They offer the home cook a motorized option for slicing, grating, and chopping with a variety of blades and discs. They are safe to use and easy to clean in the dishwasher.

POTATO GRATIN GRUYÈRE

Yukon Gold potatoes and fresh thyme are superb in this classic dish.

1 tablespoon butter	1/2 teaspoon freshly ground pepper
4 pounds Yukon Gold potatoes	1 1/2 cups chicken stock
1/2 cup finely chopped onion	1 1/2 cups heavy cream
2 teaspoons minced fresh thyme	6 ounces Gruyère cheese, shredded
3/4 teaspoon salt	

Preheat the oven to 450 degrees. Coat the bottom and sides of a 9- × 13-inch baking dish with 1 tablespoon butter. Peel the potatoes and immerse in a bowl of cold water until ready to slice.

Thinly slice the potatoes; the finest slicing blade on a food processor does this quickly. Layer one-fourth of the potato slices shingle-style in the prepared baking dish. Sprinkle with some of the onion, thyme, salt, and pepper. Repeat the sequence with three more layers. Pour the stock and heavy cream over the layers. Bake for 45 to 60 minutes or until the potatoes are tender. Sprinkle with the cheese. Briefly return to the oven until the cheese melts. Let stand for 10 minutes before serving.

Serves 6 to 8

SOUBISE

Richer than rice pilaf, soubise complements a wide variety of entrées. The rice can be molded into small ramekins and turned out onto the plates for a beautiful presentation.

2 tablespoons butter
1/2 small onion, finely chopped
3/4 cup white rice
   (not quick-cooking)
2/3 cup chicken stock
2/3 cup water
1/4 cup sauvignon blanc or another
   dry white wine

1/2 teaspoon salt
1/2 bay leaf
1/4 cup heavy cream
2 tablespoons freshly grated
   Parmesan cheese
Chopped fresh parsley, or sprigs of
   fresh herbs

Heat the butter in a heavy 2-quart saucepan. Add the onion. Sauté over medium-low heat until translucent. Stir in the rice. Increase the heat to medium. Cook the rice, stirring constantly, until it changes in color from white to translucent and back to white. Add the stock, water, wine, salt, and bay leaf and mix well. Bring to a rolling boil and stir thoroughly; cover. Reduce the heat to low.

Simmer, undisturbed, for 20 minutes. Check to see if the liquid has been absorbed. If not, cook, covered, for 3 to 4 more minutes or until the liquid is absorbed. Discard the bay leaf. Fold in the heavy cream and Parmesan cheese.

If desired, coat four 4-ounce to 6-ounce cups or ramekins generously with butter. Pack the rice mixture into the cups and immediately invert onto serving plates. Garnish with chopped parsley or sprigs of fresh herbs.

Serves 4

California State
RAILROAD MUSEUM

Old Sacramento is a four-block historic district of restaurants, saloons, gift shops, and museums capturing the feel of the Old West. The California State Railroad Museum, a highlight of the district, is the largest interpretive railroad museum in North America and the most visited in the world. The main building houses twenty-three restored locomotives and train cars dating from the 1860s through the 1960s. Among them is a classic restored 1930s Santa Fe dining car, which brings back images of the days of first-class rail travel. Fine quality meals were prepared by trained chefs and served on linen tablecloths in elegant surroundings. Visitors to the museum can go on board the many restored train cars and imagine the travel of yesteryear.

On scheduled weekends the Sacramento Southern Railroad excursion steam train leaves from the nearby Central Pacific Passenger Depot, taking passengers on a ride through the scenic foothills of the Gold Country. Unique theme train rides offered seasonally include the "Goosebump Express," "Santa's Yuletide Express," and the "New Year's Eve Train."

Carols in the Caves

The Carols in the Caves series consists of simple, informal concerts held in the wine-aging cellars of Sonoma and Napa every weekend from Thanksgiving into the New Year. Locations vary from week to week and year to year. Founder and performer David Auerbach chooses caves in a variety of wineries in Napa and Sonoma based on the caves' distinctive acoustic characteristics and personalities. During the first half of his show, Auerbach weaves storytelling and historical lore into unique performances of old-world carols accompanied by over fifty rare and exotic instruments. At intermission, guests have an opportunity to tour the winery and sample its wines. The audience returns to the cave ready to participate in a sing-along of well-known traditional carols. A popular new addition to Auerbach's performance schedule is a four-course Twelfth Night Feast of Fools dinner concert.

SAVORY POLENTA WITH ASIAGO CHEESE

Rich and satisfying, this side dish is perfect with saucy meat or vegetable entrées. While delicious freshly made, this recipe can also be made ahead successfully.

2 cups water	$1/4$ teaspoon freshly ground pepper
2 cups milk	1 cup coarse ground cornmeal
$1/2$ cup (1 stick) butter	(polenta)
2 garlic cloves, minced	$1/2$ cup grated asiago cheese
1 teaspoon salt	

Combine the water, milk, butter, garlic, salt, and pepper in a heavy saucepan. Bring to a boil. Add the polenta gradually, stirring constantly.

Continue to stir frequently while cooking over low heat for 20 minutes. Taste to determine if the polenta grains are tender. If still a bit grainy, continue to cook until tender, stirring constantly. Remove from heat. Stir in the cheese. Serve immediately.

Note: The finished polenta quickly firms up. If preparing ahead, oil an 8- × 8-inch baking pan and pour the hot polenta into it, smoothing the top. Press a piece of plastic wrap directly on the surface and refrigerate until firm, about 3 hours. Cut the cold polenta into squares or rectangles. Reheat just until warm. The pieces will become fragile if heated too hot.

Serves 6 to 8

PINE NUT BREAD

This nutty bread is wonderful with soups and stews.

2 envelopes dry yeast	1¹/2 cups unbleached all-purpose
¹/2 cup lukewarm water	flour
¹/2 cup dry white wine	2 teaspoons salt
¹/4 cup extra virgin olive oil	1 egg yolk, beaten
1¹/2 cups whole wheat flour	¹/2 cup chopped pine nuts

Sprinkle the yeast over the lukewarm water in a small bowl. Stir and let stand for 10 minutes. Add the wine and olive oil and mix well.

Fit an electric mixer with a dough hook. Combine the whole wheat flour, all-purpose flour, and salt in a large mixing bowl and mix well. Remove 1 cup of the flour mixture and set aside. Add the yeast mixture to the remaining flour mixture, beating constantly at low speed until blended. Add the reserved flour mixture gradually, beating constantly. Knead with the mixer on medium speed for about 10 minutes. Test by pressing fingertips into the dough; the indentations will spring back when the dough has been kneaded long enough.

Turn the dough onto a lightly floured surface. Knead by hand for 2 minutes. Shape the dough into a ball. Place in an oiled bowl, turning to coat the surface. Let rise, covered with a damp tea towel, for 3 hours or longer. Punch the dough down. Knead for 2 minutes. Shape the dough into a round loaf. Brush the surface with the egg yolk. Coat with the pine nuts. Place the loaf on a greased baking sheet. Let rise, covered with a damp cloth, for 1¹/2 hours or until doubled in bulk.

Preheat the oven to 350 degrees. Score the top of the loaf with the tip of a sharp knife. Bake until the loaf sounds hollow when lightly tapped, about 45 minutes. Remove to a wire rack to cool. Serve warm or at room temperature.

Serves 6

Oakland

Oakland is a truly diverse and culturally rich city with plenty to see and do. Back in the 1930s when Gertrude Stein lamented about her native Oakland, "There's no there there," she should have taken a second look. Just east of downtown, joggers, babies in strollers, and bird-watchers each find their pace around the three-mile footpath tracing Lake Merritt. If romance is in the air, a gondola can be hired to skim the lake in style. The Oakland Museum of California, an impressive collection of art, natural science, and history, houses everything from Native American paintings to a fire engine that came to the rescue during the blazing aftermath of the 1906 earthquake. The Paramount Theatre is a monument to gilded, ornamented architecture. It still showcases current musical acts, as well as occasional Classic Movie Nights, where vintage cartoons, black-and-white newsreels, and concerts on the Wurlitzer organ entertain before the show. The hills of Oakland boast spectacular Bay views from forested paths in regional parks, such as Joaquin Miller and Redwood, as well as the state-of-the-art Chabot Space & Science Center that has a mission control simulator and planetarium. Oakland offers something for everyone, and just might be the perfect alternative to a foggy day in the other city by the Bay.

Walnuts

The walnut has been an important trade item over the centuries. Dating back to 7000 B.C. in Persia where it originated, the walnut is the oldest tree food to be harvested. Franciscan Fathers introduced walnuts to California in 1770, having acquired the versatile nut in South America. Northern California produces over 99 percent of all walnuts grown in the U.S. Much of the crop is exported to other states, as well as Germany, Italy, Spain, Japan, Taiwan, and Israel.

Walnut trees take six to eight years to mature and produce a crop, but once established the trees will continue to bear for nearly one hundred years. Walnuts are harvested from September through November. Gone are the days of the roving walnut crews with their bamboo poles. Now, mechanized shaking machines loosen the nuts from their branches.

Walnuts purchased in the fall and winter tend to be the freshest. Buy walnuts that have shells with no holes or cracks. Store walnuts in their shells at relatively low temperatures and low humidity. Shelled walnuts may be frozen in plastic bags for up to six months, unshelled for up to one year.

Ardenwood Farm in Fremont, California hosts a variety of harvest celebrations, including walnut harvesting programs on weekends in October and November. The historic ranch, established in 1849 by the Patterson family, is now run by the California State Park system, which maintains the family mansion and Victorian gardens. Visitors can enjoy wagon and train rides and blacksmith and farm activities.

The town of Walnut Creek, California has held its annual Walnut Festival since 1936. Once a small time event held downtown to celebrate the harvest season, the festival has expanded to include culinary contests, major bands, and the Walnut Festival Parade led by the legendary King Walnut. The three-day festival held in September boasts an annual attendance of nearly 50,000 people.

Photo Opposite: Walnuts, Diamond of California Processing Plant, Stockton, California

WALNUT BAKLAVA

Relax with a great cup of Tully's coffee and their delectable baklava.

1 pound walnuts, finely ground
2 teaspoons cinnamon
4 cups sugar, divided
2 cups (4 sticks) butter, melted
1 pound phyllo pastry, thawed
Whole cloves
1 1/2 cups water plus 1 tablespoon, divided
Juice of 1/2 lemon
4 ounces honey

Preheat the oven to 300 degrees. Combine the nuts, cinnamon, and 1 cup sugar. Brush a 10- × 15-inch pan with melted butter. Cut 1 sheet of the pastry to fit the pan. Brush with butter and repeat with four more buttered layers. Add a thin layer of the walnut mixture. Repeat the sequence until all ingredients are used, ending with 2 sheets of pastry. Brush the top generously with butter. Make lengthwise cuts about 1 1/2 inches apart, through the top few layers. Cut diagonally at 1 1/2-inch intervals to make a diamond pattern. Center a clove in each diamond. Sprinkle with 1 tablespoon water and bake for 1 hour. Combine the remaining water and sugar in a saucepan and boil, stirring occasionally. Add the lemon juice and boil 5 minutes longer. Stir in the honey and pour the warm syrup over the baklava immediately when it is done baking. Once cool, cover loosely and let stand for 8 hours. Cut completely through the layers to serve.

Serves 30

Walnuts

The flavor of walnuts is dependent upon their freshness. Farmers' markets are an excellent source for just-picked walnuts. The difference in flavor from store-bought nuts is surprising. When buying unshelled nuts, choose those that are heavy for their size, with solid shells without cracks or holes. The nutmeat inside should not rattle when shaken. Shelled nuts should be plump, crisp, and uniform in color and size.

Because of their high fat content, rancidity is always a hazard with nuts. To prevent spoiling, walnuts should be stored in airtight containers in a cool place or frozen. Shelled walnuts can be stored in the refrigerator for up to four months or frozen in plastic bags for up to six months. As a general rule (and depending on their freshness at the time of purchase), unshelled nuts will keep about twice as long as shelled.

As spoiled nutmeats will ruin any dish they flavor, smell and taste nuts before adding them to foods. Most nuts benefit from a light toasting before serving or using in recipes. Spread in a single layer on a baking sheet and toast for about ten minutes at 350 degrees.

CARAMEL WALNUT TORTE

This decadent torte is a work of art. Make the syrup and génoise in advance to cut down on last-minute preparation.

Simple Syrup
1 cup sugar
1/4 cup white corn syrup
1/2 cup water

Génoise Cake
6 eggs, separated, at room temperature
1 teaspoon vanilla extract
1 cup sugar
1 cup sifted flour
1/2 cup (1 stick) unsalted butter, clarified, plus additional clarified butter for pan preparation
1/2 cup finely ground walnuts, lightly toasted before grinding
11/2 teaspoons dark rum
2 tablespoons Simple Syrup

French Buttercream Frosting and Assembly
1 cup (2 sticks) unsalted butter, very soft
2/3 cup Simple Syrup, room temperature
1/2 cup high-quality caramel sauce
2 tablespoons dark rum
11/4 cups finely ground walnuts, lightly toasted before grinding
Walnut halves, lightly toasted

For the syrup, combine the sugar, corn syrup, and water in a medium saucepan. Cook over low heat until the sugar dissolves, stirring constantly. Dip a brush in water and wash down any sugar crystals that may have collected on the side of the saucepan. Increase the heat to high. Boil for 5 minutes; do not stir. Let stand until cool. Store at room temperature.

For the cake, preheat the oven to 350 degrees. Brush the sides and bottoms of two 9-inch cake pans with clarified butter. Line the bottoms with baking parchment paper and brush the parchment with clarified butter. Flour both pans, tapping out the excess.

Combine the egg yolks and vanilla in a bowl and mix well. Place the egg whites in a separate mixing bowl and beat with an electric mixer until soft peaks form. Add the sugar to the egg whites 1 tablespoon at a time, beating constantly for 31/2 to 5 minutes or until stiff peaks form. Fold one-fourth of the egg whites into the egg yolk mixture.

Place the remaining beaten egg whites in a wide bowl. Pour the egg yolk mixture over the top; do not stir. Using a sieve, sprinkle the flour lightly on top. Fold the yolk mixture and flour into the whites, adding a portion of the 1/2 cup of clarified butter and ground walnuts after every few folds. Fold until the additions just disappear.

Transfer the batter to the prepared cake pans and smooth the tops gently. Bake on the center oven rack for 20 to 25 minutes or until the layers pull from the sides of the pans and the centers are springy when lightly touched. Immediately remove the cakes from the pans and cool on a wire rack. The layers may be prepared in advance and frozen, well-wrapped. Thaw before frosting.

For the frosting, beat the butter in a mixing bowl with an electric mixer fitted with a paddle attachment until light and fluffy. Add 2/3 cup Simple Syrup in a thin, steady stream, beating constantly. Beat in the caramel sauce and rum. Add the ground walnuts. Beat at low speed until mixed. Do not chill the frosting before spreading on the cake. Combine 11/2 teaspoons rum with 2 tablespoons Simple Syrup and brush the tops of the cake layers with the mixture.

To assemble, spread one-fourth of the frosting between the layers, then frost the top using a long metal cake spatula. Frost the sides with the remaining frosting. Arrange the walnut halves in a decorative pattern over the cake. Store in the refrigerator, well-covered to avoid picking up other flavors. Remove the cake about 1 hour before serving to enhance the flavor.

Serves 10 to 12

Valentine's Day Dinner

*Spend the evening enjoying a fabulous meal for two very special people.
A sophisticated hors d'oeuvre of blini with crème fraîche and caviar sets the tone for
a most romantic meal. Honey and orange-dressed salad, filet mignon topped with
mushrooms, and potato gratin make the meal and evening one to savor.
A slice of caramel walnut torte is a sweet finale.*

Blini with Caviar & Crème Fraîche 172

•

Lettuces with Honey-Orange Dressing 177

•

Filet Mignon with Savory Mushrooms 186
Potato Gratin Gruyère 196

•

Caramel Walnut Torte 202

Caramel Walnut Torte

Alembic Brandy
DISTILLERY

A thirty-minute tour of the RMS Alembic Brandy Distillery offers olfactory rewards that far surpass the sniff and sip of wine that is common in the nearby Wine Country. Situated off Highway 121 between Napa and Sonoma, the Remy Martin-owned Alembic Brandy Distillery is the largest and oldest alembic distillery in California. Rarely used in commercial distillation today, an alembic is a vessel with a beaked cap or head used in distilling. A free tour of RMS Alembic Brandy Distillery is offered several times daily. It includes a walk through the semi-subterranean barrelhouse and the cavernous still house, where eight copper alembic stills hold wines made from six different types of grapes that over time will become rich and mellow brandy. Housed in the cave-like warehouse, North America's largest collection of aging brandy is stored in four thousand ninety-gallon oak casks. Whiffs in the aroma room are free for the taking, although tasting is against the law. There is a gift shop at the distillery where several of the award-winning cognac-style brandies are available for sale. The Beverage Tasting Institute has named the RMS Alembic Brandy Distillery's fruit liqueur, Pear de Pear, best in the world.

CURRANT PEAR CRISP

*A rustic, rich dessert best served with a dollop of
whipped cream or French vanilla ice cream.*

4 cups peeled sliced ripe Bosc pears
   or another firm pear
3/4 cup dried currants
1/3 cup sliced almonds, lightly
   toasted
1 cup rolled oats (not instant)
1 cup packed dark brown sugar

3/4 cup flour
1 teaspoon cinnamon
1/4 teaspoon salt
1/2 cup (1 stick) chilled butter,
   cut into pieces
Whipped cream or French vanilla
   ice cream

Preheat the oven to 350 degrees. Coat the sides and bottom of a 9- × 13-inch baking pan with butter. Arrange the pears in the prepared baking pan. Sprinkle with the currants and almonds.

Combine the oats, brown sugar, flour, cinnamon, and salt in a bowl and mix well. Cut in the butter until crumbly. Sprinkle the crumb mixture over the fruit and nuts. Bake for 40 to 45 minutes or until brown and bubbly. Spoon the crisp into individual dessert bowls. Serve warm topped with whipped cream or vanilla ice cream.

Serves 8

MEYER LEMON CHEESECAKE

Meyer lemons give this silky cheesecake a delightful flavor.

Crust
3 cups graham cracker crumbs
3 tablespoons sugar
1/2 teaspoon cinnamon
1/8 teaspoon nutmeg
1/2 cup (1 stick) butter, melted

Filling
20 ounces cream cheese, softened
2 cups sour cream (not lowfat or nonfat)
1 cup sugar
1/3 cup Meyer lemon juice (see note)
Zest of 4 Meyer lemons, finely chopped (see note)
4 eggs

For the crust, process the graham cracker crumbs, sugar, cinnamon, and nutmeg in a food processor until mixed. Drizzle the butter over the crumbs. Process briefly until the dry ingredients are moistened. Pat the crumb mixture over the bottom and three-fourths of the way up the side of a buttered 10-inch springform pan. Chill for 15 minutes or longer.

For the filling, preheat the oven to 325 degrees. Process the cream cheese and sour cream in a food processor just until smooth. Add the sugar and process briefly. Add the lemon juice and lemon zest and process briefly. Add the eggs one at a time, processing until just blended after each addition.

Pour the batter into the chilled crust. Bake for 1 hour or until the sides are set and an area in the center of the cheesecake the size of an orange still jiggles when the pan is gently nudged. Cool completely at room temperature in the pan on a wire rack. Chill, covered, until serving time.

Note: If Meyer lemons are not available, substitute with the more common Eureka lemon juice for the Meyer lemon juice and increase the sugar by 1/4 cup.

When zesting the tender-skinned Meyer lemon, be careful to avoid cutting into the bitter white pith.

Serves 10 to 12

Meyer Lemons

Much like Key limes are distinctively different from traditional limes, Meyer lemons are different from the standard Eureka lemons most commonly found in the grocery store. Meyer lemons are much rounder in form and have smooth, unpitted deep yellow skin. They prefer colder climates than Eurekas, which thrive in subtropical climates. Meyer lemons are prized for their sweetness, mild acidity, and floral aroma. Thought to be a combination of mandarin orange and lemon, the Meyer lemon is a unique blend of tangy and sweet and adds wonderful flavor to sauces, dressings, desserts, and drinks. Meyer lemonade requires less sugar than traditional lemonade and is one of life's great pleasures. Pastry and dessert chefs are delighted when these lemons are in season. Meyer lemon tarts, sorbets, and mousses abound in the restaurants of the San Francisco Bay Area. Meyer lemons are available from fall to late spring, mostly from backyard gardeners. Their juice may be frozen and used throughout the year. Eureka lemons may be substituted in most recipes calling for Meyer lemons, but add a little fresh-squeezed orange juice and increase the specified sugar by 30 to 50 percent.

San Francisco
BELLE

Hornblower Cruises & Events'
new vessel, *San Francisco Belle*, is
destined to become a San Francisco
waterfront landmark. Built in 1994
and patterned after a classic stern-
wheeler, *San Francisco Belle* is 292 feet
long and will accommodate up to
2,000 passengers, twice the capacity
of Hornblower's next-largest vessel,
California Hornblower. Belle features
three spacious, fully enclosed decks,
wide wraparound outer decks, and a
spacious sun deck with a canopy cover.
In the style and charm of the Barbary
Coast days, she has a grand staircase
in her entryway and her interior design
is art nouveau. This unique vessel is
perfect for large private events or a
Hornblower special event cruise.
Annual events on the Bay include
Valentine's Day, Easter, Mother's Day,
Father's Day, Fourth of July, New Year's
Eve, and the popular Fleet Week cruises
in October. *San Francisco Belle* is
docked on the Embarcadero at Pier 3 in
San Francisco.

POACHED PEARS IN RED WINE

*The deep burgundy color of these pears makes them a
beautiful holiday dessert. They are also wonderful sliced over
mixed salad greens with toasted nuts and Gorgonzola cheese.*

3 large ripe Bosc pears
1 (750-ml) bottle cabernet
  sauvignon or merlot wine
1/2 cup sugar
1 whole vanilla bean, cut
  lengthwise into halves

1 whole cinnamon stick
Peel of 1 orange (see note)
Peel of 1 lemon
2 whole cloves
1 star anise
1 bay leaf

Peel the pears. Cut the pears lengthwise into halves and remove the core with a melon baller.
Arrange the pears cut side up in a skillet just large enough to accommodate the pears in one
layer. Combine the wine, sugar, vanilla bean, cinnamon stick, orange peel, lemon peel, cloves,
star anise, and bay leaf in a bowl and mix well. Pour over the pears. Add just enough water to
cover the pears.

Bring to a boil over high heat; reduce heat to low. Simmer for 15 minutes or until the pears
are easily pierced by a knife. Remove from heat. Let the pears stand in the poaching liquid
until cool. Remove the pears using a slotted spoon and store in an airtight container.

Pour the poaching liquid through a sieve into a bowl, discarding the solids. Return the
poaching liquid to the pan and bring to a boil. Cook for 45 minutes or until the mixture is
reduced to a syrupy consistency thick enough to coat a wooden spoon. Let stand until cool.
Drizzle the syrup over the pears just before serving.

Note: Remove just the colored portion of the orange and lemon peel in strips with a vegetable
peeler or sharp paring knife. The white pith is bitter and should not be used.

Serves 6

PANETTONE BREAD PUDDING

Panettone is a rich Italian Christmas bread studded with raisins and candied citron. Its distinctive flavor adds something special to traditional bread pudding.

1 (17.5-ounce) loaf Italian Panettone bread	1/8 teaspoon salt
3/4 cup sugar	4 cups whole milk
5 eggs	1 cup heavy cream
4 egg yolks	1 1/2 teaspoons vanilla extract
	Confectioners' sugar

Preheat the oven to 350 degrees. Place the oven rack in the center of the oven.

Cut the crust from the bread. Cut the loaf vertically into halves. Arrange each half round side up on a cutting board. Cut into 1/2-inch slices. Fit the slices snugly into a large soufflé dish or baking dish. There will be several layers.

Whisk the sugar, eggs, egg yolks, and salt in a bowl until blended. Heat the milk and heavy cream in a saucepan until almost boiling. Transfer the milk mixture into a heatproof glass measuring cup. Pour the hot milk mixture gradually into the egg mixture, whisking constantly. Stir in the vanilla. Pour gradually over the bread. Allow to soak in for 30 minutes, occasionally pressing gently on the top.

Bring a teakettle of water to a boil. Place the soufflé dish in a roasting pan on the middle oven rack. Add enough boiling water to the roasting pan to reach halfway up the sides of the soufflé dish. Bake for 45 minutes or until a knife inserted in the center of the pudding comes out clean. Cool in the dish on a wire rack for about 1 1/2 hours. Serve warm or cold in individual dessert bowls. Dust each serving with confectioners' sugar.

Serves 8 to 10

Milk

In 1993, milk consumption hit an all-time low in the United States. That all changed when the "Got Milk?" campaign was created, pulling the dairy industry out of its twenty-year slump. It was also in 1993 that California jumped into first place to become the leading milk-producing state, where it has remained ever since. With one-and-a-half million milk cows in California today, nearly one out of every six dairy cows in the U.S. resides in the Golden State.

Ever wonder why California has nonfat milk, when other states have skim? It is not just in the name; milk really is different from state to state. The federal standards for fluid milk are slightly different than the California standards, which provide for richer-tasting nonfat milk fortified with nonfat milk solids. This results in up to 33 percent more calcium than in skim milk produced in other states. There are also many other nutrients per eight-ounce serving, with minimal increases in calories and sodium.

Almost all milk and cream sold commercially today has been pasteurized, meaning that it has been heated and quickly cooled to eliminate the possibility of disease and to increase shelf life. Most milk is also fortified with vitamins A and D.

The Painted Ladies

Much of original San Francisco was built between 1860 and 1900, when Victorian-style architecture was popular. However, many of the Victorian homes were destroyed in the fire that engulfed the City after the 1906 earthquake. Homes west of Van Ness Avenue ("the street that saved the City") were spared, as the flames did not jump the broad thoroughfare. Today, these restored Victorians are fondly referred to as "The Painted Ladies."

Head to Hayes and Steiner Streets to see the Victorians set against the backdrop of the City's spectacular skyline often pictured in photographs of "Postcard Row." The Convention and Visitors Bureau offers a map outlining a six-and-a-half-mile loop where the most brightly colored restored homes and office buildings are found. Sightseers can also tour the Haas-Lilienthal House to view both the intricate interior and exterior Victorian embellishments, or join a two-hour "Heritage Walk" through Pacific Heights sponsored by the Foundation for San Francisco's Architectural Heritage.

SUGAR & SPICE WALNUTS

These sweetened walnuts are a treat by themselves or as a topping for ice cream.

2^1/$_2$ cups walnut halves	1 teaspoon cinnamon
1 cup sugar	^{1}/$_2$ teaspoon salt
^{1}/$_2$ cup water	1^1/$_2$ teaspoons vanilla extract

Preheat the oven to 375 degrees. Arrange the walnut halves in a single layer on a baking sheet. Toast for 5 minutes, stirring once. Let cool.

Butter a clean baking sheet; set aside. Butter the sides of a heavy 2-quart saucepan. Add the sugar, water, cinnamon, and salt. Cook until the sugar dissolves and the syrup comes to a boil, stirring constantly. When the mixture reaches a boil, stop stirring and cook undisturbed to 236 degrees on a candy thermometer. Remove from heat.

Beat the syrup with a wooden spoon for 1 minute or until mixture just begins to get creamy. Add the walnuts and vanilla and stir until the walnuts are coated and the mixture is creamy.

Turn the walnuts onto the prepared baking sheet and immediately separate them using two forks. Let stand until cool.

Makes 1 pound

CARAMELS

Caramels are a favorite confection and perfect to give as a hostess gift. Enlist family members or friends to individually wrap these treasures.

2 cups sugar
1³/4 cups light corn syrup
2 cups heavy cream
1 cup (2 sticks) butter
1 cup coarsely chopped pecans,
   toasted (optional)

2 teaspoons vanilla extract
150 (4- × 4-inch) waxed paper
   squares

Coat the bottom and sides of a 9- × 13-inch pan with butter. Combine the sugar, corn syrup, 1 cup of the heavy cream, and butter in a large heavy saucepan. Cook over medium heat until the mixture comes to a boil. Stir in the remaining heavy cream gradually.

   Stirring constantly, cook for 30 to 40 minutes or until the mixture no longer wants to boil over. Continue cooking to 246 degrees on a candy thermometer (almost hard-ball stage). Remove from heat. Stir in the pecans and vanilla.

   Pour the mixture into the prepared pan and let stand until cool. Cut into bite-size squares. Wrap each caramel in a waxed paper square, twisting the ends to seal.

Makes 150

Whale Festival

Each year as winter passes and the flowers begin to peek through the hardened ground 150 miles north of San Francisco, something special heralds the dawn of a new season in historic Fort Bragg. The annual migration of the California gray whale, a true wonder of nature, is cause for celebration along the Mendocino coast. Held every year on the third Saturday of March, the Whale Festival in Fort Bragg provides an opportunity to celebrate the marvel of the whales' journey. Visitors can observe the beauty of the whales as they breach and spout their way north along the California coastline in one of nature's more spectacular shows. A 42-foot-long model whale called Mindy, with movable parts, is on display throughout the entire weekend. Great seafood dishes from local chefs are available for tasting, along with cold beer from many of Northern California's leading microbrewers. The festival also offers a 10K run, 5K walk, and an opportunity to enjoy Fort Bragg's many wonderful shops and galleries.

Tahoe Queen

The *Tahoe Queen* is an authentic Mississippi stern-wheeler offering scenic cruises on Lake Tahoe. A glass bottom allows remarkable views of the underwater scenery in a lake of legendary clarity. During the summer months, a number of daily sightseeing departures are offered in addition to a sunset dinner-dance cruise.

Since Lake Tahoe is so deep that it never freezes, it is navigable throughout the winter. The *Tahoe Queen* provides a ferry service across the lake from the South Shore to Homewood on the North Shore, where a shuttle is waiting to transport riders to and from Squaw Valley and Alpine Meadows ski resorts. Skiers can fill up on breakfast during the twenty-five-mile morning ferry ride. After a full day of skiing, cocktails, appetizers, and a band welcome skiers aboard for the two-hour return trip.

TRADITIONS' ENGLISH TOFFEE

For years, this English Toffee has been a big seller in the "Pantry" of the Junior League of Oakland-East Bay's Traditions fundraiser.

1 cup sugar
1 cup (2 sticks) butter
1 teaspoon vanilla extract
1 cup (6 ounces) semisweet chocolate chips
1 cup finely chopped walnuts or pecans, lightly toasted

Butter a baking sheet with sides. Heat the sugar, butter, and vanilla in a heavy saucepan until the butter melts. Stirring constantly, bring the mixture to a boil over high heat and boil for 5 minutes. Cook to 300 degrees on a candy thermometer, hard-crack stage. Test by drizzling a string of the candy into a glass of ice water. If the string immediately becomes brittle and cracks, the candy has reached the proper temperature. The color will also start to change from light yellow to a golden brown. Immediately remove from heat and pour on the prepared baking sheet. Let stand for 20 minutes or until hardened.

Place the chocolate chips in a microwave-safe bowl. Microwave just until melted; stir occasionally. Spread the melted chocolate over the toffee with the back of a spoon or spatula. Immediately sprinkle with the toasted nuts. Let stand until set. Break into bite-size pieces. Store in an airtight container. The toffee may be frozen for up to two weeks.

Makes 5 dozen pieces

TOFFEE BUTTER COOKIES

*This will be a new favorite for the cookie jar or
a holiday cookie exchange.*

3 cups flour
1 teaspoon salt
1/2 teaspoon baking soda
1 cup (2 sticks) butter, softened
1 cup sugar

2 eggs
1 tablespoon vanilla extract
1 (10-ounce) package toffee bits
   (Hershey's Skor preferred)

Combine the flour, salt, and baking soda in a bowl and mix well. Beat the butter and sugar in a mixing bowl until creamy, scraping the bowl occasionally. Beat in the eggs and vanilla. Add the flour mixture gradually and beat until well-blended. Stir in the toffee bits. Form the dough into several logs, 2 inches in diameter. Chill, wrapped in plastic wrap, until firm.

   Preheat the oven to 375 degrees. Cut the logs into 1/4-inch slices. Arrange the slices 2 inches apart on a greased cookie sheet. Bake for 8 to 10 minutes or until the edges are light brown; do not overbake. Cool on the cookie sheet for 2 minutes. Remove to a wire rack to cool completely. Store in an airtight container.

Note: Coconut-Macadamia version—omit the toffee bits and add 1/2 cup shredded coconut and 1/2 cup chopped macadamia nuts and proceed as directed in the recipe. Bake on an ungreased cookie sheet.

Makes 4 dozen cookies

Coffee
IN THE BAY AREA

The Bay Area has a rich history brewing when it comes to coffee. William Bovee opened San Francisco's first coffee roasting plant in 1850. J.A. Folger, an early employee, bought out Bovee in 1865, and changed the name of the coffee mill to J.A. Folger & Co. In 1878, brothers Austin and Rueben Hills purchased Arabian Coffee & Spice, which later became Hills Brothers Coffee, still in San Francisco today.

A century later in 1966, a Dutch immigrant, Alfred Peet, revolutionized the stagnating coffee industry by popularizing specialty roasting at his small store at Walnut and Vine Streets in Berkeley. John Baldwin, a Peet protégé, headed to Seattle, with beans originally supplied by Peet, to start Starbucks Coffee in 1970. When Peet retired in 1984, Baldwin purchased his former mentor's company and later sold Starbucks. While Starbucks rapidly expanded to over three thousand locations centered around the "coffee bar concept," Peet's remains focused on selecting, blending, and roasting the finest beans, averaging sales of over one thousand pounds a week at each of its stores.

Teddy Bear Tea

The Teddy Bear Tea at the Ritz-Carlton Hotel in San Francisco is an enchanting holiday event. Each year from Thanksgiving through Christmas week, children are invited to a special late-morning seating of the hotel's world-class tea service in the lavishly decorated Lobby Lounge. Elf Binky shares holiday stories and sings carols at the grand piano, while passing out balloon characters alongside Teddy, the life-size bear. Dainty tea sandwiches, pastries, sweets, and hot cocoa are served in exquisite fashion to children of all ages dressed in their holiday finery. The morning concludes with a festive conga line around the room and souvenir pictures with Teddy. A cuddly teddy bear is sent home with each child as a memento from the special event. Of note, a portion of the price of each child's tea service benefits The Greater Bay Area Make-A-Wish Foundation.

CRANBERRY WALNUT SCONES

These scones are perfect for a holiday brunch or tea.

3 cups flour
1 tablespoon baking powder
1/4 teaspoon salt
1 cup (2 sticks) butter, softened
1/3 cup plus 2 tablespoons sugar, divided

1/2 cup plain yogurt
2 eggs
1/3 cup dried cranberries
1/3 cup chopped walnuts, lightly toasted
1/2 teaspoon cinnamon

Combine the flour, baking powder, and salt in a bowl and mix well. Combine the butter and 1/3 cup sugar in a mixing bowl. Beat until light and fluffy. Add the yogurt and eggs and beat for 5 minutes, scraping the bowl occasionally. Add the flour mixture and mix just until incorporated. Stir in the cranberries and walnuts.

Drop the dough by 1/3 cupfuls 2 inches apart onto an ungreased cookie sheet. Chill, loosely covered with plastic wrap, for 45 minutes.

Preheat the oven to 350 degrees. Combine 2 tablespoons sugar and cinnamon in a small bowl and mix well. Sprinkle the sugar mixture over the tops of the scones. Bake for 25 minutes, then reduce the oven temperature to 325 degrees. Bake for 10 minutes longer. Cool on the cookie sheet for 2 minutes. Remove to a wire rack to cool completely.

Makes 1 dozen

Seasons' Walnut Tart

Created by Tami Jewett, Chef-Owner of Seasons, an Oakland catering company, this dessert is a showstopper.

Crust
2¹/2 cups flour
¹/4 cup sugar
¹/8 teaspoon salt
1 cup (2 sticks) chilled butter, cut into pieces
1 egg yolk
1 tablespoon water
1 teaspoon vanilla extract

Walnut Filling
1¹/2 cups sugar
¹/3 cup water
¹/2 cup heavy cream
¹/2 cup (1 stick) butter, cut into pieces
2 cups walnut halves, lightly toasted

Garnish
³/4 cup heavy whipping cream
1 tablespoon sugar
¹/2 teaspoon vanilla extract

To prepare the crust, combine the flour, sugar, and salt in a food processor. Pulse several times to mix. Add the butter. Pulse until the mixture resembles bread crumbs. Whisk the egg yolk, water, and vanilla in a bowl until blended. With the motor running, add the egg yolk mixture to the flour mixture. Process until the mixture forms a ball. Flatten into a disk and wrap in plastic wrap. Chill for 30 minutes.

Preheat the oven to 375 degrees. Roll the dough ¹/4-inch thick on a lightly floured surface. Fold the dough in half carefully and place in the center of a 9-inch tart pan with removable bottom. Fit the dough into the pan and trim the edge. If the dough cracks, just patch with a bit of excess dough. Line the dough with foil and fill with rice or dried beans. Bake in the lower third of the oven for 15 to 20 minutes. Remove the rice or beans and foil. Bake for 15 minutes longer or until golden brown. Cool on a wire rack.

For the filling, place the sugar in a large heavy saucepan. Pour the water over the sugar, and without stirring, heat over low heat until the sugar dissolves. Using a pastry brush dipped in water, wash any sugar crystals clinging to the side of the saucepan into the sugar water. Increase the heat to high and boil until the syrup is medium brown in color. Remove from heat. Add the heavy cream all at once, stirring constantly. The steam from the cold cream will make the hot sugar sputter and pop, so be careful. Stir until blended and then add the butter and mix well. Quickly fold in the walnuts and pour into the baked tart shell. The mixture will look lumpy and rustic. Quickly spread the walnut mixture evenly in the tart shell with the back of a spoon. Let cool to room temperature. Do not chill.

For the garnish, combine the heavy whipping cream, sugar, and vanilla in a mixing bowl. Beat until soft peaks form. Chill, covered, until serving time. Whisk lightly and top each serving with a spoonful of the whipped cream.

Serves 10

Año Nuevo
STATE RESERVE

Located off the Pacific Coast Highway between Half Moon Bay and Santa Cruz is the largest mainland breeding colony in the world for the Northern elephant seal. First sighted in 1603, Punta de Año Nuevo (New Year's Point) was named for the day on which it was discovered. Now a state reserve, Año Nuevo is host to a mass migration of the elephant seals onshore during mating season between December and March. During the winter months, massive three-ton males battle for mates on the beaches, while the females give birth to their pups on the dunes. Most of the adult seals return to the sea by early March, leaving behind the weaned pups that remain through April. The elephant seals return to Año Nuevo's beaches during the spring and summer months to molt. Guided walking tours are available year-round at the reserve. During the breeding season access to the reserve is by reservation only.

California Fresh Harvest

HARVEST CHART

	MARCH	APRIL	MAY	JUNE	JULY	AUG.	SEPT.	OCT.	NOV.	DEC.	JAN.	FEB.	PAGE	RANK IN U.S.	CALIF. % OF U.S. PRODUCTION
Almonds, Shelled						●	●	●					159	1	99.9 %
Apples					●	●	●						157	3	8.7 %
Apricots			●	●	●								43	1	95.2 %
Artichokes	●	●	●	●	●	●	●	●	●	●	●	●	27	1	100.0 %
Asparagus	●	●	●	●								●	37	2	38.0 %
Bell Peppers					●	●	●	●	●				127	1	46.0 %
Broccoli	●	●	●	●	●	●	●	●	●	●	●	●	191	1	93.0 %
Brussels Sprouts	●				●	●	●	●	●	●	●	●	195	1	93.0 %
Carrots	●	●	●	●	●	●	●	●	●	●	●	●	79	1	59.0 %
Cauliflower	●	●	●	●	●	●	●	●	●	●	●	●	184	1	84.0 %
Cheese	●	●	●	●	●	●	●	●	●	●	●	●	151	2	16.6 %
Chicken Eggs	●	●	●	●	●	●	●	●	●	●	●	●	15	1	8.6 %
Chinook Salmon			●	●	●	●	●						45	3	28.8 %
Dungeness Crab	●	●	●						●	●	●	●	179	3	19.8 %
Fresh Market Spinach	●	●	●	●	●	●	●	●	●	●	●	●	175	1	69.0 %
Garlic		●	●	●	●	●	●						139	1	88.0 %
Head Lettuce	●	●	●	●	●	●	●	●	●	●	●	●	115	1	72.0 %
Honeydew Melon				●	●	●	●	●					63	1	76.0 %
Kiwifruit	●	●	●				●	●	●		●		18	1	99.5 %
Leaf Lettuce	●	●	●	●	●	●	●	●	●	●	●	●	115	1	83.0 %
Milk & Cream	●	●	●	●	●	●	●	●	●	●	●	●	207	1	16.8 %
Mushrooms	●	●	●	●	●	●	●	●	●	●	●	●	186	2	17.0 %
Olives	●						●	●			●	●	167	1	100.0 %
Peaches, Clingstone					●	●	●						101	1	100.0 %
Peaches, Freestone			●	●	●	●							101	1	64.8 %
Pears						●	●	●					124	2	38.6 %
Raspberries						●	●	●					104	3	26.0 %
Rice							●	●	●				146	2	21.9 %
Romaine Lettuce	●	●	●	●	●	●	●	●	●	●	●	●	115	1	78.0 %
Spot Prawns	●												89	1	100.0 %
Strawberries	●	●	●	●	●	●	●	●				●	51	1	83.6 %
Sweet Cherries			●										56	3	15.9 %
Sweet Corn			●	●	●	●	●	●	●				96	2	16.0 %
Table Grapes			●	●	●	●	●	●	●	●			34	1	90.2 %
Tomatoes			●	●	●	●	●	●	●				70	2	31.0 %
Turkeys	●	●	●	●	●	●	●	●	●	●	●	●	135	5	6.8 %
Walnuts							●	●	●				201	1	99.5 %

Sources: California Statistical Abstract 1998, Section G, Pages 90-96; California Statistical Abstract 1999, Section G, Table G32; Patricia Unterman's Food Lover's Guide to San Francisco, "Fish and Shellfish Available in the Bay Area" by Paul Johnson, The Monterey Fish Company, pages 20-23; National Marine Fisheries Service, Southwest Region, 1999 Landing Statistics; California Milk Advisory Board

PHOTO CREDITS

Garden Tea Party, pages 10 & 11
Wallunas Home & Garden, Diablo, California
Kaitlyn Haithcock, age 4
Emma Sonnenschein, age 2
Joshua Wallunas, age 20 months

•

Chicken Eggs
Page 17, Fresh Tomato
Breakfast Strata
Italian Pottery by Amalfi

•

Artichokes
Page 28, Artichoke Soup with
Parmesan Croutons
Artichoke Plate by Raynaud
Flatware by Scof
Bowls & Glass Plate by Mariposa

•

Asparagus
Page 38, Asparagus with Sun-Dried
Tomatoes
Plates by Studio Bormioli Rocco

•

Strawberries
Page 53, Chocolate-Dipped Strawberries
Plate by Raynaud
Basket by Warwick Silver
Plateholder by Saint Hilaire Silver

Field of Wild Mustard, Mt. Diablo Foothills, Tassajara Valley, California

Beach Picnic, pages 58 & 59
Carmel River State Beach,
Carmel-by-the-Sea, California
Xander Fischer, age 9
Madeline Fischer, age 7

Honeydew Melon
Page 64, Honeydew Melon with Fresh Berries
Dinnerware & Wine Glass by Mariposa
Sterling by Reed & Barton

Carrots
Page 81, Citrus Carrot Salad
Star Servers by Mariposa
Bowl by Lindt-Stymeist
Linens by India Overseas

Prawns
Page 91, Skewered Chipotle Shrimp
Plate by Mariposa Asia Collection
Margarita Glass by Bormioli Altea
Reed Mat by India Overseas

Peaches
Page 102, Candied Ginger Shortcakes
with Peaches
Plate by Lindt-Stymeist
Flatware by Scof

Fall

PHOTO CREDITS

Pumpkin Patch, pages 110 & 111
Smith Family Farm, Brentwood, California
Rob Alfeld, age 4
Sally Alfeld, age 2
Connor Christiansen, age 4
Dean Christiansen, age 2
Nicole Hope, age 9
Bradley Hope, age 6
Chad Sonnenschein, age 9 months
William Yeack, age 14
Michael Yeack, age 10
Madison Yeack, age 5

•

Lettuce

Page 116, Leaf Lettuces with
Orange-Cumin Dressing
Handpainted Bucket by Joanne Hurley
and 18th Century American Dough Bowl
from the private collection of Kathleen Tabor
Plates by Vietri
Glassware by Luminarc France

•

Bell Peppers

Page 129, Swordfish with
Roasted Peppers on Arugula
Plates by Izabel Lam

•

Garlic

Page 141, Duck with Dried Cherry Port
Sauce and Roasted Garlic Thyme Custard
Plate & Covered Box by Mariposa
Flatware by Scof

•

Cheese

Page 152, Goat Cheese Tart with
Lavender Honey
Plates by Mariposa
Champagne Flutes by Sasaki

Kiwifruit, Crow Canyon Gardens, San Ramon, California

PHOTO CREDITS

Tree Farm, pages 162 & 163
Alhambra Valley Tree Farm,
Martinez, California
Libby Ogro, age 11
Hilary Ogro, age 8
Connor Ogro, age 15 months

•

Olives
Page 169, Niçoise Olive & Onion Appetizer
Plate by Mariposa
Stemware by Royal Danube

•

Dungeness Crab
Page 180, Cioppino
Covered Casserole by Mariposa

•

Broccoli
Page 192, Warm Broccoli with
Mustard Dressing
Italian Pottery by Amalfi

•

Walnuts
Page 203, Caramel Walnut Torte
Glass Plates by Studio Bormioli Rocco

Apple Blossoms, Sebastopol, California

Albertson's
1701 Marina Boulevard
Post Office Box 5008
San Leandro, California 94577
(800) 835-8259 toll free
www.albertsons.com
Full service grocery stores located throughout Northern California.
Page 32

Alhambra Valley Tree Farm
Corner of Alhambra Valley Road and Reliez Valley Road
Martinez, California 94553
(925) 228-5324
A choose-and-cut Christmas tree farm open during the holiday season.
Pages 162 and 163

Andronico's Market
1109 Washington Avenue
Albany, California 94706
(510) 559-2800
www.andronicos.com
A 70-year-old, family-owned group of innovative, premium grocery markets located in Berkeley, Danville, Emeryville, Los Altos, Palo Alto, San Anselmo, San Francisco, and Walnut Creek.
Pages 150 and 166

B3 Design
Barbara B. Breashears
Post Office Box 94
Walnut Creek, California 94597
(925) 947-6179
www.b3-design.com
barbara@b3-design.com
Packaging design for food manufacturers, importers, brokers, and ad agencies since 1983.

Berkeley Farms
25500 Clawiter Road
Hayward, California 94545
www.berkeleyfarms.com
A complete line of California fresh dairy products.
Page 155

Steven Brandt
Master of Photography
(925) 735-8007
(877) 735-8007 toll free
www.brandtphoto.com
brandt@best.com
Fine portraiture of families and children.

California Sun Dry Foods
177 Front Street, Suite L
Danville, California 94526
(925) 743-9973
www.calsundry.com
A full line of sun-dried tomato products available at neighborhood grocery stores.
Page 174

The Course at Wente Vineyards
5050 Arroyo Road
Livermore, California 94550
(925) 456-2475
www.wentevineyards.com
Designed by two-time British Open Champion Greg Norman, The Course is located less than an hour's drive from both San Francisco and San Jose.
Pages 4 and 5

Crow Canyon Gardens/Crow Canyon Institute
10 Boardwalk Place
San Ramon, California 94583
(925) 820-7471
www.mudds.com/gardens.htm
Community gardens providing environmental education to promote the ideals of land stewardship, ecological responsibility, and small-scale biological agriculture.
Cover photos, title page, and pages 62, 78, 126, and 218

Diamond of California
Post Office Box 1727
1050 South Diamond Street
Stockton, California 95201
(209) 467-6000
www.diamondofcalifornia.com
World leader in culinary and in-shell nuts.
Page 200

Dunworth de Denus
Paul de Denus and Jane Dunworth
1402 Sunset Loop
Lafayette, California 94549
(925) 930-9193
Beautiful handpainted children's furniture.
Page 11

The Edible Schoolyard Project
1781 Rose Street
Berkeley, California 94703
(510) 558-1335
www.edibleschoolyard.org
info@edibleschoolyard.org
A project at Martin Luther King, Jr., Middle School in Berkeley, California, in which students are involved in all aspects of growing and preparing organic foods.
Page 193

FRP
2451 Atrium Way
Nashville, Tennessee 37214
(800) 358-0560 toll free
www.favoriterecipespress.com
A full-service publisher of cookbooks for companies, individuals, and nonprofit organizations nationwide.

Full Bloom
2956-F Treat Boulevard
Concord, California 94518
(925) 685-3067
Fine flowers, plants, and gifts.
Page 10

Gallo of Sonoma
Healdsburg, California
www.gallosonoma.com
World class wines produced from the grapes of Dry Creek Valley, Russian River Valley, Alexander Valley, and Sonoma Coast, Sonoma County's most renowned viticulture areas.
Pages 7, 28, 116, 141, and 180

Garlic Festival Foods
Post Office Box 1145
Gilroy, California 95021
(408) 842-7081
(888) GARLICFEST (427-5423) toll free
www.garlicfestival.com
A gourmet garlic store that produces a line of more than 25 products and gift baskets which are shipped worldwide.
Page 139

Garlic World
4800 Monterey Highway
Gilroy, California 95020
(408) 847-2251
(800) 537-6122 toll free
www.garlicworld.com
Products range from garlic braids and gifts, gourmet items, dried fruits and nuts, to fresh produce, fine wines, and souvenirs.
Page 138

It's-It Ice Cream Company
868 Burlway Road
Burlingame, California 94010
(650) 347-2122
A delicious Bay Area ice cream confection since 1928.
Page 108

Jack London Square Farmers' Market
At the foot of Broadway at Embarcadero
Oakland, California
(800) 949-FARM (3276) toll free
www.jacklondonsquare.com

A Sunday farmers' market featuring fresh fruits and vegetables, cut flowers, baked goods, and more.
Pages 36, 50, and 190

Jamba Juice
1700 17th Street
San Francisco, California 94107
(800) 545-9972 toll free
www.jambajuice.com
Serving fresh fruit smoothies, hot vegetable soups, high-nutrition breads, and pretzels for a healthy fast food alternative.
Page 80

Joe Pucci & Sons Seafoods
678 Third Street
Oakland, California 94607
(510) 444-3769
(800) 427-8224 toll free
www.jpseafood.com
Suppliers of fresh crab and other seafood, as well as everything needed for crab feeds.
Pages 179 and 181

Mallonee Associates
Joyce Mallonee
(925) 299-8887
joyce@foodstrategies.com
Marketing and merchandising strategies for the food industry.

Morgan & Company
888 Brannan Street, Suite 534
San Francisco, California 94103
(415) 437-6560
Manufacturers' representative of fine gift and tabletop merchandise to the retail trade.

Nabisco Biscuit Company
6140 Stoneridge Mall Road, Suite 400
Pleasanton, California 94588
www.nabisco.com
International manufacturer of biscuits, snacks, and other premium food products.
Page 156

Gwen Prichard, CWA
Post Office Box 345
Moraga, California 94556
Original watercolors

Smith Family Farm
Sellers Road between Sunset & Delta Roads
Brentwood, California
(925) 634-4759
(925) 625-3544
A working farm with a pumpkin patch, hayrides, and entertainment open to the public and school groups during the month of October.
Pages 110 and 111

Straus Family Creamery
Post Office Box 768
Marshall, California 94940
(415) 663-5464
www.strausmilk.com
Award-winning organic dairy products.
Page 151

wine.com
570 Gateway Drive
Napa, California 94558
(877) Say-Wine (729-9463) toll free
www.wine.com
On-line wine shopping with expert help.
Pages 17, 38, 53, 64, 81, 102, 129, 152, 169, 192, and 203

Zacky Farms
2000 North Tyler Avenue
South El Monte, California 91733
(626) 443-9351
(800) 888-0235 toll free
www.zacky.com
Suppliers of fresh, naturally grown turkey and chicken.
Page 132

Source Guide

Contributing Chefs & Restaurants

Absinthe Brasserie & Bar
Ross Browne, Chef
398 Hayes Street
San Francisco, California 94102
(415) 551-1590
www.absinthe.com
Located in the heart of San Francisco, Absinthe Brasserie & Bar recreates the romance and mystery of the bygone Belle Époque.
Page 131

Chez Panisse Café & Restaurant
1517 Shattuck Avenue
Berkeley, California 94709
(510) 548-5049 Café
(510) 548-5525 Restaurant
www.chezpanisse.com
Alice Waters' famed restaurant, which creates daily menus appropriate to the season, composed to show off the finest ingredients obtainable.
Pages 51, 167, and 191

El Charro Mexican Dining
3339 Mount Diablo Boulevard
Lafayette, California 94549
(925) 283-2345
A local favorite, El Charro has been serving Mexican food in Lafayette since 1946.
Page 127

Garibaldi's on College
5356 College Avenue
Oakland, California 94618
(510) 595-4000
This Mediterranean restaurant is a sophisticated neighborhood spot with good food and a fab martini.
Page 37

Hornblower Cruises & Events
Daniel B. Smith, Executive Chef
Pier 3 on The Embarcadero
San Francisco, California 94111
Public Cruise Reservations: (800) 668-4322 toll free
or (415) 788-8866 ext. 7
San Francisco Charter Sales: (415) 788-8866 ext. 6
California's premier fleet of luxury dining yachts.
Pages 77, 88, and 206

Ingredients Cooking/Lifestyle School at Andronico's Market
Sandy Sachs, Executive Chef
345 Railroad Avenue
Danville, California 94526
(925) 314-4362
www.andronicos.com
Hands-on cooking and entertaining classes.
Pages 23, 98, 122, and 183

Tami Jewett
(510) 339-7537
tamijewett@earthlink.net
Recipe development and food styling.

Mudd's Restaurant
10 Boardwalk Place
San Ramon, California 94583
(925) 837-9387
www.mudds.com
Farm fresh cuisine, artfully inspired.
Cover photo and title page

Postrio
Wolfgang Puck, Mitchell & Steven Rosenthal, Chefs
545 Post Street
San Francisco, California 94102
(415) 776-7825
www.postrio.com
Postrio's repertoire of California cuisine is a carefully executed layering of Asian and Mediterranean influences that are a tribute to San Francisco's multicultural roots.
Page 115

Spenger's Fresh Fish Grotto
Steve Connolly, Executive Chef
1919 Fourth Street
Berkeley, California 94710
(510) 845-7771
An historic restaurant serving high quality, fresh seafood in a setting of eclectic memorabilia.
Pages 89 and 185

Swan Oyster Depot
1517 Polk Street
San Francisco, California 94109
(415) 673-1101
San Francisco's retail source for fresh oysters, clams, and Dungeness crab, along with whatever else the boat brings in each day.
Page 178

Tully's Coffee Corporation
3100 Airport Way South
Seattle, Washington 98134
(800) 968-8559 toll free
www.tullys.com
Specialty coffee retailers and roasters, Tully's Coffee currently has locations in Washington, California, Oregon, Idaho, Sweden, and the Pacific Rim.
Page 201

Wente Vineyards Restaurant
Kimball Jones, Executive Chef
5050 Arroyo Road
Livermore, California 94550
(925) 456-2450
www.wentevineyards.com
Wente Vineyards Restaurant's philosophy is one of honesty, simplicity, and integrity: use the best possible ingredients, treat them with respect, and focus menus around the seasons.
Page 66

Tabletop Displays

Refer to Photo Credits on pages 222 and 223

Amalfi
3871 Piedmont Avenue
Oakland, California 94611

India Overseas Traders
325 North 13th Street
Philadelphia, Pennsylvania 19107

Izabel Lam New York™
Pier 41, 320A
204 Van Dyke Street
Brooklyn, New York 11231

Lindt-Stymeist
484 Bloomfield Avenue, Suite 9
Montclair, New Jersey 07042

Mariposa and Scof
The Barn
5 Elm Street
Manchester, Massachusetts 01944

Raynaud Limoges and Saint Hilaire
c/o Devine Corporation
1345 Campus Parkway
Neptune, New Jersey 07753

California Fresh Harvest

Test Kitchen Participants

Kristin Alexander
Lou Alfeld
Rob Alfeld
Sally Alfeld
Stefanie Alfeld
Susan Alfeld*
Kathy Anderson
Mary Ardell
Eric Ardell
John Armstrong
Sandy Armstrong*
Laura Balma
Elaine Barakos
Kim Barentsen
Krista Bauer
Diane Beck
Art Bell
Carol Bell
Sabrina Benjamin
Karen Berg
Jeanne Berres
Jacqui Berry
Jim Bitzer
Kelly Bitzer
Leslie Bond*
Erin Boyd
Galen Bradford
Louise Bradford*
Margaret Bradford
Andrew Brazil
Chelsea Brazil
Larry Brazil
Madeline Brazil
Nancy Brazil
Darrell Bridgeford
Kristin Bridgeford*
Dave Brockbank
Terri Brohard
Kristin Brown
Ross Brown
Peggy Bruckner-Marani*
Barbara Bruner
Greg Buchholz
Kristi Buchholz
Jane Burch
Mindy Bush
Candy Caldwell
Ken Caldwell
Barbara Calhoun*
Duane Callahan
Cheryl Campo
Steve Campo
Bob Canepa
Jean Canepa
Christy Cannon
K.C. Cannon
Barbara Cappa*
Caitlin Cappa
Gary Cappa
Mark Carter
Toinette Carter
Jackie Cate
Barbara Chaconas*
Stan Chaconas
Melissa Chambers
Michelle Chambers
Scott Chambers
Julie Christiansen

Bob Christopher
Christine Christopher*
Christine Clakley
Nathan Clakley
Lisa Clark*
Grace Clement
Lisa Clement*
Mark Clement
Dorothy Cobbledick*
Debbie Cole
Shirley Conner
Megan Conway
Cyndy Cotton
Linda Coyne
Denis Cuff
Kevin Dangers
Marilyn Daughters
Jackie Davis
Jiggs Davis
Keith Dayton
Erin Decker
Maureen Deierling
Danny Dempsey
Maria Dempsey
Dean Denhart*
Susan Denhart
Tina DeSalvo
Courtney Dettlinger*
Steve Dettlinger
Celia Dietz
Kari Dimler
Kevin Dimler
MJ Dodds*
Wendy Dooley*
Stacie Drese
Sherry Dumke
Andrew Eakin
Susan Eakin
Lee Eisman
Monika Elek*
Karen Emery
Martha Erisman
Tim Erisman
Amor Esteban
Patty Esteban
John Estes
Lisa Estes
Pat Everett
Barbara Fairchild
Dan Fairchild
John Fiero
Julie Fiero*
Betsy Fischer*
Conrad Fischer
Larry Fischer
Maddie Fischer
Ned Fischer
Sonja Fischer
Xander Fischer
Joni Fisher
Mark Fisher
Sue Flautt
Anita Fligge*
Lisa Foley
Peter Frazier
Robin Frazier
John Freeman
Mindy Fry

Grett Gaunt
Stuart Givot
Ann Goldfarb*
Larry Goldfarb
Barbara Goodman
Glenn Gould
Marci Gould
Meredith Graham
Jennifer Graves
Paul Graves
Kim Greer*
Steve Greer
Jane Grieb
Mary Griffin
Dale Haithcock
Lyn Haithcock
Robin Halloran*
Tom Halloran
Christine Hammond
Eileen Hammond-Cuff*
Karol Hansen
Sally Harper
Bob Harris
Lori Harris*
Marylou Harris
Tony Hart
Carol Hartman*
Craig Hartman
Kate Hartman
Jack Havens
Maxine Havens
Shirley Hays
Lynn Hernandez
Shay Hogan
Brad Hope
Craig Hope
Jan Hope*
Nicole Hope
Christy Hoyne
Mike Hreha
Tina Hreha
Mary Ann Hughes
Joy Hunt
Sara Hutchinson
Christina Huvelle
Carolann Ianora
Joe Ianora
Suanne Inman
Stephanie Janssen*
Alan Jewett
Jane Jewett
Tami Jewett
Anne Johnson*
Bob Johnson
Dave Johnson
Emily Johnson
Meghan Johnson
Molly Johnson
Vera Kajtar
Leslie Kalish
David Kaplan
Elizabeth Kaplan
Joan Kaufmann
Coralie Kenton
Sandy Killoran
Tim Killoran
Shannon Kirby*
Adam Kovar

Set Kwan
Carolyn La Follette
Donna Lacy
Linda La Fleur
John Leonard
Mary Beth Leonard
Karen Leser
Larry Leser
Carol Leslie
Pam Lewerenz
Claire Lindauer
Cyndy Lindauer
Christian Linderoth
Ann Marie Listek
Debbie Llama
Brian Locher
Marian Locher
Ruth Locher*
Stacey Logan
Tom Logan
Ruth Lorber
Carole Lutz
Alissa Mahoney
Kevin Marani
Julie Marquart
Murray Marsh
Natalie Marsh
Kelley Masuda
Elizabeth McCormick*
Kelly McCormick
Amy McDaniel
Stacy McGihon
Shauna McGlynn
Lila McIntire
Elizabeth Mead
Thomas Mead
Tommy Mead
Sally Mead
Angela Meaney
Kathy Mendel
Michelle Merkel
Bee Gee Millinich
Bob Millinich
Bob Miller
Mary Miller
Bryan Mings
Chris Mings
Eric Mings
Susan Mings*
Steve Mink
Ann Monty
Bill Monty
Debbie Morgan
Nancy Morgan
Kelly Moriarty*
Brian Mulligan
Peggy Mulligan
Molly Natsues
Peter Nguyen
Kathie Nicosia*
Heather Nielsen
Margaret Nielsen
Norm Nielsen
Heather Noel*
Inez Noel
Erika Odell
Mike Ogles
Rosanne Ogles

California Fresh Harvest

Test Kitchen Participants continued

Hilary Ogro
John Ogro
Libby Ogro
Molly Ogro*
David Olson
Dolores Olson
Jessica Omano
Nov Omano
Michelle O'Reilly
Bill Overholt
Mark Panella
Sue Panella
Alexandra Pappas
Michael Pappas
Ann Patton
Bill Pedder
Marjorie Pedder
Nancy Pedder
Shannon Pedder*
Chris Petrush
Jan Podoll
Todd Podoll
Stephanie Preston*
Karen Ramin
Beth Ratto
Kathy Ratto
Marcia Redford
Karen Redwood
Lois Regel
Sally Reimers
Fred Riedel
Judy Riedel
Patti Ringlee*
Carmen Ruiz
Kathy Runstrom
Leslie Ruth
Beatriz Sarmiento
Margaret Schaus
Linda Schilling
Jon Schroeder
Sara Schroeder
Nancy Scott
Peter Scott
Denise Shawver
Liz Sibson-Tuan
Liz Silverman
Diane Skrip
Martin Skrip
Will Skrip
Dan Smoot
Kim Smoot
David Sonnenschein
Becky Soto
Chérie Soza
Carol Spiering*
Colleen Stagg
Bonnie Stehr
Danya Stehr
Carol Stevenson*
Jim Stevenson
Sue Stiffler
Terry Stiffler
Kyra Stockton
Dana Strazza
Lori Strobbe
Martin Stryker
Nancy Stryker
Marty Stucky

Linda Studer
Rebecca Sullivan
John Sween
Lisa Barnett Sween
Kathleen Tabor
Cimarron Taylor
Sharon Taylor*
Lyndsey Tennant
Terry Tinnon
Deanne Tong
George Tong
Jennifer Tong*
Kevin Tong
Richard Tong
Bev Tornberg
Gayle Tornberg*
Terry Townsend
Linda Tsuchiyama
Ted Tsuchiyama
Bea Tuan
Bert Tuan
Cathi Tuominen
Allison Urban
Jennifer Urban
John Urban
Kathy Urban*
Catherine Van Sickle
Christine Velez
Dino Velez
Alan Vernon
Corinne Vernon*
Nicholas Vernon
Megan Vilke
Stephen Vilke
George Waidelich
Lori Waidelich
Craig Walker
Kate Walker
Jacob Wallin
Johanna Wallin
Jonathan Wallunas
Julie Wallunas
Jeff Weaver
Jodi Weaver
Barbara Wensel
Lee Wensel
Janet Wentz
Teresa Wenzel
Claudine Westra
Jill Willerup*
Cindy Wilmore
Elizabeth Wolfe
Kim Wolkenmuth
Christopher Woodland
Cynthia Woodland*
Rick Woodland
Beth Wynstra
Carole Wynstra
Maya Ynostroza
Barbara Yow
Richard Yow
Margie Zavoico
Midge Zischke*
Peter Zischke

*Head Tester

Recipe Contributors

Susan Alfeld
Katherine Anderson
Rhonda Andronico
Melinda Arentsen
Sandy Armstrong
Laura Balma
Nancy Barber
Kimberly Barentsen
Carol Barnes
Leslie Bates
Jacqui Berry
Rosemary Black
Wendy Boals
Leslie Bond
Louise E. Bradford
Kristin Bridgeford
Ross Brown
Mindy Bush
Barbara Calhoun
Christy Cannon
Cheryl Capece
Dave Capece
Shannon Carver
Jackie Cate
Michelle Chambers
Julie Christiansen
Carol A. Clazie
Lisa Clement
Dorothy Cobbledick
Nancy Combs
Cyndy Cotton
Kelly Craig
Todd Craig
Celia Dietz
MJ Dodds
Vickee Drury
Taressa Earl
Chris Eichler
Lee Eisman
Karen Emery
Martha Erisman
Julie Fiero
Betsy Fischer
Sue Fogarty
Lisa Foley
Linda Glowienka
Ann Goldfarb
Jennifer Graves
Pat Greenwood
Kim Greer
Lyn Haithcock
Trish Hannon
Karol Hansen
Nancy Happel
Lori Harris
Carol Hartman
Joanne Hartman
Lynette Hegeman
Kathleen Henne
Greg Holmes
Jan Hope
Ginger Howard
Bonnie Jameson
Alan Jewett
Tami Jewett
Anne Johnson
Elizabeth Kaplan
Susie Kevorkian

Sandy Killoran
Shannon Kirby
Katri Koehle
Jane Korinke
Mary Beth Leonard
Carol Leslie
T. Anne Harris Leslie
Pat Luvkun
Elizabeth McCormick
Jeannette McElroy
Sallie McOwen
Mary Mehlberg
Kirsten Melton
Mark Melton
Bee Gee Millinich
Kathy Marx Miron
Anne Mitchell
JoAnn Mize
Katie Morehouse
Ellen Muzzio
Diane Nelson
Judi Nishimine
Kathleen Odne
Molly Ogro
Mary O'Neill
Alexandra Pappas
Betty Paul
Shannon Pedder
Sherrie Prati
Gwen Prichard
Pam Purdum
Mollie Redwood
Patti Ringlee
Lynn Rubin
Pat Ruvkun
Lisa San Vincente
Marion Schwartz
Nancy Scott
Betty Shapiro
Steven T. Smith
David Sonnenschein
Chérie Soza
Carol Stevenson
Mary Stuart
Rebecca Sullivan
Kim Sweeney
Kathleen Tabor
Sharon Taylor
Ayn Thorne
Debbie Tills
Kathy Urban
Corinne Vernon
Lori Waidelich
Joan Waits
Julie Wallunas
Arel Wente
Jean Wieler
Jill Willerup
Molly Griffin Wilson
Bettye Wolfe
Elizabeth Wolfe
Cynthia Woodland

Acknowledgements

Junior League cookbooks, by nature, are possible to produce only with the help of many dedicated and hard working volunteers; we would like to thank all those who helped bring *California Fresh Harvest* to press. Foremost, we would like to thank our families for the sacrifices they have made and encouragement they have given throughout the entire two-year process. Our first-year committee members developed the vision and were instrumental in pushing this project forward. Our second-year committee members fine-tuned the vision, developed the cookbook's format, selected and tested recipes, planned our kick-off events, and obtained corporate sponsors; they deserve credit for turning the cookbook into reality. Our thanks to our forty test kitchens, comprised of League and non-League volunteers who worked diligently on contributing, testing, and tasting hundreds of recipes. Our copywriters and editors spent endless hours seeking out, researching, and conveying the wonders of Northern California. Sandy Sachs, our executive chef, shared with us her valuable expertise, her professional kitchen, and much enthusiasm for our project. Many individuals were involved in the visual aspects of *California Fresh Harvest,* and to them we are grateful: Steven Brandt for his beautiful photography; Gwen Prichard for her intricate watercolors and illustrations; Tami Jewett, for developing and testing numerous recipes, and preparing and styling the food for the prepared food photographs; and Joyce Mallonee for coming forward in our hour of need to help style the cover photographs and many of the prepared food shots. And finally, we extend our thanks to JLOEB President, Rosemary Black, for her continuous support for and dedication to *California Fresh Harvest.*

The Managing Editors of
California Fresh Harvest
Betsy Fischer, Molly Ogro, and
Elizabeth Wolfe

California Fresh Harvest

SPONSORS

Premier Partners
Over $5,000
Andronico's Market
Rosemary Black & Bill Yeack
Contra Costa Newspapers
Betsy & Ned Fischer
Gallo of Sonoma
Beth & Tyler Hofinga
Hornblower Cruises & Events
The Charles Schwab Corporation Foundation
Julie & Don Wallunas and Family
wine.com

Master Chef
Up to $5,000
Sonja & Conrad Fischer
Elizabeth Wolfe & David Sonnenschein

Executive Chef
Up to $2,500
Albertson's
Berkeley Farms
California Sun Dry Foods
The Clorox Company Foundation
Brooke & Robert Ferguson
Lyn & Dale Haithcock
Nafiz & Cana Korustan
Nabisco Biscuit Company
Molly & John Ogro
PeopleSoft
Lynn & Gerry Rubin
Joe Pucci & Sons Seafoods
Marsha & Dick Servetnick
Betty & Hort Shapiro
Zacky Farms

Sous Chef
Up to $1,000
Kelly & Jim Bitzer
Jeannette & Jim Cox
Anne-Marie & Lawrence Frank
Kelly & Brad Irving
J. Edgar Monroe Foundation
KPMG
The Mechanics Bank
Justine & Steve Noonan
Spenger's Fresh Fish Grotto
Tully's Coffee Corporation
Bettye & Lee Wolfe

Culinarian
Up to $500
Sandy & John Armstrong
Carol & Jim Barnes
Nancy & Jack Bates
Laura & Tom Beaty
Cheryl & Dave Capece
Toinette & Mark Carter
Susan & Rand Chritton
MJ & Chris Dodds
Carol & Craig Hartman
Johnson Lyman Architects
René Rambo-Rodgers & Billy Rodgers
John Simon
Chérie & Mike Soza
Tricia & Zack Stenger

Gourmet
$250
Kelsey & Kristopher Bauer
Kristina & John Botsford
The Clorox Company
Sharon & Dale Crandall
Susan & Dennis Gildea
Elizabeth & Thomas Henry
Mr. & Mrs. Kurt Herzog
Jan & Craig Hope and Family
Susie & Kevin Kevorkian
Carla Koren & Neal Parish
Terry Mack Magnin
Susan & Christopher Mings
Gala & Bruce Mowat
Diane & Scott Nelson
Kathleen & John Odne
Bridgette & Rick Porterfield
Karen Redwood
Elizabeth & Walter Schymik
Sharie & Clement Shute
Sharon Stegmuller Sievers
Sycamore Valley Day School
Dorothy & William Trautman
Carole & Dave Wynstra

California Fresh Harvest

COOKBOOK ORDER FORM

Name

Street

City

State   Zip

Daytime Telephone (   )   Evening Telephone (   )

Fax (   )   E-mail Address

Ship To *(attach list if additional shipping addresses)*

Name

Street

City

State   Zip

Telephone (   )

METHOD OF PAYMENT

Check *(payable to California Fresh Harvest)* ❏   MC ❏   Visa ❏

Name as it appears on card

Card Number   Expiration Date

Signature

		Quantity	Amount Due
California Fresh Harvest–Cookbook	$26.95		$
California Fresh Harvest–Six-book case	$150.00		$
California Fresh Harvest–Giftwrap	$2.00/book		$

SHIPPING & HANDLING

$4/book OR $3/book for 2 to 5 books OR $12/six-book case	$
Subtotal	$
Sales Tax *(CA residents add 8.25% on Subtotal–no tax if mailing out of state)*	$
TOTAL	$

Please photocopy, complete this form, and return to:
California Fresh Harvest P.O. Box 442, Lafayette, CA 94549-0442
or call (510) 346-COOK(2665) to order by credit card,
or fax to (925) 284-5221
To purchase on-line, visit our website at www.cafresh.com

This form is intended to be photocopied

The Junior League of Oakland-East Bay, Inc.

Since 1935, the women of the Junior League of Oakland-East Bay, Inc. have made a significant difference in the lives of children and their families in Contra Costa and Alameda Counties. Our members share an abiding belief that women have the power and the responsibility to improve our communities through individual and collective action.

Each year, the Junior League of Oakland-East Bay provides a range of services to East Bay communities. Our efforts include long-term community projects utilizing League resources and volunteers over a period of three to five years, enrichment grants to nonprofit agencies for their special projects, and short-term volunteer-only projects such as staffing a children-focused conference, developing graphic materials for a partner agency, or painting a homeless shelter. Since 1992, our League has focused its funding and volunteer power on improving the lives of *Children at Risk*.

At times, new nonprofit organizations are formed to meet critical needs or to expand cultural opportunities. Recognizing these community needs, League members have developed partnerships, raised funds, provided expertise, and garnered support to establish community agencies. These organizations continue to thrive and contribute to the well being of our communities, children, and families.

The Junior League of Oakland-East Bay returns 95 percent of proceeds from our fundraisers to our community fund to finance our community grants, volunteer projects, and community leadership training courses. Proceeds from the sale of *California Fresh Harvest* will support on-going children's services and implement important new programs for *Children at Risk*.

The Junior League of Oakland-East Bay, Inc. is an organization of women committed to promoting voluntarism, developing the potential of women, and improving the community through the effective action and leadership of trained volunteers. Its purpose is exclusively educational and charitable. The Junior League of Oakland-East Bay, Inc. reaches out to women of all races, religions, and national origins who demonstrate an interest in and commitment to voluntarism.

Proceeds from the sale of this cookbook benefit the charitable endeavors of the Junior League of Oakland-East Bay, Inc.

California Fresh Harvest

BIOGRAPHIES

Alice Waters, *Foreword Author*
Alice Waters is the chef-owner of the world-renowned Chez Panisse Café & Restaurant in Berkeley, California. Inspired by the abundance of readily available fresh ingredients, as well as the relationship of food to family and community, Alice opened Chez Panisse in 1971, serving a prix-fixe menu that changes daily and is based on simple preparations of the highest quality seasonal ingredients. In 1980, an á la carte bistro was opened upstairs from Chez Panisse, and in 1984 Alice opened a stand-up café that serves breakfast and lunch, named Café Fanny after her daughter. The Chez Panisse concept of food revolutionized American cooking and has received the highest accolades. In 1986, the magazine *Cuisine et Vins du France* named Alice as one of the ten best chefs in the world. In 1992, the James Beard Foundation honored her as Best Chef in America, and named Chez Panisse Best Restaurant in America. In 2000, Alice received the Lifetime Achievement Award at the *Bon Appétit* American Food and Entertaining Awards. Alice Waters has written several Chez Panisse cookbooks, as well as a story-book with recipes for children titled *Fanny at Chez Panisse.* She is a very active promoter of community-supported, organic agriculture. She has taken her vision into the community in many ways, most notably by developing The Edible Schoolyard Project at Berkeley's Martin Luther King, Jr., Middle School.

Gina Gallo, *Foreword Author*
Whether talented winemakers are made or born, Gina Gallo has the credentials to fill the bill. She is the granddaughter of California wine pioneer Julio Gallo and represents the third generation of Gallo family wine makers. As one of the bright young stars of the "Sonoma style" of crafting wines to delight the senses, Gina has the training, the experience, and the resources to make landmark wines. After college, Gina tried out various aspects of the wine industry, including sales, to learn the business from the ground up. She then went on to study wine-making at the University of California, Davis. Gina was apprenticed to Marcello Monticello, one of the most respected of the Gallo winemakers and a trusted friend of her father and grandfather. Today she can be found at the Gallo of Sonoma winery in Healdsburg, California, making world-class wines.

Steven Brandt, *Photographer*
Steven Brandt began his career as a commercial photographer and filmmaker producing ski films and television commercials. But after studying with some of the finest portrait photographers in the country and gaining inspiration from the work of fine art portrait artists, today Steve designs and creates high quality portrait art of families and children throughout the United States. He also accepts a limited number of weddings and commercial clients to help him keep his creative edge. Steve is a Certified Professional Photographer and a Master of Photography, the highest degree awarded by the Professional Photographers of America. He is also a Fellow of the Professional Photographers of California. Steve has photographed thousands of weddings, families, and children over the last twenty-five years. He feels those years have helped to prepare him for his biggest and most rewarding challenge to date, having a son of his own in the year 2000. He is now based in San Ramon, California, where he lives with his wife, Anne, and son, Chase.

Gwen Prichard, *Illustrator*
Gwen Prichard, a Signature Member of the California Watercolor Association, has had many of her paintings accepted into juried shows and has received several awards, including the Academy of Art Award in the 1999 CWA Annual Open National Exhibition. She began painting in 1987, just prior to her early retirement from a career in social work, and has been painting ever since. She has studied watercolor and drawing locally and has attended workshops taught by nationally known watercolorists. What began as a hobby quickly evolved into a devotion to the medium and a desire to learn and achieve. In her work, Gwen likes to experiment with color, shapes, composition, and design. She also welcomes the challenge of showing her works in juried competitions and has sold a number of her paintings. Her watercolors and line drawings in *California Fresh Harvest* are her first venture into the world of book illustration. She resides in Moraga, California, with her husband, Al.

Sandy Sachs, *Recipe Consultant*
As the Executive Chef for Ingredients Cooking/Lifestyle School at Andronico's Market in Danville, California, Sandy Sachs is responsible for continuing the Andronico's tradition of innovation in the Bay Area's newest and most diverse culinary center. There she delivers more than just lectures by having students participate in hands-on professional techniques and learn about regional produce and products, while preparing the latest recipes and time-honored favorites. Her class sizes are limited to twenty-four people so that her students can be immersed in the topic in an intimate, never intimidating, environment. Previously, Sandy has been a culinary instructor with Sur La Table, Gelson's Market, Bristol Farms Market, Let's Get Cooking, and Lazarus Department Store.